Routledge Philosophy GuideBook to

Hegel
on history

D0024397

'McCarney is a lucid and reliable guide to the complexities of Hegel's philosophy of history. He makes a substantial contribution to our understanding of Hegel's thought and its relevance to our own time.'

Michael Inwood, University of Oxford

Hegel's *Introduction to the Philosophy of History* remains one of the most profound and influential books on the philosophy of history. This GuideBook is intended to to be used with any of the standard translations of that work. In clear and cogent terms it

- examines the ideas and arguments of the *Introduction to the Philosophy of History*
- explains the key concepts of Hegel's system, a knowledge of which is essential for fully understanding his philosophy of history
- assesses the continuing relevance of Hegel's work to contemporary debate about the nature of history.

Joseph McCarney is Senior Lecturer in Philosophy at South Bank University

Routledge
Philosophy
GuideBooks

Edited by Tim Crane and Jonathan Wolff
University College London

LONDON AND NEW YORK

Routledge Philosophy GuideBook to

Hegel
on history

■ Joseph McCarney

First published 2000
by Routledge
11 New Fetter Lane, London EC4P 4EE

Simultaneously published in the USA and Canada
by Routledge
29 West 35th Street, New York, NY 10001

Routledge is an imprint of the Taylor & Francis Group

© 2000 Joseph McCarney

Typeset in Times by Taylor & Francis Books Ltd

Printed and bound in Great Britain by Clays Ltd, St Ives plc

British Library Cataloguing in Publication Data
A catalogue record for this book is available from the British Library

Library of Congress Cataloging in Publication Data
McCarney, Joe.
Hegel on history / Joseph McCarney.
p. cm. – (Routledge philosophy guidebooks)
Includes bibliographical references and index.
1. History – Philosphy. 2. Hegel, Georg Wilhelm Freidrich, 1770–1831 –
Contributions in philosophy of history. I. Title. II. Series.
D16.8 .M3856 2000   99–059383
901–dc21

ISBN 0–415–11695–3 (hb)
ISBN 0–415–11696–1 (pb)

In memory of my parents

I often used to see him looking around anxiously as if in fear he might be understood. He was very fond of me, for he was sure I would never betray him. As a matter of fact, I then thought that he was very obsequious. Once when I grew impatient with him for saying: 'All that is, is rational', he smiled strangely and remarked, 'It may also be said that all that is rational must be'. Then he looked about him hastily; but he was speedily reassured, for only Heinrich Beer had heard his words. It was not till later that I understood these expressions. Not till later did I understand what he meant when he declared in his *Philosophy of History* that Christianity represents progress because it teaches the doctrine of a God who died; while heathen gods knew nothing of death.

Heinrich Heine

Contents

Acknowledgements

This book has taken a good deal longer to write than I envisaged at the start. Its publishers, and the editors of the Routledge Philosophy GuideBooks series, deserve to be thanked with more than usual warmth for their understanding and patience. More specifically, I am indebted to Jonathan Wolff for his early encouragement of the project and to Tim Crane for valuable practical criticism. I greatly benefited from comments on substantial portions of the work in progress from Chris Arthur, Andrew Chitty, Richard de Zoysa, Gregory Elliott and Tony Smith. In addition, Andrew Chitty generously made available the results of his own work in correlating the English translations of the *Introduction*. I am grateful to Hugh Atkinson for making it easier for me to devote time to the demands of the book. I am grateful also to Ashley Price for the professional skill and good humour with which he processed a difficult manuscript. Finally, I wish to thank my wife for her unfailing and indispensable support.

Chapter 1

Introduction

Georg Wilhelm Friedrich Hegel was born on 27 August 1770 in Stuttgart and died, of cholera, on 14 November 1831 in Berlin. He led a relatively uneventful life in an eventful time, a time of what have to be called, in the language of his philosophy of history, 'world historical' events. In particular, there was the French Revolution and the rise and fall of Napoleon. Hegel is supposed to have hailed the first of these events as a young student by participating in the planting of a tree of liberty. Although he came to deplore, and to give in his *Phenomenology of Spirit* a profound analysis of, the excesses of the Revolution, he never ceased to regard it as having a positive historical significance. It always remained for him a vital moment in the realisation of human freedom, a view symbolised in his reported habit of raising a celebratory glass each year on the anniversary of the fall of the Bastille. Napoleon, the child of the Revolution, was to figure for Hegel as the central example in the modern world of those he terms the 'world historical individuals'. His attitude is captured vividly in a letter that reports on the sight of the Emperor, 'this world-soul', riding out of the city of Jena after his victory in battle there: 'It is indeed a wonderful sensation to see such an individual, who, concentrated here at a single point, astride a horse, reaches out over the world and masters it' (HL: 114). The note of awe and reverence is struck again when, nearly ten years later, Napoleon came to fulfil the tragic destiny characteristic of the world historical individual. It is, Hegel observes, 'a frightful spectacle to see a great genius destroy himself', allowing 'the entire mass of mediocrity' to bring him down (HL: 307).

Hegel's response to such public events sheds, one might suggest, more light on his thought than do any details of his private life. This is not simply because of the uneventful nature of that life. It has also to do with the somewhat uncanny objectivity he cultivated or found natural, his determination not to allow the merely personal and particular to intrude into philosophy. With this in mind, it should suffice for the purposes of the present inquiry if the circumstance of his life are recounted in broad outline.

Life and influence

Hegel was the oldest of three children of a minor public official in the service of the Duchy of Württemberg and his wife. He attended school in Stuttgart and, from 1788, the *Stift* or seminary at Tübingen, an institution primarily intended for training pastors of the Lutheran Church. It was in his time an extraordinary cradle of achievement, for there he formed close friendships with Friedrich Hölderlin, later to become one of the greatest German poets, and with the celebrated philosopher to be, Friedrich Schelling. These relationships were not sustained in later years, in the one case because of Hölderlin's mental collapse and withdrawal from the world, and in the other because of intellectual and personal estrangement. On graduating from the *Stift*, Hegel spent some eight years as a tutor in families in Bern and Frankfurt am Main, before becoming a *Privatdozent* or unsalaried lecturer, and, briefly, a salaried lecturer at the University of Jena. On 5 February 1807 his landlady in Jena, Johanna Burkhardt, born Fischer, gave birth to his illegitimate son, apparently the third child born to her out of wedlock. Hegel's conduct in this, the most dramatic episode of his private life has been interpreted with varying degrees of sympathy. He may at least be said to have behaved with minimal decency in ensuring that the child, who was given the name Ludwig Fischer, was cared for, and in 1817, after his marriage, in taking him into his own household. It may well be, however, that Ludwig did not receive the same affection or consideration as the children of the marriage, being, for instance, frustrated in his desire for a medical career. At any rate the letters, written some years later, before his departure overseas in Dutch military service, in which he complains of his treatment and declares his devotion to his sister, the daughter of Johanna, are among the most moving items in the mass of documentation relating to Hegel. Ludwig died of fever in Djakarta on 28 August 1831, though the news did not reach Berlin before his father's death later that year.

With the closure of the university as a result of the French occupation of Jena, Hegel became for a year the editor of a newspaper sympathetic to Napoleon in Bamberg, and from 1808 the rector of a boy's secondary school in Nuremberg. In 1811 he married Marie von Tucher, a woman twenty years younger than himself, and three children were born in a happy and enduring relationship. Their daughter, Susanna, died in infancy, but two sons, Karl and Immanuel, enjoyed long lives and successful careers. Karl became a historian and was one of the first editors of his father's lectures on the philosophy of history. In 1816 Hegel became professor of philosophy in the University of Heidelberg, and two years later was called to be professor at Berlin. There he remained until his death, at the pinnacle of his profession and, apparently, snugly placed near the heart of the Prussian establishment. Those years also saw his growing fame as a philosopher and the development of a Hegelian 'school'. In truth, however, his position was less assured and comfortable than it seemed. This was owing in part to the suspicions aroused by his efforts on behalf of his students and others who were accused of political offences. He was, moreover, subject to persistent charges of religious unorthodoxy by the powerful evangelical faction at court. It was, ironically, his old college friend Schelling who, ten years after his death, was summoned by the new king, Friedrich Wilhelm IV, to take up his chair in Berlin with a commission to root out 'the dragon-seed of the Hegelian pantheism'.

It remains the case that before Hegel's death he had come to be generally regarded as the greatest German philosopher of his time. For varied and complex reasons the regard in which he was held was shortly thereafter to go into steep decline. This no doubt reflected a familiar cyclical pattern in the natural history of reputations. It also owed something to the fact that the Hegelian school failed to maintain itself for long as a coherent entity. As early as the mid-1830s it began to split into 'Old' or 'Right' Hegelians, 'Young' or 'Left' Hegelians and an embattled 'Centre'. Although the lines of demarcation were by no means precisely drawn, it was plain that a certain aspect of Hegel's legacy was crucially at stake. This was the degree to which it should be seen as having conservative or radical implications in the sphere of religion on the one hand and of politics on the other. For all the debilitating effects of the conflict, Hegel continued to wield considerable intellectual influence, even at his lowest posthumous ebb. This is most obviously shown by the development of Marxism. Karl Marx's intellectual career began in the Young Hegelian group, and later he declared that at a time when Hegel was being treated as a 'dead dog' in Germany, he had openly avowed himself 'the pupil of that mighty thinker'. In the work of Friedrich Engels there is a still more explicit and methodical recourse to a version of Hegel's thought. Even in academic circles in Germany, Hegel's standing was to revive towards the end of the century. A key figure in the revival was Wilhelm Dilthey, a thinker for whom the strategic philosophical role Hegel gave to history was especially congenial. Elsewhere, important work was being done in this period by philosophers more or less avowedly under Hegel's influence. They include F. H. Bradley, Bernard Bosanquet and J. M. E. McTaggart in Britain, Benedetto Croce and Giovanni Gentile in Italy and C. S. Peirce and Josiah Royce in the United States.

A particularly striking development of the twentieth century was the upsurge of interest in Hegel from the 1930s onwards in France. It was inspired in large part by Alexandre Kojève's interpretation of the philosophy of history, and flowered creatively in the work of Jean-Paul Sartre, and, in terms of scholarship, in that of Jean Hyppolite. In Britain Hegel's influence was to decline sharply from its late Victorian and Edwardian heyday under the impact of the rejection by G. E.

Moore and Bertrand Russell of what they took to be his philosophy, and later of the still more fanciful interpretation of it by Karl Popper. From the late 1950s, however, the tide began to turn with a succession of works that have done much to establish a sober and defensible view of his achievement. Taken together with a parallel development in the United States, it has become usual to refer in this connection to a Hegel revival in the Anglophone philosophical world. In Germany he has, as one might expect, continued to maintain a substantial presence in the academy, resulting in many advances in historical and textual scholarship. His exemplary significance as a metaphysician, by way of both warning and inspiration, in the work of the most important German philosopher of the century, Martin Heidegger, should also be remarked. It is a significance intriguingly mediated by the central role that came to be occupied there by the figure of Hölderlin. In all of these ways, and in others that cannot be detailed here, Hegel's influence on intellectual history has been pervasive and profound. The briefest sketch of it will testify to the deep truth in the remark attributed to Kojève's pupil, Jacques Lacan, that it is just when we think we may be moving away from him that he is most likely to be sneaking up behind us.

Scope of the inquiry

In view of Hegel's long and active life as a philosopher it is perhaps surprising that there are only four large-scale works that he wrote directly for publication and saw through the press himself. They are *Phenomenology of Spirit* (1807), *Science of Logic* (issued in successive volumes 1812, 1813 and 1816), *Encyclopaedia of the Philosophical Sciences* (1817, with new editions in 1827 and 1830) and *Philosophy of Right* (1830). In the various collected editions of his writings approximately half of the material consists of the lecture series on aesthetics, the history of philosophy, the philosophy of history and the philosophy of religion. This book is in essence a study of and commentary on the text that is referred to in its pages as *Introduction*; that is to say the introduction to the *Lectures on the Philosophy of History*, hereafter referred to as *Lectures*. It will also pay special attention to the main body of that work. For although it is true that most of what is of theoretical interest in it is to be found in the *Introduction*, this is not quite true of everything. In any case the outline of world history that follows the *Introduction* serves indispensably to illustrate, flesh out, develop and apply its themes. Even when taken as a whole *Lectures* is, however, far from providing all that the student of Hegel's philosophy of history needs to consider.

Most obviously, there is the explicit treatment of the subject elsewhere in his writings, especially in the final volume of the *Encyclopaedia* and in the *Philosophy of Right*. Indeed, he commended the relevant portions of the latter work to the students on his philosophy of history course as their nearest approach to a textbook (H, 3: 11; M, 11: 1, 3). Where the *Phenomenology* is concerned it is not necessary to accept entirely Royce's description of it as 'a sort of freely told philosophy of history' to hold that it contains much that is indispensable for such a philosophy. In particular, there are arguments that may, as will appear later, be said to have a foundational role. Hegel's logical writings, the *Science of Logic* and the first volume of the *Encyclopaedia*, have to be invoked in any attempt to outline his metaphysics.[1] That the philosophy of history must be situated against this metaphysical background is a truth that will emerge decisively only in the course of the discussion. Some pointers to it are, however, visible even now. Hegel is, by express and fixed design, a systematic thinker for whom 'the true' is comprehensible only as 'the whole'. The philosophy of history is indisputably an element of the system, as is straightforwardly shown by its presence in the *Encyclopaedia*, and in the encyclopaedic prototypes produced earlier in Heidelberg, and, though in still more shadowy form, in Nuremberg. It seems natural to suppose that its grounding and vitality will largely depend on its position there.

The point now at issue does not, however, have to rely on such general considerations. The *Introduction* makes clear very early on that it presupposes certain theses which have been proved elsewhere by 'speculative cognition', and which accordingly figure as the legacy of philosophy to historical understanding (H, 28: 27; M, 20–1: 9, 11, 12). If the present inquiry is to achieve its object it will have to draw on whatever resources are available in Hegel's work to elucidate and justify these presuppositions. In doing so it seems unavoidable that it should yield just the kind of outline of his metaphysics referred to earlier. Indeed, to pursue his philosophy of history unrestrictedly is, as will be shown, to arrive at the heart of his metaphysical enterprise. For he is, beyond all comparison, the historical philosopher, the one for whom history figures most ambitiously and elaborately as a philosophical category. This, however, is also a claim that must await vindication in the course of this inquiry.

Text of the *Introduction*

An issue that has to be dealt with in advance of the main discussion is that of the precise status of the text which is its central concern. Hegel delivered his lecture course on the philosophy of history in the University of Berlin on five occasions in all, from the winter semester of 1822–3 at two-yearly intervals until the winter semester of 1830–1. The versions we have of the basic theoretical component of the lecture course, the *Introduction*, have been compiled partly from his manuscripts and partly from transcripts made by students. No fewer than four editors have worked at the task, each having somewhat different material at their disposal, and each adjusting, arranging, including and omitting in accordance with their own best judgement. They are, with the dates of their editions, Eduard Gans (1837), Karl Hegel (1840), Georg Lasson (1917) and Johannes Hoffmeister (1955). There is much scholarly disagreement over the merits of these alternatives, and, in particular, over the question of which is the most authentic and reliable presentation of what Hegel actually said.[2] Over-simplifying a little, it may be suggested that in practice the significant choice is between Karl Hegel and Hoffmeister. This is reflected in the pattern of the English translations. Karl Hegel's edition is the basis of that made by J. Sibree, as part of his translation of the *Lectures* as a whole, and of those by Robert S. Hartman and Leo Rauch, while H. B. Nisbet has translated Hoffmeister.

It will not be possible to lay out in full and adjudicate the issues at stake in this debate, nor is it necessary for present purposes to do so. The differences between Karl Hegel and Hoffmeister and, hence, their translators, seem reducible to no simple formula that would disclose their underlying principle. All that can be said in general is that there is, as one would expect, very substantial overlapping of content, especially for the manuscript material, with variations in the order of presentation. Hence it is that formulations which occur at a particular point in the one will often appear in an unexpectedly different setting in the other. In addition, Nisbet, following Hoffmeister, offers the more substantial text, containing material not to be found elsewhere. He also confers on the reader, again following Hoffmeister and, ultimately, the example set by Lasson, the benefit of distinguishing typographically between manuscript and transcript sources, with the former in italics. All of the English translations are, however, in current use, and for that reason, if no other, none may be set aside in a work such as is undertaken here. A policy of neutrality will be adopted towards them, as towards their parent editions, and page references will be given, wherever possible, to each of these sources. This should enable users of all the English versions to find their bearings. The translations from the *Introduction*, and indeed the *Lectures* as a whole, that are used in the present work are, however, by its author. This seemed to accord best with the spirit of neutrality. It was in any case required to ensure consistency, a matter of obvious importance where terms with any theoretical weight are concerned.[3]

It is plain that our central concern is with what an earlier commentator on Hegel's philosophy of history has called an 'impure text' (Wilkins 1974: 18). A reasoned case can, nevertheless, be made for taking the text we have seriously, in its two main versions and with all its impurity, and for according it a substantial authority. Readers who do not see the need for such a case, or who would be uninterested in its detail and are willing to accept its conclusion, may, however, wish to omit the rest of this section and go directly to the next. A point to be made by way of background here is that the situation with regard to the philosophy of history is by no means unique in Hegel's work. Much of our information about his thinking in aesthetics, the philosophy of religion and the history of philosophy is similarly derived from published lecture series, also reconstructed from his manuscripts and student transcripts. Yet they are routinely cited and relied on in the secondary literature and without them serious discussion of his views in these areas would be virtually impossible. That would be a high price to pay for an ideal of textual purity, especially if, as will be argued here for the philosophy of history case, it is unnecessary. A further reassuring, if unsurprising, point may be made by way of preliminary. It is that Hegel took very seriously the task of preparing his lecture course and expended his best efforts on it, as his correspondence shows:

> I greatly exerted myself this winter. My lectures on the philosophy of world history have taken up my time and reflection day and night, so that in the end I found my stomach quite upset and my mind quite exhausted.

(HL: 603)

This cry from the heart must tend to confirm the significance of the lectures in Hegel's output and enhance the respect they are due, provided, of course, that we possess a satisfactory statement of their content. To that crucial issue the argument should now turn.

The first step is to note that Hegel's seriousness is reflected in that of his student transcribers in their concern to produce an accurate record. Hence, there are grounds for reposing confidence in the basic transcript material. Lasson's verdict on the notes made by Gustav von Griesheim for the 1822–3 series, the series referred to in Hegel's letter, gives an indication of how things stand in this respect: 'His notes, already used by the first editors, fill two volumes; they are a most painstakingly written, extremely neat and legible fair copy, every line of which bears witness to the diligence of the copyist' (H, 274: 223).

This judgement is endorsed by the editors of the recently published student transcripts for the 1822–3 series. They regard, however, the verbatim record made by Heinrich Hotho even more highly, as being 'more exact and comprehensive in the reproduction of the philosophical train of thought' (VPW: 527). The notes by Friedrich von Kehler are much less detailed, but they too are said to share in the 'surprisingly large measure of agreement' that prevails among the sources (VPW: 528). In the case of von Griesheim and Hotho in particular, the recent editors find a 'wide-ranging agreement' that extends not merely to the division into individual parts, chapters and sections but also to details of expression at the level of words and sentences (VPW: 528). An agreement of this kind between independent sources serves, of course, to lend weight and credibility to each of them. It is strongly encouraging for anyone who proposes to make use of a work drawn in part from such sources.

That the work in question is drawn from them only in part must not be forgotten. Indeed, it is the second major pillar of the present argument. The manuscript content, as revealed by the choice of type-face, comprises in Hoffmeister's edition some two-fifths of the text of the *Introduction*, about seventy pages in all. If to this is added the discussion of the philosophy of history in the *Encyclopaedia* and *Philosophy of Right*, a reasonably substantial body of work of unquestionable authenticity which is directly devoted to this subject will emerge. Moreover, the manuscript element of the *Introduction* suffices of itself to sustain the main weight of the argument and to fix the theoretical character of the whole. It provides the bulk of the passages one would wish to place any reliance on in determining these matters, and everything that is indispensable. Thus, they include, as it is admittedly vital they should, the statement of philosophical presup-positions referred to earlier, a passage that may truly be said to be foundational for the entire work. There is, one should add, nothing in the student transcripts that jars with, or stands significantly apart from, the manuscript content. The one seems rather to support and supplement the other in the most natural and unforced way. So much is this the case that it seems impossible to dissent from the conclusion reached by another commentator: 'I have not been able to discern any *philosophical* difference between what is said in the notes and in the manuscript' (O'Brien 1975: 177n). This circumstance must itself, of course, reflect favourably on the merits of the notes. The task that now presents itself, in the light of all the considerations that have been advanced, is to make the best sense one can of the *Introduction* as a whole, its canonical core and the complementary record provided by the devotion and efficiency of Hegel's students.

Varieties of history

Hegel begins his lecture course by declaring its subject to be 'philo-sophical world history', and goes on to distinguish this history from other kinds which he designates as 'original' and 'reflective'. The latter is then further subdivided. The hallmark of original history, as practised by such figures as Herodotus, Thucydides, Julius Caesar and Cardinal de Retz, is that 'the spirit of the writer and the spirit of the actions he relates are one and the same' (H, 6: 13; M, 12: 2, 4, 4). 'Spirit' (*Geist*) is a term with a rich significance for Hegel, but it will suffice for now, and be justified later, to take up the clue to its meaning he himself offers in speaking in this connection of 'culture (*Bildung*) and consciousness' (H, 8: 14; cf. M, 13: 3, 5, 5). Reflective history is an untidy category, and the explanation Hegel gives of its subdivisions is too sketchy to be entirely clear and satisfying.[4] The general conception may be best understood negatively, by contrast with original history. Its distinctive feature is then the fact that the writer approaches the historical material 'in his own spirit which is different from the spirit of the content itself' (H, 10–11: 16; M, 14: 4, 6, 6). It is this that gives rise to the opportunity and the need for 'reflection'. The contrast is not to be understood as one between a history that is marked by thought and one that somehow or other manages not to be. Indeed, the whole purpose of original history is to redeem what was mere external existence by means of thought, transferring it into 'the realm of spiritual representation (*Vorstellung*)' (H, 4: 12; M, 11: 1, 3, 3). For Hegel, however, as will emerge more fully later, 'reflection' (*Reflexion*), following in his usual manner what is suggested by the etymology, must involve specifically a 'bending back' of thought from its object. Hence, it presupposes just such a distancing of subject and object as is constitutionally present in reflective, and absent in original, history. Reflective history may also be determined negatively in another way, by contrast with what follows it in the sequence. From that standpoint it is marked by a failure to rise to the level of the philosophical understanding with which world history is imbued. To this higher form Hegel quickly turns at the start of the *Introduction*, making it the virtually exclusive object of his attention thereafter, as it must be for the present discussion also. Henceforth, whenever he speaks simply of 'history' it may be assumed to be philosophical world history he has in mind. Thus, it figures as a term of art, a term whose full explication may be said to be the ultimate goal of our inquiry.

The writing, or at any rate advocacy, of philosophical world history, and the construction of philosophies of history to accompany it, were thriving enterprises in the intellectual climate of Hegel's time and place. Indeed, they may be said to have flourished there as never before or since. Hegel's work in the field is the crown and completion of a tradition of German thought whose other major figures are Immanuel Kant, Johann Gottlieb Herder, Johann Gottlieb Fichte, and his own exact, but more precocious, contemporary, Schelling. It may help to bring this tradition into focus if it is considered in relation to the distinction that has become conventional in our own time between 'critical' and 'speculative' philosophy of history. The standardly distinction is understood in the following way. Critical philosophy of history takes for its subject matter 'history' in the sense of the activities and achievements of the historian. It is in essence an inquiry into the kind of truth and objectivity he or she can attain, the logic according to which the inquiry proceeds and the nature of the explanations he or she provides. Thus, it is closely related to the philosophy of science, and, in the Anglo-American philosophical world at least, its defining concerns are often taken to be summed up in the question of whether, and to what extent, history counts as truly scientific. The subject matter of speculative philosophy of history is 'history' conceived as the actual course of events. Its aim is to display whatever meaning or pattern there may be in those events taken as a whole. It attempts, one might say, to reveal the secret of the plot that binds them intelligibly together, the nature of the mechanism through which they unfold and, usually, the conclusion towards which they tend. The attempt is characteristically accompanied by an interest in the question of whether there may be some justificatory purpose at work in them. This question gets its force from the fact that, as it has seemed to very many observers, what the record of events most obviously shows is monstrous and pervasive evil and suffering. It would not be too much to say that the will to redeem these features, and so, as far as possible, to reconcile human beings to their past, and by implication their present, has been the primary impulse of the entire enterprise.

It seems easy to say where Hegel, and the tradition he comes from, should be placed with regard to the distinction between critical and speculative philosophy of history. He belongs by the universal agreement of users of the distinction on the speculative side, usually as the outstanding and exemplary practitioner of the subject. Within the terms of the distinction such a placing is scarcely open to challenge, and is, so far as it goes, a reliable guide to the nature of his achievement. This account of the matter, however, needs to be qualified, or made more complicated, in a couple of respects. To begin with one should not overlook the simple fact that he has some substantive comments to make on the business of being a historian, comments that may thereby be taken as contributing to critical philosophy of history. The first of them is worth noting not for any fresh light it sheds on that business, but for what it sheds on Hegel's own thinking, or at least for its value in dispelling vulgar misconceptions. It is his insistence that history is an empirical inquiry and that this character determines its proper method. 'We have', he warns, 'to take history as it is, we have to proceed historically, empirically' (H, 30: 29; M, 22: 10, 12, 13). The warning is repeated in moving from generalities to particular phenomena. Thus, for instance, what constitutes the distinctive principle of a people must, Hegel declares, 'be approached empirically and demonstrated in historical fashion' (H, 168: 138; M, 87: 64, 79, 68).

In warning that we have to take history as it is, Hegel had wished to contrast his position with the practice of some 'ingenious professional historians'. These historians are, he believes, guilty of precisely what they accuse the philosophers of doing, that is of introducing '*a priori* fictions' into history. An example is the fiction of 'an original primeval people, directly instructed by God, living in perfect insight and wisdom, with a thorough knowledge of all natural laws and spiritual truth' (H, 31: 29; M, 22–3: 10–11, 12–13, 13–14). Here one comes upon the issue of greatest concern to Hegel in this area, an issue posed emphatically in the opening sections of the *Introduction* and recurring periodically thereafter. It is the charge that speculative philosophy 'constructs history *a priori*' (H, 25: 25; cf. H, 31–2: 29–30; H, 168: 139; M, 22: 10,12,13; M, 87 :64, 80, 68). In rebutting it the *Introduction* makes the second, and much more interesting, of its contributions to critical philosophy of history.

For the discussion allows, indeed insists on, what may properly be regarded as a role for the *a priori*, though not that of constructing historical fictions. Thus, it affirms that:

even the ordinary and average historian who perhaps believes and professes that he is merely receptive, merely surrendering himself to the given, is not passive in his thinking and brings his categories with him and sees what is at hand through them.

(H, 31:29; M, 23:11, 13, 14)

A little later Hegel illustrates what he has in mind by identifying the most obvious of these categories as 'importance' and 'unimportance' (H, 34: 31; M, 23: 11, 13, 14). They are essential categories if history is even to begin its task of ordering the vast domain of the past intelligibly, but they are brought to the data, not implicit in them. What is legitimately and indispensably *a priori* are such general categories, while substantive theses concerning, for example, the existence or non-existence of a primeval people lie wholly within the scope of the empirical. In all this Hegel is fully in line with the orthodox stance of later philosophy of science. More specifically, he may be said to anticipate the now commonplace view that inquiry is inherently 'theory-laden' and hence, that pure empirical givenness is a myth.

There is a second, deeper sense in which a simple assignation of Hegel to speculative, as opposed to critical, philosophy of history has to be qualified. It arises from the tendency of his thought to loosen or blur the contrast. This in turn rests on its capacity to subvert the underlying distinction between two meanings of 'history', at least in some measure. Hegel is well aware of, and draws attention to, an ambiguity in the term '*Geschichte*' (history). The term has, he observes, both 'objective' and 'subjective' sides, denoting, on the one hand, historical narrative (*Geschichterzählung*) or *historia rerum gestarum*, and, on the other, historical happenings (*Geschehene*), the actual deeds and events themselves or *res gestae*. He seems encouraged to hold that the two sides are not rigidly and exclusively opposed by his sense of the genius of ordinary language. The union of the two meanings in one word must, he believes, be viewed as belonging to a higher order than that of 'external contingency'. We should rather suppose that historical narrative and historical happenings appear simultaneously in virtue of their 'inner common ground' (H, 164: 135; M, 83: 60, 75, 64). What this ground consists of will have to be considered later. For the present one should merely note that the activity of being a historian and the existence of a subject matter to work on are, in Hegel's view, internally and inextricably connected. The implication that not all of the deeds and events of the human past count as truly 'historical' is one he willingly accepts. The form his acceptance takes, and the manner in which it is worked out, are, once again, matters that will have to be postponed for now. To note the point should, however, serve even at this stage to lend force to the warning that for him 'world history' is a term of art.

The double meaning of 'history' in ordinary usage may be taken as virtually the paradigm of a harmless ambiguity, one that should not give rise to any significant difficulty in practice. Hegel seems at any rate wholly at ease with it, and, while sometimes acknowledging it for working purposes of analysis, is usually content just to exploit the flexibility of the situation. An example at a very general level of his shifting without notice between meanings has already been given in recording the habit of characterising the *Lectures* as involving both 'philosophy of world history' and 'philosophical world history'. In the latter case it is plainly *historia*, the narrative of events, he has in mind. It is equally natural, and reasonable, to suppose that in the former he is essentially concerned with the philosophy of *res gestae*, the 'things done' in history. In relation to it his ambitions turn out to be those he inherited from his predecessors from Kant to Schelling, the ambitions that, as was noted earlier, serve to define speculative philosophy of history. It now seems quite safe to join with conventional opinion in taking him to be the representative figure of this tradition. The distinctive ways in which he represents it, some of which have already been mentioned or hinted at, may be allowed to emerge in the course of the discussion.

Predecessors

Hegel's philosophy of history, as is to be expected, is influenced by and draws on the work of his immediate predecessors. Indeed, it is not hard to find direct precedents there for many of its main contentions (Collingwood 1946: 113–14). The largest presence among these fore-runners is that of Kant, as it may reasonably be said to be for Hegel's philosophy in general. If a single thinker had to be selected for background and contrast in expounding that philosophy, Kant is the natural choice. He is the dominant figure in the German philosophical world of the time, the setter of its agenda and the authority against whom any ambitious philosopher had to turn to assert their own identity. This situation may be readily illustrated from the philosophy of history, though the point of doing so cannot be fully clear until Hegel's own position has been considered in detail. It may help to pave the way for so doing to note that a central theme of it is foreshadowed in Kant's conception of universal history as the development of the rational capacities of the human species (Kant 1991: 42–3). Since reason manifests itself in human life as freedom, it is therefore 'the history of freedom' (ibid.: 227). Moreover, the achievement of freedom takes a distinctively political form for Kant, as it was to do for Hegel: 'The history of the human race as a whole can be regarded as the realisation of a hidden plan of nature to bring about ... [a] perfect political constitution' (ibid, 50). If one looks beyond the overall shape of the story and the manner of its culmination to the processes at work in it, the affinity is equally striking. A clue is given in the reference to the 'hidden' character of nature's plan; hidden, that is to say, from the human agents through whom it is implemented. Nature, or, as Kant says indifferently elsewhere, 'providence', works out of their sight, turning their actual motives and intentions to instruments of its purposes. This, as Kant emphasises, is to make use of base means, 'social incompatibility, enviously competitive vanity, and insatiable desires for possession or even power', for higher ends beyond their compass (ibid.: 45). Here he seems to anticipate the Hegelian notion of the 'cunning of reason'.

None of this is seriously at odds with or diminishes Hegel's true originality. So much is in effect conceded by the critic who has reminded us most sharply of his debts to his predecessors in the philosophy of history: 'he has combined their views with extraordinary skill into a theory so coherent and so unified that it deserves independent consideration as a whole' (Collingwood 1946: 114). The point will stand even if one assumes, as this critic does, that Hegel has taken over the views of others substantially unchanged and only the combination is novel. The assumption is itself, however, quite untenable. In truth, Hegel has so transformed the content of the doctrines in question that the similarities that remain are largely, though not entirely, formal, as the case of Kant will show. For, although Hegel's conception of freedom has plain, and plainly acknowledged, roots in Kant's thought, it also differs significantly in ways that will later be explored. This is true also of the character of the political setting in which freedom is to be realised through history. Moreover, even if one were willing to speak of a cunning of nature or providence in connection with Kant's view, it is by no means to be equated with Hegel's cunning of reason. Apart from all other considerations, this view is itself so lightly sketched as to provide little concrete guidance for any successor. Thus, it is entirely characteristic that Kant should hold that 'we', the philosophical historians, 'are too short-sighted to perceive the hidden mechanism of nature's scheme' (Kant 1991: 52). For better or worse this modest and sober assessment is far removed, as will become abundantly clear, from the spirit of Hegel's approach to such matters.

The basic difference between the philosophies of history of Kant and Hegel lies, however, beyond all variations of detail. It lies in the fact that these philosophies belong within, and depend upon, systematically different framework of thought. Kant and Hegel differ philosophically in quite fundamental respects, in the theory of knowledge, or epistemology, and the theory of being, or ontology. That is to say, they differ in their view of the nature and scope of human knowledge and in their view of what the universe essentially consists in, of what there is. Hegel's constant complaint is that Kant limits our knowledge to appearances, putting the true nature of reality, of 'things-in-themselves', beyond its reach. The complaint is, of course, supported by detailed arguments, but beneath them and pervasively there is a deep impatience and lack of sympathy. Hegel regards Kant's modesty and sobriety as a wholly unnecessary concession to scepticism, a wilful, pusillanimous failure of nerve, almost as a betrayal of philosophy on the part of a great philosopher. There is, Hegel insists, no unknowable realm of 'things-in-themselves' behind the phenomena to which alone we have access. What precisely is at stake in this insistence will become clearer in the course of the discussion. For the present it may serve to capture the tone of Hegel's own approach if one notes how the *Introduction* declares, taking advantage of St Paul in an uncharacteristic moment, that 'the spirit leads into truth, knows all things, and penetrates even the depths of the Godhead' (H, 40–1: 36; M, 26–7: 14, 16, 17; cf. Corinthians 2: 10).

The difference in epistemological ambition between Kant and Hegel is easy to illustrate from the philosophy of history. Kant regards the central principle that history is the development of human rationality and freedom as not itself capable of theoretical proof, and, hence, as not, properly speaking, an item of knowledge at all. Instead it is an assumption urged upon us by what might be termed practical considerations. For without it the ways of nature or providence cannot be supposed to be justified and we might 'turn away in revulsion' from the spectacle history affords of folly and wickedness (Kant 1991: 53). To avoid such an outrage to our moral sense we must adopt the central principle to regulate our thinking, even though we cannot know it to be true. Hegel is content with no such qualified satisfaction of the primary impulse of speculative philosophy of history. For him nothing needs to proceed in the Kantian 'as if' mode. The central principle, as he understands it, can, he is convinced, be properly established by reason, and counts as wholly genuine knowledge. This contrast gives a radically different significance to his philosophy of history in general, one that ensures its distinctive identity and true independence of its great precursor.

Structure of the inquiry

This book consists of two parts with a bridging section, a structure suggested by the way the text of the *Introduction* is arranged. The first part deals with the philosophical groundwork, the meaning and derivation of the theses that, we are told at the outset, philosophy brings to historical understanding. It offers, as one might suppose it must, an account of Hegel's chief metaphysical notions, of 'reason' and 'the Idea' and their religious representation as 'God', of 'the concept' and of 'spirit' and of the concept of spirit; that is to say, 'freedom'. It is here that the outline of Hegel's metaphysics referred to earlier is to be found. There follows the bridging discussion that tries to connect in general terms the metaphysics with the interpretation of the course of world history, an interpretation in which that course essentially figures as the progress of the consciousness and of the realisation of freedom. In the second part of the book the influence of the actual sequence of topics followed in the *Introduction* is more directly evident. It is, as will appear, a rationally intelligible sequence, thereby giving support to the view that the work we have exhibits a certain formal unity and design. The first topic to be considered is what Hegel terms the 'means' of world history, the activities driven by 'passion' of human beings, with those he declares to be the 'world historical individuals' as particularly important and instructive exemplars. The discussion goes on to focus the kind of 'dialectic' Hegel discerns in history in terms of the device of 'the cunning of reason'. It then turns to consider the 'material' of history, the peoples and states in and through which spirit works its passage to freedom. The distinctive features of this achievement, the lineaments of the society of freedom, are examined with particular attention to the question, much discussed in recent years, of whether Hegel is committed to holding that history has an end, or that it has already ended. Finally, the inquiry draws out the implications of Hegel's own description of his philosophy of history as a 'theodicy', a 'justification of God'. It concludes by asking what it could mean for readers of Hegel today to come to accept the forms of understanding his philosophy of history embodies. Kierkegaard famously observed, with Hegel in mind, that 'In relation to their systems most systematisers are like a man who builds an enormous castle and lives in a shack close by'. The philosophy of history must be the core of Hegel's defence to this brilliantly unfair charge, for it is, once it is seen in its true character and dimensions, the indispensable key to understanding how his system can be inhabited.

PART 1

PHILOSOPHICAL FOUNDATIONS

Chapter 2

Presuppositions

The philosophical framework of the *Introduction* is composed of a relatively small group of elements. Those that must figure in the basic list are 'reason', 'the Idea', God', 'the concept, 'spirit' and 'freedom'. They have this status because each seems at different times to be cast in the role of the central, organising category of the philosophy of history. For each is taken in turn as identifying the subject responsible for world historical development, or the object that undergoes it, or both. These identifications are made in a series of striking pronouncements.

> reason rules the world, and ... world history has therefore been rational in its course.
>
> (H, 28: 27; M, 9: 11, 12, 20)

> In world history we have to deal with the Idea as it manifests itself in the element of human will, of human freedom ...
>
> (H, 83: 71; cf. M, 38: 23, 29, 26)

History is the unfolding of God's nature in a particular, determinate element …

(H, 48: 42; cf. M, 28: 15, 18, 18)

[In world history] the concept in general … determines itself, posits determinations in itself and then sublates (*aufhebt*) them …

(H, 167: 138; M, 86: 63, 78–9, 67)

World history in general is the exposition (*Auslegung*) of spirit in time …

(H, 154: 128; M, 96–7: 72, 87, 75)

World history is the progress of the consciousness of freedom …

(H, 63: 54; M, 32: 19, 24, 22)

To grasp these propositions with their implications and interconnections is to grasp the basic structure of Hegel's philosophy of history. Much then remains to be done by way of assimilating its detailed content, but a vital step will have been taken. Showing how to take it is the task of the first part of the present inquiry.

The best starting point is clearly indicated in the *Introduction*. When it formulates the 'only thought' that philosophy brings to the understanding of history, it does so in terms of 'reason'. This formulation, together with the key proposition about reason cited above, occurs in a passage of great interest and importance from the opening pages of the work. It may truly be said to be foundational for the work as a whole, and the discussion will come back to it frequently. For convenience, and to mark its special significance, it should, in spite of its length, be quoted in full.

The only thought which philosophy brings with it is the simple thought of reason, that reason rules the world, and that world history has therefore been rational in its course. This conviction and insight is a presupposition in regard to history as such. In philosophy itself, however, it is not a presupposition; it is proved in philosophy through speculative cognition that reason – and we can stand by this term without considering its connection and relation with God more closely – is substance as well as infinite power, that it is itself the infinite material of all natural and spiritual life, as well as the infinite form, the actualisation of itself as content. It is the substance, that through which and in which all reality has its being and subsistence. It is the infinite power, for reason is not so powerless as to arrive at what is only an ideal, an ought, outside reality, who knows where, indeed as something particular in the heads of a few people. It is the infinite content, the essentiality and truth of everything, and is itself the stuff which it works up through its own activities. Unlike finite activity, it does not require the condition of external materials, of given means from which to get its nourishment and the objects of its activity. It lives in itself, and is itself the material upon which it works. Just as it is its own presupposition and its end is the absolute final end, so it is itself the activation and the bringing forth from inwardness into appearance, not only in the natural universe but also in the spiritual, in world history. That this Idea is the true, the eternal, simply the powerful, that it reveals itself in the world, and that nothing is revealed there except it, its glory and honour – this, as we have said, is what was proved in philosophy and is here presupposed as proved.

(H, 28–9: 27–8; M, 20–1: 9–10, 11, 12)

This is an exceedingly rich passage which will reveal its full meaning only gradually. There is, however, a simplifying and clarifying step it points towards that may be taken straight away. The pointer lies in the way it invokes the first three of the basic elements listed above. Its invocation of the Idea seems almost a rhetorical variation on that of reason, so similar are the roles assigned to them. This is fully in keeping with their relationship throughout the *Introduction* and elsewhere in Hegel's work. The most succinct statement is in fact to be found elsewhere, in the remark that the Idea is 'the proper philosophical meaning of "reason"' (EL: 288). This seems to license the complete substitutability in philosophical usage of the one for the other. Here one should note also that the *Introduction* passage sidesteps any closer consideration of the relationship between reason and God. Yet once again a shortcut may be taken, this time by referring to the assertion later in the work that 'God and the nature of his will are one and the same, what we call in philosophy the Idea' (H, 52: 46). There has now emerged a kind of triple identity, in which 'the Idea' figures as the philosophically favoured term for reason and for God. With this identity one reaches rock bottom, the deepest layer of thought, in the intellectual scheme of the *Introduction*.

The chief occupants of that layer are the various propositions advanced initially in the foundational passage in the name of 'reason'. They affirm that reason is substance and infinite power, the infinite content and the infinite form, the essentiality and truth of everything, the absolute final end. It would be hard surely to exceed the metaphysical sweep and boldness of these presuppositions of understanding world history. Indeed, they might well be thought to constitute the central theses of Hegel's metaphysics. At any rate it appears that, as it were, some vital preliminaries to the action of the *Introduction* have already taken place off-stage. They will have to be recapitulated if that action is to be fully intelligible. In particular, one must ask how precisely it is that the propositions listed above are proved through speculative cognition.

Logic of consciousness

In trying to answer this question a particular work has a special claim on one's attention. For, if the kinds of arguments now being sought are not to be found in the *Phenomenology of Spirit*, one might well despair of finding them anywhere. Its standing in the matter seems to be endorsed explicitly by what Hegel says of it in the 'Introduction' to the *Science of Logic*.

In the *Phenomenology of Spirit* I have exhibited consciousness in its movement onwards from the first immediate opposition of itself and its object (*Gegenstandes*) to absolute knowing. The path of this movement goes through every form (*alle Formen*) of the *relation of consciousness to the object* (*Objecte*) and has the concept of science for its result. This concept therefore ... cannot be justified in any other way than by this emergence in consciousness, all the forms (*Gestalten*) of which are resolved into this concept as into their truth. ... The concept of pure science and its dedication is therefore presupposed in the present work in so far as the *Phenomenology of Spirit* is nothing other than the deduction of it. ... Thus pure science presupposes liberation from the opposition of consciousness. It contains *thought in so far as this is just as much the object (Sache) in its own self, or the object (Sache) in its own self in so far as it is equally pure thought*.

(WLI: 42–3; SL: 48–9)

This is a dense passage, but with a little patience it should be possible to get it to yield up its main message. The *Phenomenology* is, it appears, essentially concerned with the relationship of consciousness and object. It arrives at a particular view of the relationship, a view referred to, seemingly indifferently, as 'absolute knowing' and as 'the concept of science'. This result is achieved by an exhaustive enumeration of alternatives: the path to it goes through 'every form' of the relationship. The justification of it is identical with, 'nothing other than', the phenomenological movement of its 'emergence in consciousness'. Thus, to grasp the justification is to climb for oneself what Hegel refers to elsewhere in the *Phenomenology* as the 'ladder' to the standpoint of science or absolute knowing which that work provides (PS: 14). The climber is thereby liberated from the opposition of consciousness and object in coming to see that its two poles are really one. Thought emerges as the object in its own self and the object is equally pure thought. This outcome is what Hegel standardly refers to as the 'identity of subject and object'. The *Phenomenology* grounds the identity by showing that all conceptions that treat the object as merely external to, and other than, the subject are untenable and have successively to be abandoned. This deduction of the concept of pure science is presupposed in the *Science of Logic* and, one may add, in the Logic that deals with the same content in the first volume of the *Encyclopaedia*. Thus, the detailed exposition of Hegel's system in these works begins with a movement of thought that is curiously analogous to what one finds in the *Introduction*, a displacing elsewhere of responsibility for justifying the basic premises of the discussion. As the *Science of Logic* makes plain, it is ultimately displaced on to the *Phenomenology*. There, it appears, is where all the ladders start.

The way in which the *Phenomenology* achieves its results should be looked at more closely. Its significance for the philosophy of history is twofold. There is its vital role in proving the presuppositions of the entire enterprise, and, equally vital, its role in the elaboration of the detailed content. For it enshrines a logic of consciousness that, suitably enriched and expanded, will provide the key to understanding the course of world history as conceived by Hegel. To make a start in exploring this aspect, one should note that the progress to absolute knowing in the *Phenomenology* has its own inner dynamic, or – in his distinctive language – dialectic, and needs no input from without: 'Since what consciousness examines is its own self, all that is left for us to do is simply to look on' (PS: 54). It is not 'we', the philosophers or phenomenological observers, who refute the pretensions of the successive shapes of consciousness: in true Hegelian manner they refute themselves. They prove to be unsustainable by their own immanent standards, those implied in, or projected by, their self-understanding. An illustration may help to focus this conception.

The starting point of the entire process, the 'first immediate opposition' of consciousness and object, is called by Hegel 'sense certainty' (PS: 58–66). This is supposed to be immediate in the sense of not being mediated by any moment of reflection. It steps forward as the most direct, purely receptive kind of sensory awareness of particular things. When, however, sense certainty tries to meet the minimal requirement for knowing an object, the ability to identify what is known, it cannot do so in its own terms. Instead it is obliged to identify the object not as a bare particular but as an object of a certain kind. It is obliged, that is to say, to apprehend it as an instance of what Hegel, following the philosophical tradition, terms a 'universal'. The idea of a universal is the idea of whatever can take instances while retaining its identity throughout all of them and being definable independently of any particular ones. Its entry on the scene here spells the doom of any claim to pure sensory immediacy. Sense certainty as direct appropriation of particulars turns out to be incoherent and is subverted from within: 'So it is fact the universal that is the true [content] of sense certainty' (PS: 60). This outcome prepares the way for the next stage of the dialectic. The natural way to grasp the object in the guise of a universal is to see it as a thing possessed of properties. For properties – redness, roundness and so on – are paradigmatically universals, ranging indifferently over their instances. The apprehension of the object as a thing with properties is called by Hegel 'perception'. At the next dialectical stage this shape of consciousness too will examine itself and, finding itself wanting, make way in turn for its successor.

This illustration of phenomenological method has another feature of general significance. It lies in the idea that the outcome of one dialectical stage paves the way directly for the next. Thus, the collapse of sense certainty enforces a lesson about the role of universals that is then taken up in perception. In Hegel's technical language, one may say that the negation of each stage is a *determinate* negation. It never leaves one with mere vacancy or variousness but with a quite specific content that furnishes the means of continuing the story in a particular way. The *Phenomenology* insists strongly on this feature:

> The necessary progression and interconnection of the forms of the unreal consciousness will by itself bring to pass the *completion* of the series ... [When] the result is conceived as it is in truth, namely, as a *determinate* negation, a new form has thereby immediately arisen, and in the negation the transition is made through which the progress through the complete series of forms comes about of itself.
>
> (PS: 50–1)

To the themes of immanent self-movement and the completeness of the series of transformations, this passage adds that of the necessity of the transforming movement. It is a theme with a central place in the dialectical procedure. Thus, the surrender to the life of the object is said to amount to the same thing as 'confronting and expressing its inner necessity' (PS: 32). Determinacy of negation is clearly essential if such claims are to have any force. For it serves to ensure the element of inner connectedness and continuity in which, in principle, the notion of necessity can take root. The issues at stake are no less vital for the philosophy of history. Thus, in the *Introduction* the 'inner or conceptual necessity' by which historical transitions are governed is strongly emphasised (H, 72: 62; M, 104: 78, 94, 81). It is, therefore, a topic that will recur in the course of this discussion.

The character of at least the first stage of Hegel's foundational argument should now be clear in broad outline. The exposition of his system presupposes the standpoint of absolute knowing or pure science, as deduced in the *Phenomenology*. The deduction starts from the 'first immediate opposition' of consciousness and object, and goes through the inner contradictions of all such oppositions until the series is exhausted. What results is the overcoming of opposition in the identity of consciousness and object. The authority of this argument rests on certain key assumptions. It depends in the first place on the assumption that the starting point has been correctly identified, that sense certainty really is the primitive relationship of consciousness and object. Second, it requires the truth of the contention that, once the movement gets under way, the forms of consciousness succeed one another of determinate necessity. These conditions are in turn needed to ensure that, provided the movement flows unrestrictedly, the series of forms is complete and nothing of significance is left outside. An independent study of the *Phenomenology* would be needed to establish that all of these requirements have indeed been satisfied. The present discussion will largely have to be content with revealing the strategy of the argument. There are, however, two aspects of it that should be investigated further. They correspond to its twofold significance for the philosophy of history. It has to be asked how the strategy deals with the spectre of scepticism, a question that must arise for any foundational arguments in philosophy. The second aspect arises from the possibility that in due course the logic of the phenomenological process will have to be invoked to explicate Hegel's historical dialectic. With that in view, one needs to look more closely at the source of the abounding and unquenchable energy of the movement.

Scepticism

Both aspects may be introduced by noting some dramatic claims made in the *Phenomenology*. Hegel tells us there that the path taken by 'the natural consciousness which presses forward to true knowledge' can be regarded as 'the pathway of *doubt*, or more precisely as the way of despair' (PS: 49). The first of these descriptions raises the question of scepticism, while the second raises that of how the natural consciousness finds the strength to persevere with its journey. Hegel goes on at once to say that what happens on the journey is not 'what is ordinarily understood when the word "doubt" is used: shilly-shallying about this or that presumed truth, followed by a return to that truth again'. On the contrary, the path is, he assures us, one of a 'thorough-going scepticism' (PS: 49–50). At this point one seems to be on familiar epistemological ground, inescapably part of the landscape of modern philosophy since Descartes. Hegel's relation to that ground may suggest another way of characterising his foundational argument. To develop the suggestion it may be helpful to consider how he introduces the claims that have just been cited. He does so by observing that, on the phenomenological path, natural consciousness will show itself 'not to be real knowledge'. Since, however, 'it directly takes itself to be real knowledge', this path has a 'negative significance' for it, counting for it as the loss of its own 'self' and of its 'truth' (PS: 49). Hence it is that the path is one of doubt and despair.

For present purposes the significant assertion is that natural consciousness takes itself to be real knowledge. This sense of itself is crucial for dialectical movement. If it were to be lost, one pole of the contradictions that fuel that movement would fall away, and it must cease. This should become clearer if one tries to express the form of the incoherence that emerges to crown the episode illustrated above. It would have to be in some such terms as the following: 'There is knowledge, but sense certainty, or perception, is not it'. That 'there is knowledge' is the key to the entire structure. Thus, the scepticism involved is plainly some way from being 'thoroughgoing', as the tradition of modern philosophy would understand that label. It is indeed permitted to destroy 'this or that presumed truth' without shilly-shallying or any subsequent return to it. What it does not, and cannot, do however, is to impugn the general conviction of the possession of truth: rather it is assumed. At every stage a truly thoroughgoing scepticism that could challenge that conviction has to be set aside. This is not to employ such scepticism, still less to refute it, but simply to repudiate it and to set one's course by the repudiation.

It should be possible to generalise the point. A chain of reasoning draws its strength from that of the individual links and cannot be categorially stronger than they are. If the individual stages of Hegel's argument work only by bracketing scepticism, such bracketing may be said to be a condition of the argument as a whole. This is so at any rate if the brackets are never removed in some decisive settling of accounts with the sceptical challenge. That encounter does not take place in the *Phenomenology*, nor does it, one might add, anywhere else in Hegel's writings. Scepticism is in one sense of great importance for him, and his work may be seen as a systematic response to it. The awareness of it as a limiting possibility hovers perpetually on the margins of the discussion. Unlike Descartes, however, and perhaps instructed by what he took to be the failure of Descartes' programme, he does not seek to meet it head-on and demolish it by argument. His strategy is just to remove it to the margins of discourse, to discount it as an option for serious thought. In carrying this out, scepticism comes to be variously represented as pointless, empty, barren, tedious and in poor intellectual taste. It comes, that is to say, to be the target of Hegel's ample powers of rhetoric. The results do not, however, amount to anything like a formal refutation.

At this point the character of Hegel's foundational project may be reformulated. The project is, it now appears, one of persuading us that his position is the only feasible alternative to scepticism. In phenomenological mode the message is that one either rejects the very possibility of human knowledge or sets out on a course that leads to absolute knowing. Less phenomenologically, it may be put in hypothetical terms: 'if there is any knowledge, there is absolute knowing'. Whether Hegel actually succeeds in demonstrating the truth of this hypothesis in detail is once again a question that would require a full-scale study of the *Phenomenology* to settle. For the present what matters is the logical form of the argument on which the presuppositions of the *Introduction* are founded. Providing any such foundations is a hazardous enterprise, as the history of philosophy will testify. Yet, Hegel's approach has certain advantages. The robustness of one's conclusions in philosophy, as that history also shows, is, in general, inversely related to the degree of certainty with which one is entitled to hold them. Hegel's position may surely be said to represent a defensible point of trade-off between these variables. It shows intellectual economy in its ability to dispense with large, contestable assumptions. Yet it avoids the opposite trap of professing to offer something for nothing, complete theoretical security at no cost. It makes plain that there is a price to be paid. Given that scepticism remains an unrefuted, if merely formal, possibility, it is that of renouncing any prospect of an irresistible proof of one's central philosophical theses. Hegel's approach seeks to show that the price is modest and would be paid by any reasonable person, indeed by anyone who is not already a committed sceptic, if there are any. To put aside the essentially non-serious option of thoroughgoing scepticism and take up philosophy is to embark on a path that leads to the standpoint of absolute knowing.

The second aspect to be considered comes into view when one asks how it is that the traveller on the way to despair, the subject consciousness, finds the strength to complete the journey in spite of the relentless capsizing of all the hopes reposed in the successive forms. What makes it credible, or even intelligible, that, so to speak, it simply picks itself up and carries on each time? It seems that one has to postulate some kind of aspiration to higher levels of consciousness that nothing can extinguish. This is what Hegel refers to in the *Phenomenology* as an 'instinct of reason' and as an 'instinct to get to the concept' (PS: 149, 463). It is the factor which the *Introduction* generously characterises as a 'universal unconscious instinct of humankind' (H, 90: 76; M, 45: 31, 39, 32). The idea that reason has its unconscious and instinctual side is entirely characteristic of Hegel. Hence the need to explain how rational and, what are usually held to be, quite irrational or non-rational elements come together in his philosophy of history will have eventually to be confronted. The immediate effect is to introduce an element of will and feeling into the dialectics of the *Phenomenology*. This element soon forces its way to the surface once the opening arguments are out of the way. The dialectic changes from one of pure cognition involving familiar epistemic forms to one of 'desire', and seems for a time to lead outside epistemology, as traditionally conceived, altogether. When desire comes to be focused on another consciousness, which takes on the role of object, the path to absolute knowing begins to assume an interpersonal dimension and to open up in the direction of human society and history. This is, however, to anticipate. What has to be noted at present is the need to assume some rooted and enduring striving towards the light if the subject consciousness is to persist on its way of despair.

Idealist metaphysics

This reconstruction of Hegel's foundational argument may now be said to have arrived at the standpoint of absolute knowing. The next step is from there to the content of his metaphysics, the immediate ground for his philosophy of history. In characterising that content a number of familiar terms almost unavoidably suggest themselves. Most obviously, one may characterise it, as Hegel does himself, as 'idealism'. This is, it might be supposed, an appropriate label for a philosophy that takes 'the Idea' to be what is truly real. Moreover, it will not mislead, provided one remembers that it is 'objective', and not 'subjective', idealism that is in question. Hegel's idealism is the doctrine that whatever there is, all that has objective existence – and including for this purpose the knowing subject – is in a sense that it is the task of the present discussion to uncover, ideal or rational. It is not the doctrine that the existing world is somehow constituted, and has its reality conferred, by the knowing subject. It may help to clarify matters if one adds that, thus understood, idealism is a form of what may be called, in a surely central use of an admittedly slippery term, 'realism'. For it is committed to the existence of a reality that is fully independent of what is known or believed about it by consciousness. To be an idealist in this sense is indeed to take a step beyond the bare standpoint of absolute knowing, to give a particular interpretation to the metaphysical insight it discloses.

What that standpoint discloses is the identity of subject and object as the outcome of a process in which all attempts to conceive them otherwise have foundered in incoherence. Thus, to accept the phenomenological deduction is to be committed to monism; that is to the view that the universe, the totality of subjects and objects, comprises just one kind of basic stuff or, in metaphysical language, 'substance'. Thus, for instance, an ontological dualism of mind and matter is thereby excluded. This position does not as yet, however, necessarily yield idealism. A materialist monism seems in principle to be just as eligible. Hence, one might conclude, anachronistically in terms of Hegel but making the point of principle, that consciousness is itself but a brain process, a configuration like everything else, though no doubt extraordinarily complex, of purely physical elements. In fact, however, Hegel shows no inclination whatever to take materialism seriously as an option in philosophy. This is scarcely surprising in view of the philosophical tradition he inherited and in certain essentials never ceased to accept. The key figures in that tradition are Descartes and Kant. It had, ever since Descartes' discovery that what is most immune to sceptical doubt is his own existence as a thinking thing, focused resolutely on the primacy of the knowing consciousness. Hence, it seems inevitable that in Hegel's version the essential nature of that consciousness should pervade and fix the character of the whole. The founding argument of the *Phenomenology* shows that the only tenable epistemology takes the knower and the known to be consubstantial. The common substance of the worlds of nature and of spirit, it now appears, must in some sense be mental or ideal: just as thought 'constitutes the substance of external things, so it is also the universal substance of what is spiritual' (EL: 57).

The argument has now arrived on the ground staked out in the foundational passage of the *Introduction*. In particular, it should be clear why Hegel can assert that substance is to be identified with the Idea or reason. His conception of substance is inherited from the philosophical tradition. Thus, Descartes had declared that 'we can mean by *substance* nothing other than a thing existing in such a manner that it has need of no other thing in order to exist'. The inference he draws is also fully acceptable to Hegel: 'There can indeed be only one substance conceived as needing absolutely no other thing in order to exist; namely, God' (Descartes 1970: 192). The distinctive way in which Hegel interprets this doctrine will emerge in the course of the discussion. For the present one should merely note that the universal common substance that grounds the identity of subject and object, thought and being, is divine as well as rational and ideal. It may also be well to take a hint from Descartes' sense of God as needing 'absolutely' no other in order to complete the characterisation of Hegel's ontological ground. In addition to reason, the Idea and God, he routinely refers to 'the absolute' in this connection (e.g., H, 126: 106; H, 146: 178; H, 182: 150). The appropriateness of the term should now be evident. Substance, 'that through which and in which all reality has its being and subsistence', is 'absolute' just in the sense that there is nothing outside it to which it could possibly be 'relative'. It is fully self-sufficient, existing unqualified and undetermined by anything other than itself. At least half of the meaning of Hegel's idealism is constituted by the thesis that this absolute substance is reason or the Idea.

Double meanings

There is a final step to be taken if idealism is to be a philosophically fertile position. Its character can be indicated here only in schematic terms. The identity of thought and being must, if it is to be a substantial thesis, be taken as implying a structural congruence, and so the possibility of mapping one dimension in terms of the other. More concretely stated, it signifies that what we are obliged of conceptual necessity to think must be true of the world too. The responsibility for working systematically through what we are obliged to think belongs to logic. Its task is to reveal and work through the succession of forms that thought must assume when it commits itself to unrestricted development. The premise of identity, which, Hegel assures us, it presupposes, serves to guarantee that reality cannot fail to mesh with, and still less run counter to, its deliverances. Thus, he can assert that 'the true objectivity of thinking consists in this: that thoughts are not merely our thoughts, but at the same time the *In-itself* (*Ansich*) of things and of whatever else is objective' (EPW 1: 116; EL: 83). Seen in this way, logic is also ontology, a general theory of what there is. Hence, Hegel's two major works on the subject take the form, as he frequently reminds us, of a series of definitions of the absolute, from Being as the most abstract and least adequate to the Idea as the concrete culmination of the series (EL: 135, 139, 158, 170, 175, 237, 257, 272, 286). Such a logic, he declares, takes the place of the 'former metaphysics', the metaphysics that was demolished by Kant's critical philosophy. A detailed examination of this logical–ontological project lies beyond our present scope. There is, however, an implication of it that should be noted for its bearing on our understanding of the basic categories of Hegel's philosophy of history.

It is in virtue of his fundamental project that these categories are endowed with a 'double aspect', at once 'objective' and subjective'. They figure both as concepts of 'a type or grade of object' and as concepts of 'a stage of knowing', as determinations alike of thought and of being (Royce 1901: 456). Thus, to take a central case, the double aspect of 'the dialectical' is proclaimed as follows: 'It is in general the principle of all motion, of all life and of all activation in the actual world. Equally, the dialectical is also the soul of all genuinely scientific cognition' (EL: 128–9).

The dialectical is, it appears, the dynamic principle both of the actual world and of all genuine knowledge of that world. In a similar way the categories listed earlier as comprising the philosophical framework of the *Introduction* serve to identify both the organising elements of historical knowledge and the forces that drive the actual processes of history. It should be added that, while some are more or less evenly balanced or neutral between their objective and subjective sides, others tend naturally, as it were, to one or the other. They present themselves as primarily either 'categories of fact' or 'categories of knowledge' (Royce 1901: 456). Moreover, the need to face two ways at once, or tread a tightrope between two spheres of reference, places considerable strain on Hegel's language. The result for many of his readers has been a sense of pervasive ambiguity and tolerance of ambiguity. Matters are not helped by the fact that in this regard, as in others, Hegel is by no means adept at signalling his intentions. He tends rather to shift back and forth with little or no warning between objective and subjective forms of discourse. This is one of the factors that make the reading of him an exercise calling for more than usual alertness. It should already be clear, however, how one might hold that ultimately the system is not ambiguous. The two sides are but aspects of a unitary whole, alternative facets of a coherent vision of the unity of thought and being. A proper vindication of this claim must, however, await the working out of our inquiry.

Chapter 3

Subject and infinite power

The justification of the theses about reason which philosophy brings to the study of history is by no means complete. Indeed, as hinted earlier, it may be said to have reached only the halfway stage. What have so far been reconstructed are the arguments to ground the conception of reason as substance, and, hence, as the infinite, that is to say absolute and unlimited, material and content. What remains to be established is its role as infinite power and the infinite form that activates the content. A starting point is provided by a remark in the *Phenomenology*: 'In my view, which can be justified only by the exposition of the system itself, everything turns on grasping and expressing the True, not only as *Substance* but equally as *Subject*' (PS: 9–10). The remaining task, it might be said, is one of demonstrating that reason, 'the truth of everything', is subject, as well as substance. This, as the remark in the *Phenomenology* suggests, is for Hegel what is distinctive in his way of grasping and expressing 'the true'. Substance is, after all, a central category of the traditional metaphysics, and his understanding of it as rational or ideal may, broadly speaking, be said to be shared with many thinkers in the tradition. His individual contribution consists, in its self-understanding, in the doctrine of reason as subject. This doctrine is, however, the site of the oldest and most intractable disagreement concerning the interpretation of his thought. In view of the crucial importance of the debate for the philosophy of history in particular, it is one in which the present inquiry can scarcely avoid taking sides. No progress can be made in explicating that philosophy without declaring, and attempting to vindicate, where one stands on the issues at stake in it. This is a nettle that simply has to be grasped.

The obvious way to fix the issues is by invoking a contrast between a 'transcendent' and an 'immanent' reading. The alternatives present themselves in these terms for all the basic ontological categories that help to form the groundwork of the philosophy of history. In order to do full justice to the side of the debate which will not ultimately be taken here, they will be developed initially with reference to God. It may be in any case that the simplest, most direct, way of grasping the absolute as subject is in terms of the notion of a transcendent deity. This is God as an autonomous, personal being, distinct from, superior to, and in no way dependent on, the created world, the God of traditional theism. In the alternative view, God's existence is immanent within, indeed is constituted by the domains of nature and human society, and has no reality apart from them. Such a view tends naturally towards pantheism; that is, the doctrine that God is identical with the universe, conceived not as a mere aggregate of particulars but as an impersonal, unified totality. In so far as Hegel adopts this position he will be taking the universe as such to be the ultimate ontological subject. For such a conception to have any relevance or authority for his philosophy of history, it would, in ways that will shortly emerge, have to be mediated by spirit.

The disagreement sketched above has its origins in the earliest responses of Hegel's contemporaries to his work, and it shows no sign of being laid finally to rest in our own time. As might be expected in such circumstances, both sides can appeal to seemingly authentic textual support. Hence, the debate can be sustained indefinitely on a diet of suitable quotations. It is also only to be expected that some critics should conclude that Hegel is systematically ambiguous on the key issues, and that no unitary reading of him is really possible. This is a conclusion that will be resisted in what follows. It will not be possible, however, within the confines of the present inquiry, to provide anything like a full survey of the arguments on each side of the debate. The question of knock-down proof either way can, in any case, scarcely arise, given the nature of the textual appearances. Nevertheless, an attempt will be made here to show that the balance of argument, of considerations capable of determining an unbiased intellect, favours the immanent view. That weighting, it will be contended, is especially persuasive for anyone whose primary concern is to do justice to Hegel's philosophy of history.

Preliminary observations

There are, to begin with, some factors which, though not, objectively speaking, of great moment, have undoubtedly influenced Hegel's readers. Among such influences may be cited a concern for his enduring relevance and reputation. A system of thought that depends crucially on a transcendent personal deity can scarcely hope, it may be supposed, to engage with the central concerns of contemporary philosophy. It is not by any means the case that all serious thinkers have abandoned belief in such a being. Their religious views are generally, however, no longer required to be integrated with, and help to determine, their work in philosophy. At a different level rather similar influences affect those who hold that Hegel's philosophy of history might yield a theoretical framework within which the historical events of our own time might be situated and understood. Such a project seems wholly in the spirit of his own attitude to current affairs and his constant concern for the empirical dimension of his thought. These matters will come up for more sustained discussion later. For the present it suffices to note that, if the Hegelian scheme has to depend on the irruptions into human history of a superhuman subject, the attempt to construe world events in the light of it is not likely to be widely persuasive. These are, of course, not very telling considerations in an argument about the merits of theoretical alternatives. There is, after all, nothing that guarantees Hegel's enduring significance for philosophy and for historical understanding. If it cannot be demonstrated on the basis of the best available reading of his work, that, one would have to say, would be just too bad. It is natural, however, that sympathetic readers should seek an interpretation of it which would avoid such a conclusion.

There is another line of thought that bears with similar weight on our concerns. It starts by observing that a metaphysics of transcendence tends to drain the philosophy of history of even partial autonomy, and hence, of much of its interest and significance. The court of appeal on all problems that arise within it will lie ultimately in the workings of an irresistible will that shapes human history to its own preformed ends. There will, of course, be issues that arise over the mediations linking that will to the actual course of events, but these will be essentially of a technical nature. In principle, the answer to all philosophical questions will be known already, derived from a single, totalising principle of explanation. An immanent approach, by contrast, leaves the philosophy of history with everything to do, using only the indigenous resources of the human world. It is then a rich and complex subject, not the mere outpost of a metaphysical empire in which all explanatory energy is concentrated at the centre. None of this, however, can be in any way decisive, not even if it could be shown that the immanent approach is virtually a condition of the possibility of studies such as the present. It remains the case that the mere wish to exhibit the philosophy of history as a spacious domain, teeming with its own distinctive philosophical problems, should not be allowed to infect the interpretation of Hegel's ontology.

A final preliminary observation has to be made. It is to suggest that there is an asymmetry of perspectives so far as making sense of the textual evidence is concerned. Such asymmetry is often thought to offer a way of ranking interpretative possibilities in order of rational preference. The contention in the present case is that from the standpoint of immanence one can situate and account for, in a way that is not possible in reverse, the evidence favouring its rival. Here one needs to invoke the fact, referred to earlier, of the difficulty, indeed precariousness, of Hegel's personal situation in the final period in Berlin. This showed itself in, for instance, his vulnerability to the charge of pantheism, a charge virtually indistinguishable from atheism in the eyes of his enemies at Court. If his actual metaphysical beliefs were incompatible with Christian orthodoxy it would, nevertheless, not be hard to see why, in the circumstances of the time, he should seek in some degree to placate the orthodox. If, on the other hand, he really did believe in a transcendent personal deity, it seems almost inexplicable that he should lay an elaborate trail of materials for a radically non-theistic interpretation of his system. He might surely have been content to be the official philosopher, the Aquinas as it were, of Lutheranism, and we would not then have the troubled legacy we do. It has to be admitted that considerations of this kind lead easily into well-trodden and unrewarding areas of debate concerning his alleged opportunism and time-serving. Without wishing to take that path, one might still allow a sense of the background sketched here to inform in some measure the attempt to evaluate the textual evidence. To that crucial task the discussion should now turn.

The claim that will be advanced is that the immanent view should be judged, just on the basis of that evidence, to have the better of things, both, as it were, quantitatively and qualitatively. This is, and must be, the core of the case for it. The correctness of the claim will emerge only in the long run, in the course of the discussion as a whole. It may be useful, however, to offer, as part of what has to be vindicated, a preliminary general characterisation of the evidence falling on each side. For transcendence there are various individually striking but relatively isolated formulations of a programmatic kind whose programme is never carried through in substance and detail by Hegel. They are couched overwhelmingly in the language of religious representations rather than of speculative thought. On the other side there is a more numerous, more theoretically infused and weighted, more integrally related, set of propositions. They seem to testify to a ramified logical structure, already visible in part and for the rest needing to be drawn actively into the light of day. They provide the basis for a coherent and comprehensive reading of Hegel's thought that readily accommodates and does full justice to his philosophy of history. Such claims cannot, of course, be justified all at once and in advance, but only, in the spirit of Hegel's own procedure, through the exposition of the reading in question.

If immanence can yield such a reading there emerges a final reason for preferring it which is especially significant for the philosophy of history. It will be preferable on familiar methodological grounds of economy. The principle is that of Ockham's Razor; that entities should not be multiplied beyond what is strictly necessary in explanation. Thus, if one can dispense with the extravagant ontology of the superhuman personal subject, one should do so. The philosophy of history is a crucial test for such a policy. It is the challenge of deciphering meaning in the seemingly chaotic manifold of history that chiefly tempts one to reach for the most powerful weapon imaginable, a theistic conception of providence. Its assistance comes, however, at the price of grounding inquiry in an element that, for Hegel, is not itself fully permeable by reason. For he does not suppose that the existence of a transcendent deity can be rationally demonstrated.[1] His philosophy of history will commend itself all the more if it can avoid having to pay the price of such an ungrounded ontological commitment. Moreover, the ability to do so in this important field would give strong support to viewing the system as a whole in terms of an immanent metaphysics.

Immanence and transcendence

The *Introduction* is as good a means as one can find of showing the dual character of the evidence. It is particularly useful as a source of items to be placed on the transcendent side. Indeed, there is scarcely another text which is its equal in that respect, and many readers have taken it as speaking univocally for transcendence. Though this is not so, it is easy to see how the impression arises in the light of such passages as the following:

> Christians ... are initiated into the mysteries of God, and so the key to world history is also given to us. Here there is a definite knowledge of providence and its plan. It is a leading doctrine of Christianity that providence has ruled and continues to rule the world, that whatever happens in the world is determined by and commensurate with the divine government.
>
> (H, 46: 41; cf. M, 27: 15, 16, 17)

The insight of philosophy is that no force can surpass the power of goodness or of God ... that world history displays nothing other than the plan of providence. God rules the world; world history is the content of his government, the execution of his plan. To comprehend this is the task of the philosophy of world history ...

(H, 77: 67; cf. M, 53: 36, 47, 39)

It seems especially significant that in these passages the model for providence should be government, political rule. For few political thinkers have been more sharply aware than Hegel of the distinction within the state between rulers and ruled (H, 139: 117; M, 139–40: 44, 58, 47). Moreover, it is an autocratic form of personal government that is in question, the government of a being whose will must always in the end prevail. Translated into a metaphysical setting the weight of this conception must surely fall on the transcendent side of the fence. The most striking formulation that the *Introduction* can set alongside it there invokes the Idea as well as God. It tells us that the Idea is 'the eternal life of God in itself, as it were before the creation of the world, the logical nexus' (H, 91: 77). This seems to echo a remark in the *Science of Logic* which is itself perhaps the most often cited item of evidence for taking Hegel transcendently. The remark refers to logic as 'the system of pure reason' whose content is '*the presentation (Darstellung) of God, as he is in his eternal essence before the creation of nature and a finite spirit*' (WL 1: 44; SL: 50). It is natural to suppose that Hegel has some version of traditional theistic views of creation in mind here. This suggestion raises, however, some very large issues, and it may be best to take it up again when the argument has made further progress. In this preliminary registering of evidence it is clear enough where these statements should, at least initially, be placed.

The *Introduction* is also rich in signs of immanence, as passages such as the following attest:

The kingdom of the spirit is created by human beings. Whatever representations we may form of the kingdom of God, it is always a kingdom of the spirit which is realised in human beings and which they should bring into existence.

(H, 50: 44)

The precise significance of the reference to spirit will become clear later, but supporters of immanence can surely draw some comfort even now. The emphasis is on the kingdom of God and the spirit as a purely human achievement, confined to, and exhausted by, a human frame of reference. There seems little room for anything of divine or spiritual significance outside that could be transcendent in relation to it.

Elsewhere a more extended discussion offers a kind of encouragement to the immanent side which is in general familiar from Hegel's writings. It consists in a scathing criticism of what is plainly a transcendent view of God. In the case of religions with a spiritual understanding of God, everything depends, Hegel declares, on whether they know 'the truth, the Idea, only in its division or in its true unity'. In the former case, and specifically, it seems, in Judaism and Islam, God is regarded as 'an abstractly highest essence, Lord of heaven and earth, over there beyond and from whom human reality is excluded'. In the latter case, that of the Christian religion, 'the finite and the infinite are united'. The divine Idea is revealed as 'the unity of divine and human nature', and this is 'the true Idea of religion' (H, 126: 106; M, 70: 50, 64, 53). It seems reasonable to suppose that the contrast between the two kinds of spiritual religion may be aligned with that between a transcendent deity existing above and beyond the world and one dwelling immanently in unity with it.

In speaking of the unity of the finite and the infinite and of divine and human nature, Hegel may perhaps have been conscious of entering sensitive ground. For there follows one of his conventional and unsatisfactory disavowals of pantheism. As with similar attempts elsewhere, it conveys a sense of unease and misdirection, of an energetic assault on the wrong target and of punches being pulled when an appropriate one is in view. Pantheism is, we are told, the view that 'represents the universe as nature'. Such a view has, however, 'no content', for in it 'God, the subject, disappears' (H, 127: 106). This objection seems, strictly speaking, to be directed not at pantheism as such, but quite generally at any view that fails to grasp the true as subject. Hence, while it may have force against a pantheism such as that of Spinoza, 'the philosophy in which God is determined only as *substance*, and not as subject and spirit', it can have none against one that avoids this error (EPW 1: 20; EL: 8). Such a pantheism of substance and subject seems by no means inconceivable. For one thing it might well prove more faithful to the injunction to grasp the true in both of these aspects than any form of theism can readily manage. It is plainly one and the same object of reference 'the true', that is in question. Since for theism, however, God is emphatically not to be identified with the world, it seems to prise subject and object apart in a way that makes the injunction hard to follow, A pantheist view, on the other hand, might well require the assumption that the God who is subject is identical with the universe conceived as a unified totality. The obvious analogy is with the human person as a subject which is standardly conceived as more than the sum of its limbs and organs, more than the body as such, while yet being nothing apart from them. A conception of the totality as subject will be filled out in certain respects in the discussion that follows. For the moment one should merely note that, if its viability in principle is accepted, it is by no means ruled out of court by the attack on pantheism in the *Introduction*. Indeed, that attack, for all its heat and bluster, seems almost expressly designed to avoid doing so. Hence, the friends of a Hegelian, as opposed to a Spinozan, pantheism need not think themselves confounded by it.

They may even take heart from a reference that follows immediately. It is to what is offered as an alternative to pantheism but seems in truth to gesture towards a better understanding of its nature. This is the conception of 'the unity of God and the world'. It is said to be present in the Indian doctrine of incarnation, the art of the Greeks and, in a much more refined sense, the Christian religion. In the latter 'the unity of divine and human nature is made manifest in Christ', thus pointing to 'the true Idea of God' (H, 127: 106). The Christian incarnation is a doctrine to which Hegel is partial for its ability to represent a speculative truth, that of the unity of universal and particular or infinite and finite. Yet here, as elsewhere, he conspicuously fails to endorse what is surely the simple essence of the matter for ordinary Christians, the unique status of Jesus as the incarnate second person of the Trinity. His role for Hegel is that of making manifest a universal truth rather than of personally embodying a singular one. Jesus is the emblem of and witness to the unity of the divine and the human, not its sole exemplar and meeting point. It follows that, however outstanding he may be in that role, he does not partake essentially of the divine nature in any qualitatively different sense from any other member of the human race. A shift of perspective on the traditional Christian doctrine of incarnation may be said to have taken place, one that subverts it utterly. Instead of being a doctrine of God taking on human form, it becomes the revelation of humanity as the highest expression of the divine, thus turning the central drama of Christian theism against its origins.

This initial survey of the guidance the *Introduction* provides in interpreting Hegel's ontological categories is now concluded. It is already plain that the work's reputation as speaking unambiguously for transcendence is undeserved. There are, it is true, formulations such as those concerning providence in history, which are most naturally taken in that sense. In the case of what seems theoretically the most significant of them, the reference to divine creation, this impression will later be shown to be unfounded. It should be added that, while the presentation of the evidence for transcendence is now more or less complete, the main weight of that for its rival will be felt only over the course of the discussion. That course will also, as noted earlier, have to be relied on for what is for present purposes the best vindication of an immanent reading, its ability to yield a comprehensive, economical and coherent reconstruction of Hegel's philosophy of history.

Chapter 4

Concept and spirit

The first test for an attempt to read Hegel's philosophy of history through an ontology of immanence is that of dealing with the basic categories listed earlier. This has already begun in the case of reason, the Idea and God, and will be taken further with them as the discussion proceeds. Beyond that, the hitherto shadowy items of concept and spirit have to be moved into the spotlight. A starting point is offered by the foundational passage of the *Introduction*, and, specifically, by its reference to reason as 'the infinite material of all natural and spiritual life'. This reference is later spelled out in terms of the Idea:

> The purest form in which the Idea reveals itself is thought itself, and it is thus that the Idea is regarded in logic. Another form is that of physical nature, and finally the third is spirit in general.
>
> (H, 53: 46)

Thus, the Idea, or reason, reveals itself as thought, as nature and as spirit. Hence it is that the *Encyclopaedia* exposition of the system begins with logic and proceeds in turn to the philosophies of nature and spirit. The transitions from logic to nature and from nature to spirit are both of great interest to the present inquiry. The first will enable it to redeem a promise made earlier, that of dispelling the air of transcendence around the reference in the *Introduction* to the Idea in its creational role.

The *Encyclopaedia* account of the transition from logic to nature is noteworthy for the resolute way in which it distances itself from the language and thought patterns of traditional theism. Thus, it refers critically to the posing of the question of creation in which God is imagined to be 'a subject, an actuality for himself and remote from the world', that is, an 'abstract infinitude and universality'. The correct conception is sketched as follows:

God has two revelations, as nature and as spirit, and both manifestations are temples which he fills, and in which he is present. God as an abstraction is not the true God; his truth is the living process, the positing of his other, the world, which, comprehended in its divine form, is his son.

(EPW 2: 23; HPN: 204)

This strikes the authentic note of Hegel's religion, of what might be called, were it not for its air of paradox, his Christian pantheism. God's truth is the positing of the world of nature and spirit that is also in another aspect, his son. He fills these temples of his manifestation, and is, one may infer, filled by them. For apart from them he is but an empty abstraction. The conception is one that Hegel captures epigramatically elsewhere: 'Without the world God is not God' (ICR: 308n).

It is wholly in line with this conception that the *Encyclopaedia* account should go on to affirm that the world 'is created, is now being created, and eternally has been created'. For 'creating is the activity of the absolute Idea', and so 'the Idea of nature is, like the Idea itself, eternal'. The chief point Hegel insists on by way of clarification is that by 'eternal' he does not have in mind temporal duration, however prolonged, not even 'an infinitely long period of time'. Eternity, we are told, is not 'before or after time', but rather 'absolute present, the now'. As the medium of existence of the Idea it is 'sublated time', 'absolute timelessness' (EPW 2: 26,50; HPN: 207, 231). The cautionary note struck by the 'as it were' (*gleichsam*) in the *Introduction*'s reference to the eternal life of God before the creation of the world can now be properly appreciated. For it is not with the obvious sense of 'before' – that is, temporal priority – that one has to deal. Neither, it appears, can the priority be straightforwardly onto-logical: God is not God without the world. Indeed, the ontological sequence is most naturally taken as running the other way. With a slight shift of perspective it will appear that it is nature and spirit that have the primacy and fullness of being from which the Idea as logical nexus is but a bloodless abstraction.

The priority this nexus has can only be conceptual and epistemo-logical. It is conceptual just in the sense that the logical Idea is the fundamental pattern inscribed in the real, the template to which all determinations of nature and spirit must conform. Nothing exists or occurs in contravention of logic. To approach the matter epistemolog-ically is to arrive at the starting point for Hegel's elaboration of his system. This is, as was noted earlier, the thesis that what we are truly compelled to think must also characterise the objective world. The primary constraints on what we think, the forms of conceptual neces-sity, are the requirements of logic. From this standpoint talk of the priority of the logical Idea is simply a reiteration of the founding prin-ciple of Hegel's idealism, the principle that makes it a fertile and expansive philosophical position. It now appears that what seems the most theoretically awkward formulation in the *Introduction*, as well as its counterpart in the *Science of Logic*, should be read in a way favourable to immanence. The language of creation, and of what there is before creation, is but a picturesque way of referring to the conceptual and epistemological priority of logic. It is not the invoca-tion of a transcendent personal subject, and such a subject would in any case be an idle wheel in the mechanism.

Idea and concept

The Hegelian concept has so far lurked in the wings of this discussion. Indeed, where the *Introduction* is concerned, it is, one has to admit, the least prominent of the basic categories. Nevertheless, it has there, as elsewhere, an indispensable role, and we are given precise indications of its identity. They include the assertion that 'the Idea is the reality which is merely the mirror, the expression, of the concept' (H, 61: 53). To this should be added the key proposition concerning the concept that was cited at the start, and may now be given a fuller statement:

> The logical, and still more the dialectical, nature of the concept in general is that it determines itself, posits determinations in itself and then sublates them, and through this sublation wins for itself an affirmative, and truly richer, more concrete determination.
>
> (H, 167: 138; M, 86: 63, 78–9, 67)

The lessons to be drawn immediately from these remarks are that the concept is progressively self-determining and that the Idea is its reality.

The second of these lessons may be taken as a variation on Hegel's stock formula for the relationship of Idea and concept. This is that the Idea is 'the unity of the concept and reality' or 'the unity of the concept and objectivity' (SL: 756, 757, 758, 806, 843; EL: 238, 274, 288). A simple, yet serviceable, transposing of terms gives the result that the concept is the Idea shorn of reality or objectivity. It emerges as the principle which is realised or objectified in the Idea, while, seen from the other end, the Idea is that principle encased in objective reality. This is, one should note, an area in which Hegel's usage is even more than usually fluid. The Idea and the concept frequently seem to be usurping each other's functions, as delineated here, or are simply used interchangeably. Nevertheless, the functional distinction may be said to represent Hegel's dominant usage, and the one he generally proposes whenever he addresses the matter self-consciously. It also offers the advantage of a more differentiated vocabulary in which to render his thoughts, and will be adopted in the present discussion.

The two features of the concept which the *Introduction* highlights are intelligibly connected. For if it is the unrealised Idea, it is natural to think of it as inherently restless and dynamic, ever striving to fulfil itself in reality. This primal tension of Idea and concept is what essentially sets Hegel's idealism apart from that of his predecessors from Anaxagoras to Spinoza. It introduces the element of inner-directed self-movement into a static universe. The metaphysical vision of idealism is then one of a cosmic process of becoming. So powerful is its grip on Hegel that the characteristic imagery of self-movement and self-making may be said to pervade his dealings with his basic onto-logical categories in general. The concept may, nevertheless, be properly seen as its chief focus and vehicle. It may then be said to represent the subjectivity of the Idea in two related senses. It is the Idea as subjective, lacking objective embodiment, and, moreover, it bears the main responsibility for sustaining our sense of the Idea as subject. To avoid any paradoxes in the latter role of seeming to be both creator and created, it may be thought of in terms of the emer-gence of successively higher stages of the subject's development. This notion of step-like progress opens up a space within which there should be enough differentiation of levels to justify talk of creation. On the other hand, it ensures enough continuity across the phases for the assumption of an enduring subject to get a purchase. Viewed in the largest perspective, the drive of the concept to become Idea is the cosmic mainspring of the movement.

The introduction of the concept takes this inquiry a large step closer to its central concerns. To appreciate this one has only to invoke Hegel's characteristically dramatic insistence that time is 'the existing concept itself', 'the concept itself that *is there*' (PG: 45–6, 584; PS: 27, 487). In less dramatic terms the relationship may be captured by suggesting that time is inescapably the medium in which the concept's self-movement and self-creation are enacted and fulfilled. The higher stages of the process are worked out in historical time; that is, to antic-ipate a little, the historical phase of the time of spirit. This conception is a necessary condition of rendering intelligible the thesis that history is a rational process. Moreover, it now becomes possible in principle to do justice to Hegel's status as pre-eminently the historical philoso-pher, the one for whom history has the most fundamental role as a philosophical category. This in turns opens up the prospect of situ-ating his philosophy of history in a strategic place in the system as a whole. These possibilities will be pursued, and reflected on, from a variety of perspectives in the discussion that follows. For the present it suffices to note that they presuppose the immanent reading of Hegel's ontology. On the transcendent reading, history emerges as at best a sphere of operations for an ahistorical absolute that remains untouched in its true being by what occurs there. It is only from the immanent standpoint that history can appear as an indispensable medium of the absolute's self-creation. A note of caution has to be struck here. An independent argument for immanence has not been offered in these remarks since, for all that has been said, it remains possible that history has no such strategic role in Hegel's thought. The compelling force of the view that it has will emerge only through engaging in detail with the philosophy of history. Nevertheless, the general possibilities sketched above deserve to be borne in mind, however abstract they may be at this point. For they pick out vital ingredients of the coherent, comprehensive exposition on which, as noted earlier, all hopes of vindicating one's point of view in reading Hegel must ultimately rest.

At this point another usage of 'Idea' and 'concept' has to be considered. It involves a move away from their role as terms of cosmo-logical import, the Idea or concept in general, to locutions of the form, 'the Idea of x' and 'the concept of x', where 'x' ranges over an indefinitely large set of objects. The most important cases in the *Introduction* are those where it has the values 'spirit' and 'freedom' (for example, H, 53: 47; 124: 104; 153: 127; 256: 208 and M, 29: 16, 22, 19; 68: 48, 62, 51; 39: 25, 30, 27; 94: 69–70, 85, 73). These usages should not be intuitively hard to grasp since they mirror the corre-sponding forms at the general level. Indeed they may offer an easier starting point. A definition, Hegel remarks, conventionally enough, 'includes everything which belongs to the essentiality (*Wesentlichkeit*) of the object' (M, 70: 50, 64, 53; cf. H, 125: 105). Elsewhere he elabo-rates the theme in his own way by interpreting the process of definition as a matter of 'reducing the object to its concept' (WL 2: 512; SL: 795). Thus, the concept of an object comprises whatever properties inescapably figure in the definition, those that constitute its nature or essence. The Idea of the object in question will then be its conceptual essence together with its concrete existence, the realised concept. For any existing object there must, Hegel maintains, be some measure of agreement with its concept: 'without any identity at all between concept and reality nothing can subsist' (EL: 287–8). The identity cannot, on the other hand, be complete in the case of finite things: 'they have a concept, but their existence is not adequate to it' (EL: 60). The realisation of the concept in such cases is a matter that admits of, indeed insists on, degrees. The sole concept that can be fully realised is that of an infinite object, the absolute itself. This is the concept, in general, the concept whose realisation is the Idea in general. 'God alone', Hegel declares, giving the point its religious expression, is 'the genuine agreement between concept and reality' (EL: 60). This is, to use terms introduced earlier, the only case in which the tension inherent in the double aspect of the subjective and the objective can be definitively resolved.

From nature to spirit

The transition in Hegel's system from logic to nature was considered earlier. To set the scene for the next stage of the discussion, one should turn to that from nature to spirit. A basic premise of it is that nature is, as the *Encyclopaedia* tells us, the Idea in 'the form of *otherness*' and 'the determination of *externality*' (HPN: 205). According to the *Introduction*, it is in space that the Idea 'lays itself out (*sich auslegt*) as nature' (H, 154: 128; M, 96–7: 72, 87, 75). This cannot, of course, be conceived as simple otherness, sheer spatial externality, as in a dualist metaphysics. In accordance with the monistic outlook of idealism, nature is variously said to be 'implicitly' (*an sich*) 'reason', 'the Idea' and 'divine' (HPN: 204, 206, 209). In this connection Hegel notes that 'Schelling had called it a petrified, and others even the frozen, intelligence'. It would be wholly contrary to the dynamism of Hegelian ontology to view such a condition as permanent: 'God does not remain petrified and moribund however, the stones cry out and lift themselves up (*heben sich auf*) to spirit' (EPW 2: 25; HPN: 206). The encounter of nature and spirit is the occasion for one of Hegel's excursions into erotic imagery, in this case an imagery drawn from the foundations of the Judaeo–Christian tradition: 'Spirit has the certainty which Adam had when he beheld Eve, "This is flesh of my flesh, this is bone of my bones". Thus, nature is the bride espoused by spirit' (EPW 2: 23; HPN: 204).

If nature and spirit are one flesh, that flesh has to be identified with reason, the 'infinite material'. What the groom brings to the union may be characterised in various ways. Spirit is, in one aspect, reason become conscious of itself, in contrast to the unconscious reason that is nature (PS: 263). Thus, the *Introduction* can refer indifferently to 'self-conscious reason' and to 'spirit as such' (H, 37: 34; M, 23: 11, 13, 14). In another aspect what spirit brings is a new kind of temporal dimension. Instead of the cycle of nature that always repeats itself with 'nothing new under the sun', there enters change in the sense of progress towards what is 'better and more perfect', an 'impulse of perfectibility' (H, 149: 124–5; M, 74: 54, 68, 57). At this point it may be helpful to bring together the two parts of an *Introduction* formula that have already been cited separately: 'World history in general is the laying out of spirit in time, just as in space the Idea lays itself out as nature' (H, 154: 128; M, 96–7: 72, 87, 75). With the first part of this formula we arrive back at one of the key propositions listed at the start. To grasp it fully, however, one has to look more closely at the ontological category which figures in its predicate; that is to say, spirit.

For anyone wishing to understand the nature of spirit, the *Introduction* is a helpful and suggestive text. It offers, among others, the following formulations:

> [Spirit] is entirely individual, active and utterly alive: it is consciousness but also its object – and it is the being of spirit to have itself as object.
>
> (H, 54: 47; cf. M, 30: 17, 23, 20)

> The next step is that we consider more closely spirit, which we grasp essentially as consciousness ...
>
> (H, 59: 51)

> The universal spirit is essentially present as human consciousness ... The spirit that knows itself and exists for itself as subject posits itself as immediate and existent: thus it is human consciousness.
>
> (H, 113: 95)

The chief clue to understanding spirit that is given here is its identification with consciousness. It is one with the largest significance for the philosophy of history. Indeed, when Hegel declares flatly elsewhere that 'spirit is consciousness', he glosses this by taking it to be positing 'in other words' the presence of reason in history (HPM: 281). The gloss will need some elaboration before its point is entirely clear. What should be noted at once, however, is that the *Introduction* directly warrants the view that it is specifically with human consciousness that spirit is to be identified. This is, of course, entirely in keeping with the interpretation of Hegel's ontology that has been adopted here. On that interpretation spirit is, and can only be, the human spirit. The process of elaborating the connection with reason in history may start by situating Hegel's doctrine of spirit in two large contexts of meaning. The first is that of the philosophical tradition he inherited, and the second is that of ordinary usage and belief.

The philosophical tradition

The problem of consciousness, and more especially of self-consciousness, had been central to modern philosophy ever since Descartes. His method of hyperbolic doubt had led him to find the only truly secure foundation for knowledge in the *Cogito*, the principle that 'I think, therefore I am'. In seeking to understand this 'I', it leads him further to the conclusion that 'absolutely nothing else belongs to my nature or essence except that I am a thinking thing', and, hence, that 'my essence consists solely in the fact that I am a thinking thing' (Descartes 1986: 54). What the thinking subject is most assured of, it appears, is its own existence as a thinker: the foundational consciousness is constitutively a self-consciousness. In the most general terms the story after Descartes is one of the progressive thinning out, in both his 'rationalist' and 'empiricist' successors, of this legacy. In particular, the subject consciousness becomes gradually drained of any suggestion of substantiality or 'thingness'. The crown of this development, and the most important precedent for Hegel, is the work of Kant. In his hands the 'I' becomes a purely logical subject with no more existential weight than is needed to be the admittedly indispensable, but purely formal, principle of the unity of consciousness. Hence, it is, as Hegel complains, 'totally abstract and completely undetermined' (EL: 84). What can properly be said of it is, as Kant himself explains, limited in the extreme: 'it is obvious that in attaching the "I" to our thoughts we designate the subject of inherence only transcendentally, without noting in it any quality whatsoever – in fact, without knowing anything of it either by direct acquaintance or otherwise' (Kant 1968: 337). From the fullness of Cartesian substance, the 'I' has dwindled here to a flickering and ungraspable, but also ineliminable, spectre at the feast of experience.

Hegel's verdict acknowledges both the value and the limitations of Kant's achievement: 'the Kantian philosophy leads essentiality back to self-consciousness, but it can supply no reality for this essence of self-consciousness, or this pure self-consciousness, nor can it demonstrate being in the same' (VGP 3: 332; LHP 3: 426). The Kantian philosophy, it appears, grasps the crucial significance of self-consciousness, but is unable to give the notion any content. By now the original impulse from Descartes has been whittled down almost to vanishing point. No further refinement is possible in this direction, and neither can the story be run backwards to its origins. The solution must be to escape somehow from the problematic which Descartes and Kant share, to break the grip of assumptions they take for granted. The challenge of thereby giving reality and being to self-consciousness is what creates the need and the opportunity for spirit.

The obvious place to look for the details of the genealogy of spirit is the *Phenomenology*. Spirit is not present there at the start, and yet is the centre of attention well before the end. Its birth and development are chronicled in the context of the ascent of the natural consciousness to absolute knowing. The logic of the opening arguments has already been surveyed, but to arrive at spirit one has to move the story forward a little. That logic had been epistemic in character, a matter of unmasking the pretensions of various forms of consciousness to yield knowledge of objects. When it has run its course the affective and volitional aspects of dialectic come strongly to the fore. The primitive dialectical force of negation begins to find expression in 'desire'. Indeed, at this stage, 'self-consciousness is desire', as Hegel informs us with characteristic largesse (PS: 109). Negation as desire at first takes the extremely crude form of seeking the actual destruction of the object desired. Success in this brings no lasting satisfaction, however, since it serves only to re-establish the utter dependence of consciousness on the object for the discharge of its primary impulse. The cycle of destructive desire and its inevitable frustration begins again. To escape this contradictory structure, at the next stage consciousness seeks not to negate the object directly but to have it negate itself. To be capable of doing so, however, it must in turn also be self-conscious. Thus, the process arrives at 'the duplication of self-consciousness'. This is the key moment for present purposes, the moment of the emergence of spirit. It marks the birth of a new kind of subject, one which is, 'the unity of the different independent self-consciousnesses'. It is, that is to say, a collective subject: the simple 'I' becomes an ' "I" that is "We" and "We" that is "I" ' (PS: 110). Self-consciousness can now achieve satisfaction and fullness of existence only in being recognised by another self-consciousness, and at this point the dialectical movement becomes 'the process of recognition' (PS: 111).

This has been a summary account of some steps in a complex argument. It has been given because the steps in question involve the advent of spirit, the central pillar of Hegel's philosophy of history. A good deal of work remains to be done, however, before the argument will sustain a historical dimension. Indeed, from that point of view relatively little may seem to have been achieved. The stage that has been reached is, strictly speaking, that of a dyadic relation between self-conscious subjects. This does not yet ensure the presence of truly social, still less historical, forms of interaction. Yet, in another way, what has been achieved is of decisive importance. For it breaks radically with the problematic of Descartes and Kant that dominated the tradition Hegel inherited. He has taken their solitary ego and propagated it, transforming it into an 'I' that is 'We'. This is the crucial shift from the first person singular to the first person plural standpoint that has resounded throughout later philosophy, and whose implications have been fully worked out only in the twentieth century. No longer is the entire edifice of human knowledge to be poised precariously on the ability of the lone subject to synthesise his or her own experience. The responsibility is now collective, dispersed over the entire realm of what has come to be called 'intersubjectivity' but remains in essentials what Hegel designated as the kingdom of spirit.

Ordinary usage

The complex philosophical provenance of Hegelian spirit should not be allowed to obscure its links with ordinary life and usage. The term '*Geist*' ('spirit') itself is one 'we are familiar with in everyday speech as the spirit of a people, an epoch, a team (*eines Volkes, einer Epoche, einer Mannschaft*)' (Habermas 1968: 15; 1974: 146). There is nothing high-flown or recondite about these usages, a fact that reflects the ordinariness of the phenomena to which they refer. In them, *Geist* figures as a normal descriptive term, employed to pick out important and incontrovertible aspects of social life. Its use is grounded in, and needed to do justice to, common experience. Hegelian spirit may be seen from one point of view as elaborating and systematising that experience. Theoretical burdens are, of course, acquired in the process, but always in the dialectical fashion that preserves essential features of the starting point, never simply putting aside or losing sight of them. In this perspective Hegel appears as belonging to an honourable tradition in philosophy at least since Aristotle, a tradition of working with the grain of ordinary life and seeking to articulate the wisdom hidden in it.

The standard usage of *Geist* has two features in particular that illustrate the kind of affinity between that life and speculative thought in which Hegel delights. The first is that the 'spirit' with which we are familiar in everyday speech 'always extends beyond the subjectivity of the solitary self-consciousness.' (Habermas 1968: 15; 1974: 146). At the core of its meaning there is an impulse towards what is social and public. Thus, in interpreting spirit as the collective subject that overcomes Cartesian–Kantian individualism, Hegel is, as it were, moving with the genius of the language. The other relevant feature of 'spirit' is its association with 'life, vitality', with what is 'spirited' as well as 'spiritual'. The lack or absence of spirit, the state of being *geistlos*, suggests, on the other hand, enervation or torpor (Farrell 1971: 215).

It would be hard to exaggerate the emphasis laid on the second of these features in the *Introduction*. Spirit, we are told, 'never stands still' but is 'something active' and 'activity is its essence' (H, 46: 41; 55: 48; cf. M, 30–1: 17, 23, 20–1). It is 'essentially energy' and that 'infinite movement ... which never rests' (H, 114: 96; 161: 133; cf. M, 99: 73, 89, 77). What should also be noted is that in close proximity to these descriptions there tends to be an equally typical insistence that the movement in question is self-movement and a movement of self-formation:

> The business of spirit is to produce itself, to make itself its own object, and to know itself; in this way, it exists for itself.
>
> (H, 55: 48; M, 30–1: 17, 23, 20–1)

> The differentiation of spirit is its own deed ...
>
> (H, 114: 96)

> The will of spirit is to fulfil its own concept ...
>
> (H, 152: 127; M, 76: 55, 69, 59)

> It is the drive and inherent (*in sich selbst*) impulse of spiritual life to break through the shell of naturalness and sensuousness, of the alienation of itself, and to come into the light of consciousness, i.e., to itself.
>
> (H, 157: 131; M, 78: 57, 71, 61)

These formulations, it should be observed, are far from encouraging any notion of spirit as a preformed entity, standing over and apart from the realm of human experience. Their message is rather that it exists only by virtue of its self-making activity in that realm.

The list includes what will now be familiar as a standard Hegelian use of 'concept'. The preceding discussion will also have made clear in general terms how the *Introduction* views the relationship between spirit and the other ontological categories. The characteristic theses that spirit is self-conscious reason and the Idea as it manifests itself in human life have already been introduced. Moreover, a reference has been cited to the kingdom of God as a spiritual kingdom to be realised in and through human activity. Some further statements concerning the relationship of spirit and God should be noted, not least for their strongly immanent character:

> Thus Christianity ... speaks of God. It recognises him as spirit, and this is not something abstract but the process in itself ...
>
> (H, 47: 42)

> God is the spirit in his community; he lives and is real in it. The world spirit is the system of this process whereby the spirit produces for itself the true concept of itself.
>
> (H, 262: 213)

These passages point towards two distinctive Hegelian themes, the dynamic ontology of becoming and the fundamental significance of the intersubjective and social. God is essentially process, and in his highest manifestation as spirit has reality only in and through the human community. The effect is to isolate still further the transcendently tinged remarks about providence in the *Introduction*. It brings out more sharply their position as anomalies in a theoretical framework that but for them readily accommodates the entire content of the work.

Forms of spirit

Spirit is referred to in the *Introduction* with a variety of epithets. A start should be made in reducing this to order, at least at the most general level of reference. When Hegel has in mind world history as such, he standardly refers to the spirit that animates it as the 'world spirit'. This term also figures in a series of equivalencies and parallels. Thus, we are told that 'The world spirit is the spirit in general' (H, 30: 29). Later the world spirit is said to 'correspond' to 'the divine spirit, which is the absolute spirit' (H, 60: 52). Hegel is understandably careful, however, most obviously because God is nature as well as spirit, to add that the 'universal spirit or world spirit is not synonymous with God' (H, 262: 212). This addition gives 'universal' as an equivalent for 'world', and Hegel is generally content to use the two terms interchangeably (for example, H, 60: 53). Nothing of theoretical significance depends on these shifts of terminology.

The varieties of spirit in the *Introduction* should be related to Hegel's best-known taxonomy of the field, that which forms the structure of the *Encyclopaedia* philosophy of spirit. Spirit is classified there as being 'subjective', 'objective' and 'absolute'. Subjective spirit is the sphere of individual consciousness as revealed through what Hegel somewhat idiosyncratically designates as anthropology, phenomenology and psychology. Objective spirit is spirit in its overtly social or public aspect, as embodied in the customs, laws and institutions of a human community. Absolute spirit is spirit as apprehended through the ascending triplet of art, religion and philosophy. In such a scheme it is not surprising that the *Encyclopaedia* discussion of world history should itself fall within the realm of objective spirit. There is no reason not to suppose that the *Introduction* account may be assigned there also. Yet almost nothing of the *Encyclopaedia* taxonomy survives in that work. What is plainly present is the sense of the division of labour of art, religion and philosophy. Thus, 'the true' is said to attain 'not just to representation (*Vorstellung*) and to feeling, as in religion, and to intuition (*Anschauung*) as in art', but also to 'the thinking (*denkenden*) spirit' as in philosophy, in this respect 'the highest, freest and wisest form' (H, 125: 105; M, 69: 49, 63, 52; cf. H, 123: 103; M, 73: 53, 66, 55). This rising sequence of art, religion and philosophy is frequently invoked by Hegel, and is standardly defined in terms of the shift from intuition to representation to thought.

There can be no objection to viewing the way the *Introduction* deals with art, religion and philosophy in terms of the absolute spirit of the *Encyclopaedia*, any more than to linking its discussion of world history with objective spirit. It should be remarked, however, that to have recourse to absolute spirit is by no means to leave the historical behind. This is most obviously shown by the fact that early in the *Introduction* Hegel recognises the legitimacy of histories of art and religion as providing a 'transition to philosophical world history' (H, 21: 23; M, 19: 7–8, 9, 9). Nor is he content with giving them his blessing as theoretically viable undertakings. His courses of lectures on aesthetics and the philosophy of religion provide, among other things, outline surveys of just such histories. Where the history of philosophy is concerned, Hegel's achievement is of a quite different order. He is himself one of the greatest practitioners of the subject, the first major thinker to take it with utmost seriousness as integrally bound up with the practice of philosophy. All of this is only to be

63

expected. The forms of absolute spirit are essentially communal enterprises, the achievement of traditions of intersubjectivity to which many generations of artists, worshippers and thinkers have contributed. In virtue of that they are historical through and through, even if they remain distinct from the world history with which Hegel's philosophy of history is constitutionally concerned. In a still wider sense, a sense generated by Hegel's ontological framework, there is again nothing surprising here. History is, as was suggested earlier and will be shown in more detail in the later discussion, an indispensable medium of the self-creation of the absolute, and as such no form of spirit can escape its enveloping and sustaining presence.

Chapter 5

Freedom

In turning to the topic of freedom the reader of the *Introduction* enters a different world, one that is spacious and well-lit by contrast with the admittedly incomplete dealings of the text with reason or the Idea. The widening of the thin trickle of commentary, first noticed with spirit, now forms a vigorous stream. Indeed, if the main body of the *Lectures* is included, one has a veritable ocean of material. That body, as has already been remarked, is a sketch for a philosophical history of the world. As such it is a highly thematic undertaking, and its central theme is the progress of the consciousness of freedom. This is, as it were, the backbone along which all the elements are articulated. Hence it is that, where freedom is concerned, the *Lectures* yields both conceptual comment and a mass of detail by means of which one's conceptual grasp can be tested and extended. Moreover, the *Introduction* by itself is as satisfactory an account of the basic theory as may be found anywhere in Hegel's work.

To get one's bearings, the way in which the *Introduction* situates freedom in the categorial network should be considered. It will suffice to outline its relations with the Idea and with spirit. Most of the key connections are summarily established in the following passages:

> [In world history] it is the Idea in general but in the element of the human spirit which we have to consider; more specifically, it is the Idea of human freedom.
>
> (H, 53: 46)

> we have recognised the Idea in its determinacy as the self-knowing and self-willing freedom whose sole end is itself.
>
> (M, 68: 48–9, 62, 51)

> As the substance of matter is gravity, so, we must say, the substance, the essence, of spirit is freedom … Philosophy teaches us that all the properties of spirit exist only through freedom. All are but means of freedom; all seek and produce only this. It is an insight of speculative philosophy that freedom is the sole truth of spirit.
>
> (M, 30: 17, 22, 20; cf. H, 55: 47–8)

World history, it appears, is concerned with what may be indifferently referred to as the Idea determined as freedom or the Idea of freedom. Moreover, the object of this concern is linked to spirit by a series of striking assertions. They tell us that freedom is the substance, the essence, the sole truth of spirit. It seems natural to propose, in a still more distinctively Hegelian idiom, that freedom is the concept of spirit. The effect of all this is obviously to give freedom a pivotal role in the overall scheme. Hence, it becomes essential to ask how it is itself to be defined or, in other words, what the concept of freedom is. It may be helpful to follow the example of the discussion of spirit and begin by sketching a background that contains two elements. The first is the ordinary conception of freedom obtaining in the modern world, and the second is the philosophical legacy Hegel inherited. His contribution will emerge more sharply when set against these sources of constraint and inspiration.

Everyday thought and philosophy

Hegel is, as we have seen, characteristically anxious to preserve a link between his speculative flights and everyday ways of thinking. The point of doing so might well seem especially clear where freedom is concerned. Of all the key categories of the *Introduction* it is the one with the largest presence in ordinary life. There it is in constant, concrete use, embedded in a rich network of linguistic intuitions. The core of its meaning does not, however, seem hard to formulate. Speaking somewhat roughly and provisionally, it is that to be free is to be independent of outside control. It is then a short and obvious step to the inference that it is to be dependent on, or subject to, the control of the self. If this formulation is sharpened a little, there emerges one of the definitions of freedom in the *Oxford English Dictionary*, 'the power of self-determination attributed to the will'. Here one has arrived, it might be supposed, at the heart of what is yielded by examining ordinary conceptions of freedom, their legacy, as it were, to the philosophers. It does at any rate seem to be the case that the formula that freedom is self-determination is wide enough to encompass all the serious alternatives on offer from them. The significant disagreements in the philosophical literature do not concern the question of whether it is acceptable as a general definition, but rather the question of what determination by self could mean. These differences are rooted in rival metaphysics of the self.

The tradition of thought usually labelled 'empiricism' has been constitutionally unwilling to allow any existential status to the self other than what is conferred by the empirically given and introspectable. This has tended to leave the empiricist self with a somewhat precarious hold on life. Thus, John Locke concluded that '*self* is not determined by Identity or Diversity of Substance', but only by 'Identity of consciousness' (Locke 1975: 345). The implication that it therefore leads a kind of discontinuous existence, springing into being when memory fires and lapsing out of it in the gaps between firings, has been the subject of both humorous and serious comment since the earliest reception of his work (Aarsleff 1994: 113, 262–3). David Hume for his part seems unwilling to acknowledge the self as, even intermittently, a unitary existent and genuine object of reference. It is rather 'a bundle or collection of different perceptions', for these are, he assures us, all that he encounters 'when I enter most intimately into what I call *myself*' (Hume 1888: 252). Such conceptions of the self provide the ground for a wholly accommodating and naturalistic view of what self-determination, and hence freedom or 'liberty', might mean. For Locke, and Hume's definition differs only verbally, it is a matter of 'our being able to act, or not to act, according as we shall choose or will' (Locke 1975: 248; Hume 1988: 88). This is freedom as self-determination in the sense of an ability to act, or refrain from acting, just as one chooses, and whatever one's choices may be. It seems an admirably democratic approach that takes all forms of uncoerced choice to be equally eligible as vehicles of freedom. This feature does not, however, commend it to the representatives of the main alternative tradition, that usually labelled 'rationalism'.

It should suffice for present purposes to cite the views of Spinoza, one of the philosophers of the past most admired by Hegel. Spinoza's starting point is fully in line with everyday thinking, as the relevant part of his formal definition shows: 'That thing is called free which … is determined to act by itself alone' (Spinoza 1996: 2). He is, however, utterly opposed to interpreting this as indiscriminately permitting all forms of choice. To do so would be to admit within the scope of freedom the determination of action by what he calls 'passive emotions', a process that serves rather to define the condition of 'human bondage'. In taking this view, Spinoza may said to be still in touch with our intuitions. It does seem to be at odds with them to have to admit that, for instance, such a slave to the 'passive emotions' as the alcoholic with a well-stocked cellar, could exemplify, much less be a kind of paradigm of, human freedom. In the very name of that freedom, it might be suggested, some form of ordering has to be imposed on the empirical chaos of desires. Spinoza's idea of how this is to be achieved is wholly unsurprising. For, more fully specified, freedom turns out to be for him a matter of determination through the power of reason, and, thus, a 'free man' is one 'who lives according to the dictate of reason alone' (Spinoza 1996: 151). What the rationalist philosopher now has to do, one might suppose, is to give an account of the self that exhibits the faculty of reason as an integral, perhaps constitutive, element. This would then open the way for continuing to hold that freedom as determination by reason is in principle a form of self-determination.

It is, however, just what Spinoza, at least in Hegel's view, is unable to do. This inability is part of the story of what was earlier referred to as the progressive thinning out, among both empiricists and rationalists, of Descartes' thick conception of the self. With Spinoza it has become as emaciated as with Hume, though by a quite different route, and equally incapable of constituting the ground of freedom. Hegel makes the point with heavy emphasis in declaring that, in Spinoza's way of proceeding, 'the "I" disappears, gives itself altogether up, merely withers away' (LHP 3: 286). Even more drastically, we are told that there is in his system 'an utter blotting out of the principle of subjectivity, individuality, personality, the moment of self-consciousness in being' (LHP 3: 287). This seems effectively, if crudely, directed. At any rate it surely speaks for many readers of Spinoza in voicing a sense of the absence in his thought of a satisfactory role for subjectivity. What is needed for present purposes to repair it is, one might suppose, some larger scope for individual personal initiative in relation to the dictates of reason by which free action is determined.

The account of freedom by which Hegel was most directly confronted might seem expressly designed to meet this requirement. Kant's starting point is the insight that was brilliantly formulated by Jean-Jacques Rousseau: 'the mere impulse of appetite is slavery, while obedience to a law which we prescribe to ourselves is liberty' (Rousseau 1973: 196; cf. LHP 3: 402). The first part of this formulation seems to echo Spinoza, but the second envisages a role for subjectivity that goes beyond the range of his thought. The idea of self-legislation is developed by Kant, however, in a way quite unlike that of its originator. For the escape to freedom is not essentially conceived of by Rousseau in terms of a recourse to reason, a faculty of which he is suspicious, at least in any action-guiding capacity. In his account individuals rise above the slavery of appetite by setting aside their distinctive particular interests in favour of those they share with everyone else. In doing so they come to express in their law-making the 'general will', a will directed to the common good (Rousseau 1973: 200). Kant's treatment of the theme retains by contrast something of the impulse of Spinozan rationalism. Self-legislation is to be conceived as legislation in accordance with reason, a conception made possible by the assumption that our nature is at least in part that of rational beings. Thus, to continue the political metaphor, freedom becomes self-government through reason or, in Kant's language, 'autonomy'. This is to be distinguished from any form of determination by interests or desires, even ones shared by all. Such determination is for Kant merely a servile 'heteronomy' of the will. His account of freedom might now be thought to combine the integral link with the reason of Spinoza and the scope for individual subjectivity found in Rousseau, and, hence, to be the sublation of these precursors. Yet Hegel is unable to accept the way in which Kant grasps and elaborates the basic insight that freedom is rational self-determination. In considering his criticism it should be borne in mind that our chief interest is not in its independent merits, nor in the resources Kant may have to rebut it, but rather in the part it plays in forming his own solution. As is the case generally in this inquiry, it is, so to speak, with Hegel's Kant that we have to deal.

Hegel's attack is directed at the manner in which Kant construes the determination by reason that is freedom. He interprets the essence of Kant's position in the following way: 'the rational in itself is purely *formal* and consists in that whatever should count as law must be capable of being thought of as legislation that is universally valid' (VGP 3: 366; LHP 3: 458). The basis of this interpretation, as Hegel goes on to make clear, is the formulation of Kant's fundamental principle of morality, the categorical imperative, which enjoins us to 'act on *maxims* ... which are capable of becoming universal laws' (VGP 3: 368; LHP 3: 460). The principle, as thus formulated, is 'formal' in that the test of our ability to universalise the maxims under which our actions fall is simply whether we can do so consistently. Thus, the Kantian moral life is the life of reason, and the life of reason is the life of contradiction – avoidance. This doctrine would constitute an extraordinary achievement if it could deliver what it promises. In Hegel's view, however, its formalism is nugatory in that 'the universal, the non-self-contradictory, is something empty' (VGP 3: 368; LHP 3: 460). The core of his criticism is that the categorical imperative supplies no determinate guide to action and leads in no particular practical direction:

One may indeed bring in material *from outside* and thereby arrive at *particular* duties, but it is impossible to make the transition to the determination of particular duties from the … determination of duty as *absence of contradiction*, as *formal correspondence with itself*, which is no different from the specification of *abstract inde-terminacy*…

(EPR: 162)

If this criticism is accepted, the implications for the theory of freedom are grave. For freedom consists in being determined by reason, and, it would appear, we have no way of telling just what it is that reason requires. The notion of freedom becomes as vacuously and uselessly formal as that of reason itself.

The way forward is suggested by Hegel's diagnosis of the means by which the categorical imperative is made to appear to yield determinate results. It does so by bringing in 'material from outside' to which it has officially no right. Thus, it forbids the action of keeping a deposit only by virtue of covertly presupposing the institution of depositing (NL: 77). Viewed in this way, the essence of Hegel's case is that Kant has an inadequate self-consciousness of his own procedure. The solution is to make explicit and systematic what he relies on unwittingly, the recourse to a social institution. The vehicle for doing so is indicated plainly when Hegel complains that in Kantian practical reason 'no thought is given to a system of self-realising spirit' (VGP 3: 369; LHP 3: 461). It is specifically to objective spirit, the world of social institutions and customs, that one must look to remedy the omission, and thereby give content to the notion of freedom as determination by reason.

Ethical life

When Hegel wishes to refer to objective spirit in its normative aspect, he uses the term '*Sittlichkeit*', usually translated as 'ethical life'. It denotes the ethical values and standards embodied in the institutions and customs of a society. Hence, it is to be contrasted with '*Moralität*' ('morality'), as conceived particularly by Kant but also by lesser figures whom Hegel liberally assails (EPR: 157–84). The hallmark of morality is that it is individualistic through and through, focused exclusively on the individual faculty of reason as in Kant, or on individual feelings and intuitions in other versions. The notions it typically employs include 'conscience', 'duty', 'intention', 'sincerity', 'responsibility' and an abstract 'ought' (*Sollen*) which functions in relation to the existing state of things as an aspiration or rebuke. Ethical life, on the other hand, comprises the values instantiated in, and animating, a given social world. It is as rich in content as are the normative practices of the community in question, and in a well-ordered community will be capable of yielding guidance on all but the most unusual exigencies of life. Thus, its practicality, its bearing on decisions about what to do and how to live, is not in question. What must also be shown if it is to be the proper ground of freedom is its intrinsic rationality. For that task the philosophy of history is indispensably necessary, and its being so is an important element of its strategic role in Hegel's thought.

The thesis that has to be vindicated is that concrete, substantial reason is realised in ethical life. Unless this can be done the contention that freedom should be conceived as a matter of identifying with, and conforming to, the institutions and practices of one's society must be an insupportable, indeed barely intelligible, dogma. The forms of ethical life are, for Hegel, historical forms that come into being as manifestations of spirit and pass away when the spirit in them is exhausted. If there is to be a rationality present in them, it must be a historical rationality, one for which history is a necessary dimension of existence and efficacy. Hegel's philosophy of history is expressly designed to ground such a rationality. It will suffice for present purposes to recall the basic proposition that world history is a rational process since reason inheres in it as 'substance and infinite power'. Against this philosophical background it becomes feasible and legitimate to suppose that existing forms of ethical life are vehicles of reason. Hence, there will be a presumption in favour of accepting the guidance they provide for the conduct of action. This must be rationally preferable to having recourse to individual morality with its empty formalism or unregulated emotion. Thus, the *Introduction* can assert that:

The content of what is good or not good, right or not right, is, in ordinary matters of private life, to be determined by the laws and customs of a state. There is no great difficulty in knowing it.

(H, 94: 80; M, 44: 28–9, 37, 31)

If the historical rationality of ethical life is granted, the final component of the theory of freedom falls into place. It supplies the ontological bond of individual and society that is required. In so far as my actions are determined by ethical life, they are not determined, it is now clear, by what is merely other than, and external to, my self. The determining factor is the substantial reason that is also constitutive of the individual self, 'flesh of my flesh and bone of my bones'. This may intelligibly and properly be conceived as a form of self-determination. Hence, the programme of exhibiting freedom as rational self-determination is now in principle complete. As yet, however, there is only an outline sketch, and to fill in the details one cannot do better than to turn to the text of the *Introduction*.

Objectivity and subjectivity

What is perhaps most immediately striking in the *Introduction* is an insistence that freedom is not what Hegel calls '*Willkür*', that is, as it is variously rendered, arbitrariness, self-will or caprice. Elsewhere, he explains that *Willkür* is 'being able to do as one pleases' (EPR: 48). His stance is made clear in such passages as the following:

The Orientals do not know that spirit or the human being as such are free in themselves. Because they do not know this, they are not free. They know only that One is free; but for this very reason, such freedom is mere arbitrariness (*Willkür*), savagery, dullness of passion, or a milder and tamer version of the same which is itself but an accident of nature or arbitrariness.

(H, 62: 54; M, 31: 18, 23, 21)

Hegel wishes, like his rationalist predecessors, to reject all attempts to construe freedom naturalistically as acting in accordance with whatever one happens to desire. The weakness of this model is presented succinctly as follows: 'It is inherent in arbitrariness that the content is not determined as mine by the nature of my will but by *contingency*, thus I am also dependent on this content, and this is the contradiction which underlies arbitrariness' (EPR: 49). The desires in question confront the individual as a given, an 'accident of nature', to which he or she is just as subject as if they were forms of external coercion. The arbitrary will is, one might say, a tyrannical ruler, a conclusion that is, as has already been noted, in line with everyday thinking. Our ordinary habits of thought seem to point towards the need for what one happens to desire to be subject to some form of regulation arising immanently in the nature of the self. The obvious candidate is regulation by reason, for it alone may readily be conceived as having the necessary capacity to transcend the sphere of desire. An incipient rationalism in common sense seems to force itself on one's attention here.

There is, however, an aspect in which the *Introduction* may be seen as drawing on other elements in the philosophical background, however little Hegel acknowledges his debt to them explicitly. Thus, he is quite remote from the suspicion of merely private interests one finds in different forms in Rousseau and Kant and from their asceticism with its longing to disengage from the gross particularity of individual desire. He displays no concern to set aside such interests and desires in order to arrive at an abstract purity of the will, whether conceived in terms of generality or of autonomy. On the contrary, he refers to the right of the subject to be satisfied by whatever activity or task it performs as an 'infinite right' that is an 'essential moment of freedom' (H, 82: 70; cf. M, 36–7: 22, 28, 26). Elsewhere, the 'right of the subject's *particularity* to find satisfaction' is said to be 'the right of *subjective freedom*'. As such, it is the hallmark of modernity, 'the pivotal and focal point in the difference between *antiquity* and the *modern* age' (EPR: 151). What characterises antiquity is 'objective' or 'substantial' freedom, a merely 'implicit (*an sich*) rationality of the will' in which individual subjects relate themselves to commandments and laws in 'complete servitude'. The modern world by contrast respects the subjective freedom that 'can only determine itself in the individual and which constitutes the reflection of the individual in his own conscience' (H, 243: 197; M, 135: 104–5, 93).

It is plain that Hegel is no tyrant of reason, intent on crushing the natural man and woman beneath its wheels. He cannot simply insist, as Rousseau notoriously does, that those who are recalcitrant in the face of the universal will be 'forced to be free' (Rousseau 1973: 195). Such an insistence would be bound to constitute a violation of 'infinite right'. Moreover, Hegel is keenly aware that a tyranny exercised in the name of reason will be as grievous as any other, and perhaps more grievous in being better armoured in its own conceit (PS: 355–63; EPR: 58, 277). He takes care to ensure that such a regime could claim no inner connection with, still less foundations in, his philosophy. In so doing he may be seen as drawing something from the humanism and naturalism that characterise empiricist thinking in this area.

The principle of subjective freedom was, according to the *Lectures*, introduced into world history by the sophists of Ancient Greece. With them there emerges a 'subjective independent freedom' in which 'conscience' is the test to which the individual is enabled to bring everything (M, 309–10: 253). What is chiefly reflected, and reflected on, in conscience is the universal that is concretely embodied in ethical life. Thus, the principle of subjective freedom is, as Hegel explains elsewhere, the principle whereby 'the individual's substantial activity … is mediated by his own *particular will*' (EPR: 338). Substantial activity is activity in accordance with the substantial freedom of ethical life. As a form of freedom, this is a determination of reason, but one in which reason is merely present 'implicitly' (*an sich*). Only with the emergence of subjective freedom does it come to be explicit, 'for itself' (*für sich*). There arises, in place of childlike subservience, a mediation of self-conscious reason between universal and individual, a right to reflect on, and assent to, in the light of conscience, the deliverances of ethical life. Such a right is, of course, a world away from being a licence for the arbitrary will. It is, nevertheless, empty and pointless unless it embraces the right to dissent, to conclude in particular circumstances that the presumption in favour of the rationality of the ethical is overborne. Thus, it is potentially a destructive element, and, indeed, its initial impact on the Greek spirit was that it 'plunged its world into ruin' (M, 309: 252–3). It is, in Hegel's view, the very essence of the modern age that it can, and must, accommodate this tremendous power. His conception of how it is to be achieved cannot become clear without an account of the crucial role of the modern state. There are, however, some factors that should, even at this stage, be borne in mind.

In particular, it should be noted that modern ethical life is not a totalitarian project that seeks to control the whole of private existence. This is shown in its respect for conscience as 'a sanctuary which it would be *sacrilege* to violate' (EPR: 164). Moreover, it does not even aspire to provide guidance, still less direction, on all important matters that call for practical decision, but remits them to the discretionary choice of individuals. Its doing so is a matter of principle, a manifestation of its essence. An instance of great significance is suggested by Hegel when he complains that in Plato's republic 'subjective freedom is not yet recognised, because individuals still have their tasks assigned to them by the authorities'. Such freedom, 'which must be respected', requires 'freedom of choice on the part of the individuals' (EPR: 286). That the modern world is able to respect, indeed to insist on, the freedom to choose one's occupation is itself, of course, an achievement of history. The conception of history as the development of the freedom and rationality of spirit is indispensable if one is to make sense of the claim that modern ethical life can, and must, accommodate subjective freedom. It alone can provide the assurance that the results of individual reflection will in general be consonant with the ethical substance embodied in the institutions and practices of society. There can be no systematic or inescapable tension between them since both are expressions and instruments of reason. Hegel frames the issues by invoking an antithesis, 'one side of which is God and the divine, and the other the subject as something particular'. He then inserts history into the picture in the following way:

> World history is concerned with nothing but to create a situation in which these two sides are in absolute unity, true reconciliation, a reconciliation in which the free subject is not submerged in the objective existence of spirit but arrives at its independent right, and at the same time absolute spirit achieves the pure objective unity of its absolute right.
>
> (H, 244: 198)

Being at home

With this theme of unity and reconciliation one arrives at the central image of freedom in the *Introduction*. It depicts freedom as a matter of 'being with oneself' (*Beisichselbstsein*), and, correspondingly, to be free is to be 'with oneself' (*bei sich selbst*). These are literal renderings that may strike somewhat harshly on the ear, and, not surprisingly, translators of the work have preferred such expressions as 'independence', 'self-sufficiency', and even 'self-contained existence'. The translators of other works of Hegel have sometimes rendered *Beisichselbstsein*, and its abbreviated form *Beisichsein*, as 'being at home with oneself'. It is, as will shortly appear, a strongly suggestive practice in the overall context of Hegel's thought. To begin with, however, one should register the central image in its literal guise:

> spirit is by nature with itself (*bei sich selbst*) or free.
>
> (H, 54: 47)

> Matter has its substance outside itself; spirit, on the other hand, is being with itself (*Beisichselbstsein*), and just this is freedom. For if I am dependent, I relate myself to an other which I am not, and cannot exist without such an externality. I am free if I am with myself (*bei mir selbst*).
>
> (H, 55: 48; M, 30: 17, 23, 20)

> law is the objectivity of spirit and of the will in its truth; and only the will which obeys the law is free: for it obeys itself and is by itself (*bei sich selbst*) and therefore free.
>
> (H, 115: 97; M, 57: 39, 53, 42)

The second of these passages, with its contrast between freedom and dependence, lends particular support to the preferences of the translators of the *Introduction*. It also serves to bring Hegel directly into line with what was earlier said to be the core of the ordinary meaning of being free; that it is to be independent of outside control. We enter upon distinctively Hegelian ground, however, with the hint in the passage of a connection between this meaning and the absence or overcoming of otherness. The hint is made fully explicit in such state-ments, widely separated in time, as the following:

> a freedom for which there is something truly external and alien is not freedom; its essence and formal definition is simply that nothing is absolutely external.
>
> (JS: 476; NL: 89)

> [Freedom] on its purely formal side consists in the fact that the subject has nothing alien, no barrier or limit, in whatever stands over against it, but rather finds itself therein.
>
> (VA: 134; HA: 97)

As these statements show, the achievement of freedom involves no absurd notion of obliterating externality as such. It is a matter of removing its 'truly' or 'absolutely' external, that is its 'alien', character, and so of coming to find oneself in it. This sense of the overcoming of alienation, of ceasing to be a stranger, accounts for much of the appeal of the metaphor of being 'at home'. It indicates that the free human being is at home not in a solipsistic fantasy but in an objective world that has become his or her own world. Here one seems to hover on the brink of the key formulation of the entire conceptual field. This expands 'being with oneself' to its full range of meaning by proclaiming that freedom is 'being with oneself in an other' (*Beisichselbstsein in einem Andern*). The other in whom I am freely with myself is plainly not the other 'which I am not', to whom one is, according to the *Introduction*, related rather in dependence and unfreedom. The radical implication that it is an other which, in some sense, I am is drawn explicitly elsewhere, as when Hegel explains 'just what freedom is' as follows:

> being at home with oneself in one's other (*in seinem Anderen bei sich selbst zu sein*), depending upon oneself, and being one's own determinant ... Freedom is only present when there is no other for me that is not myself.
>
> (EPW 1: 84; EL: 58)

Thus, when I am free, the other, while not ceasing to be an 'other for me', becomes also myself. If one asks how such a sublating of otherness is to be conceived, the answer must draw on the largest resources in Hegel's thought, on the metaphysics and its expression in the philosophy of history.

Consciousness and realisation

A passage from the *Lectures* sketches the metaphysical background of freedom as follows:

> The human being is not free when he does not think, for then he relates himself to an other. This comprehension, the grasping (*Übergreifen*) of the other with the most inward self-certainty directly contains the reconciliation: the unity of thinking with the other is present *in itself* (*an sich*), since reason is just as much the substantial basis of consciousness as of what is external and natural. Thus the object is no longer a beyond with a different substantial nature.
>
> (M, 521: 439)

Freedom seems to be associated here with an achievement of complete generality, a reconciliation with everything external, the object as such. The achievement is possible in virtue of the fact that reason is the substantial basis of all existence. In the light of this truth the object can no longer appear as an alien 'beyond'. The truth in question is, of course, what is disclosed from the standpoint of absolute knowing, the standpoint that overcomes the opposition of consciousness by revealing its inner unity with the object. It now appears that some such unity may be said to be at the heart of Hegelian freedom too. Indeed, it is hard to avoid being struck by the formal similarity between Hegel's characterisations of freedom and of absolute knowing. Hence, one might be led to suggest that to occupy the standpoint of absolute knowing is to be an emblem of freedom in its highest, most comprehensive form. This is what the *Phenomenology* refers to as the 'supreme freedom' of spirit, the condition in which it has completed the overcoming of its alienation from nature and from itself so as to be fully reconciled with the world (PS: 491). Such a condition may, for convenience, be referred to as 'metaphysical freedom'.

In itself this is not, of course, the freedom that constitutes the central theme of world history. The point may be reinforced in a fruitful way by referring to one of the canonical statements of the *Introduction* on the relationship between history and freedom. Having reminded us that world history 'represents the development of spirit's consciousness of its freedom', it adds at once, 'and of the realisation produced by such consciousness' (H, 167: 138; M, 86: 63, 78, 67). It would be hard to exaggerate the emphasis Hegel gives to this distinction between consciousness and realisation. Elsewhere he formulates the basic idea by contrasting the 'principle' of freedom and it 'application'; that is, 'its *introduction* and *execution* in the reality of the spirit and of life'. The distinction is, he declares, 'a fundamental determination of our science' which it is 'essential to keep in mind'. Least of all must it be overlooked by the philosophy of history, for 'the application of the principle to worldliness, the permeation and transformation of worldly affairs by it' is 'the long process of which history [is made up]' (H, 62–3: 54; M, 32: 18–19, 24, 21–2). The direction in which one must look for the working out of this process is indicated plainly by Hegel. It is towards the state as the 'realisation' or, more expansively, the 'ethical whole and the reality', of freedom (H, 116: 98; H, 124: 104; M, 58: 40, 54, 43; M, 68: 48, 62, 51). The freedom with whose consciousness and realisation history is essentially concerned is not that of absolute spirit as philosophy but that of objective spirit as politics. It is political, not metaphysical, freedom. The obvious issue that now arises is how one is to conceive of the relationship between the two kinds of freedom.

The answer seems clear enough in its general outline. The very possibility of political freedom is grounded in the truth that is captured in the concept of metaphysical freedom. It is idealist metaphysics that provides the ultimate guarantee that the world is our world and the proper setting for spirit. This is the largest possible context of meaning and justification for the doctrine that individuals will find themselves at home in the political arrangements that objective spirit, in the course of its long travail in history, comes to devise for them. Thus, the cosmic order underpins that of human history and society. The theoretical sequence involved here is assumed throughout, and constantly re-enacted in, Hegel's work. It will suffice for now to recall the fundamental inference that reason rules the world and *therefore* world history has been rational in its course.

An *Introduction* passage that encapsulates many of these themes, and signals some fresh ones, runs as follows:

> In so far as the state, the fatherland, constitutes a community of existence, and in so far as the subjective will of human beings submits itself to laws, the opposition between freedom and necessity disappears. The rational, as the substantial, is necessary, and we are free in so far as we recognise (*anerkennen*) it as law and follow it as the substance of our own existence; the objective and the subjective will are then reconciled and one and the same untroubled whole.

> (H, 115: 97; M, 57: 39, 53, 42)

In referring to the rational as the substantial, the passage is invoking the central thesis of Hegel's ontology, the thesis that reason is 'that through which and in which all reality has its being and subsistence'. Its presence here points once again to the fact that his vision of freedom in the state has a metaphysical ground. Determination by law is not other-determination but rather spells out the concrete meaning of what it is to be self-determined, and therefore free. This is ultimately because law is the embodiment of reason, the universal substance alike of nature and of spirit. The passage also serves to bring out the crucial importance of conscious awareness for Hegelian freedom, the extent to which it involves, in all its forms, a cognitive achievement. For it is only in so far as we *recognise* the rational as law that we are free. This raises some important issues that will have to come up for discussion later. In the same category are the issues raised by the insistence that the rational must be recognised as *law*. Such an insistence serves to refine and deepen the contention noted earlier that 'only the will which obeys the law is free'. Elsewhere in the *Introduction*, 'justice (*Recht*), ethical life and the state, and they alone' are said to be 'the positive reality and satisfaction of freedom' (H, 111:

94; M, 56: 38, 50, 41). It is plain that Hegel is wholly committed to the view that freedom must be embodied as an objective structure of law and justice. That view is best pursued, however, when one comes to consider the indispensable matrix of its embodiment, the state, in more detail.

INTERVAL

Chapter 6

From system to history

The preceding discussion has tried to reconstruct the formal framework of Hegel's philosophy of history, and the second part of this work will be concerned to give it detailed content. The present chapter is intended to be a bridge between these two undertakings. It will take up the lessons of what has gone before so as to leave them as well adapted as possible for what is to come. In particular, it will seek to bring the picture of the historical dialectic – of what, as it were, makes history go – into sharper focus. It is already evident that the direction in which one must look for a model of that dialectic is towards the ascent of consciousness in the *Phenomenology*. The intrinsically dynamic nature of human consciousness could scarcely be emphasised more strongly than it is there. A sense that such consciousness is itself 'the *absolute dialectical unrest*' (PS: 124) pervades the work, and its chief categories are designed in one way or another to conceptualise that unrest. When one turns from phenomenology to philosophy of history they turn out to have a role there too; indeed, to be key components of the scene. These categories may be listed as 'negation', 'contradiction', 'reflection', 'determinate negation', 'sublation' (*Aufhebung*) and 'recollection' (*Erinnerung*). They will be dealt with briefly and schematically here, for various instances of their concrete workings have already been given, and many more will emerge in the course of the discussion.

Dialectical categories

The mainspring of dialectical unrest is not in doubt: its moving principle is 'the *negative* in general' (PS: 21). It is through the workings of this principle that contradictions arise, and to think these is itself 'to think pure change' (PS: 99). The basic form such thinking takes is reflection. In grasping how it operates, the image of light waves meeting and being reflected, 'bent back', from things is helpful (Inwood 1992: 247–50). Intellectual reflection bounces thought, as it were, off its object and back into the self. A consciousness caught in this interaction is thereby released from fixity and implicated in a process of mediation and movement. In particular, it is provided with a ladder to higher levels of self-consciousness. For the reflective interaction with its object is at the same time a distancing from the self, a bringing of it under scrutiny from a new vantage point and, thereby, a means of transcending the self-conception with which the process started. This form of development will be illustrated shortly.

The unrest constituted through negation, contradiction and reflection is by no means chaotic but is inscribed with order and direction. As well as instruments for thinking pure change, the *Phenomenology* has others for organising the changes and making their sequence rationally intelligible. Some of them have already been encountered. There is, first, the insistence that what negation generates is not random otherness but a determinate other marked with the specificity of what is negated. It is a negative shaped by its opposite, and one may reasonably expect the series of such outcomes to keep a shaping pressure. However weak it becomes, the result must still differ in kind from the workings of mere chance or contingency. This expectation is reinforced by a defining feature of dialectical resolutions. It belongs to the meaning of *Aufhebung* that it preserves and takes forward something of what it supersedes, a factor that is itself an assurance of continuity in change (SL: 107). The assurance is strengthened by the strategic role of recollection, a role with a peculiarly vital significance for the philosophy of history. To obtain a preliminary glimpse of it, one may refer to the section on absolute knowing at the end of the *Phenomenology*.

There Hegel envisages the alarming possibility that spirit may have to 'start afresh' in each phase of its existence as if 'all that preceded were lost'. What prevents disaster is '*Er-Innerung*', the 'making inward' that preserves the earlier experience in consciousness. This preservation, Hegel adds, is from one point of view history and, from another, 'the science of the appearing of knowledge'; that is to say, phenomenology. Here history and phenomenology come together as 'comprehended history', the final moment of the *Phenomenology* and the signal for its rhapsodic farewell to the reader (PG: 590–1; PS: 492–3). Thus, one has here an explicit avowal of the inner bond of phenomenology and history as sealed through recollection. The detailed nature of the bond will have to be worked out later, and, in particular, it will be necessary to consider how the power of recollection achieves institutional embodiment in history. For the present it should be of value to pursue the general relationship of phenomenology and history a little further.

This is so because some findings of quite fundamental importance for the discussion as a whole are beginning to emerge. In particular, the constitutive principle of Hegelian phenomenology should now be clear in its main outline. It is that, in a sense yet to be fully explicated, human consciousness has an immanent logic of development, a logic whose bearers are the categories from negation to recollection listed above. What makes Hegelian philosophy of history possible is the thesis that this logic can, in all essentials and with due allowance for the change of setting, be transposed to history. Spirit is the indispensable medium and vehicle of the transposition, and therein lies its crucial significance for the architecture of Hegel's thought. The thesis that world history enshrines the logic of spirit is, one might now suggest, the still centre, or rather the beating heart, of his entire project in this region of philosophy. Hence it is also the core concern of the present discussion, which is in essence an attempt to clarify, elaborate, apply and vindicate it. A full understanding of the theme cannot be reached in advance of a detailed engagement with the workings of historical spirit. Some vital elements should, nevertheless, already be visible.

The root idea is that consciousness, and in due course, spirit, will, if left to itself, tend to exhibit certain patterns of development. It is essentially directed by its very nature and, hence – discounting external shocks, and assuming its biological preconditions continue to be met – is disposed to evolve by inner determinations in some sequences rather than others. In the most general terms this natural movement of consciousness may be seen to be directed towards ever more extensive assimilation of objects, greater richness and concreteness in the manner of their apprehension, and increasing reflexivity of awareness of its own character and activities. By any relevant epistemic standards such a movement must be accounted as progress, as a shift from less to successively more adequate forms of cognition. If one turns from the overall shape of the process towards its detailed mechanism it is not hard to detect what might be termed the micro-foundations. They consist in the fact that some specific transitions in consciousness are readily intelligible and only to be expected, while others may be ruled out in principle. Hence it is that immanently determined changes are unidirectional and irreversible. In this sense one may speak of the process as necessary, and the legitimacy of doing so is the ultimate ground of the necessity to be found in history. To bring out the familiar and uncontentious character of the basic idea, it may be illustrated from observers other than Hegel.

Since the field is so wide one may as well cite some of Hegel's English contemporaries who managed to capture the idea even in a language that is not the native tongue of speculative thought. It is natural to look in particular to William Blake, since he is so often, and with justice, held to be a distinctively dialectical thinker. Indeed, many of his aphorisms have a markedly Hegelian flavour, as when he proclaims that 'Without Contraries is no progression' and that 'Opposition is true Friendship' (Blake 1958: 94, 105). Against this background, it is not surprising that the sense of an in-built sequentiality in matters of the human spirit should find such frequent and varied, though almost inevitably metaphorical, expression in his work. It is not just that he was in no doubt that the songs of experience must follow those of innocence. We are also assured that 'What is now proved was once only imagined' (Blake 1958: 97), and that

> The Child's Toys & the Old Man's Reasons
> Are the Fruits of the Two Seasons
> (Blake 1958: 70)

The theme may perhaps even be detected in a grosser guise in the famous rebuke to Satan:

> Every Harlot was a Virgin once,
> Nor cans't thou ever change Kate into Nan.
> (Blake 1958: 212)

The unidirectional, irreversible sequence is from innocence to experience, imagination to proof, toys to reasons and virginity to harlotry. The underlying idea is more prosaically expressed by another English dialectician of the time. Tom Paine robustly asserts that 'though man may be *kept* ignorant, he cannot be *made* ignorant', and that 'it has never yet been discovered how to make man *unknow* his knowledge, or *unthink* his thoughts' (Paine 1958: 104).

Our own time yields no shortage of illustrations. It is commonplace to be reminded that 'one cannot unlearn what one has learnt', or that 'knowledge cannot be erased', or that 'there is no route back from reflectiveness' (Cooper 1984: 237, quoting V. S. Naipaul; Elster 1978: 149; Williams 1985: 163). The authors of these sayings are, of course, not blind to the routine, brute occurrence of unlearning, erasure of knowledge and loss of reflectiveness as the result of, among other things, accident, disease or physical decay. Indeed, anything that causally undermines the sustaining power of recollection will have these consequences. Their point is rather that there is no *route* back in the sense that there is one forward, no intelligible series of internally related, inner-directed steps.

At this stage one may invoke a more formal context that is also more obviously attuned to the concerns of the present discussion. The idea that consciousness should be credited with its own temporal logic is a familiar one in the work of historians of science. It is routinely assumed there that science by its very nature, and by virtue of the institutionalised forms of critical discourse that express it, tends to develop towards ever more comprehensive, integrated and economical structures of explanation. Hence, the overall order of changes one is empirically confronted with in the history is also a rationally intelligible order. Newton could not have come before Kepler or after Einstein. It would, of course, be a mistake, even in the strictest Hegelian terms, to depict the history as the pure unfolding of an immanent logic of science. For one thing, there can be no absolute necessity in the process since it depends on favourable material conditions and the absence of external shocks, factors that, so far as its immanent logic is concerned, are unbiddable contingencies. The necessity that is in question is, as it is in philosophical world history itself, the necessity that belongs to whatever is rationally intelligible and is, other things being equal, rationally only to be expected. Nevertheless, the general point will stand: the dialectic of scientific consciousness, however weak its impulse or intermittent its efficacy, is an integral part of the historical understanding of science. More generally still, one seems entitled to conclude even from this brief survey, that Hegel is not grappling here with phantoms created by his own style of thinking but with realities that anyone interested in the field must have some means of conceptualising. The means he offers, in the form of the categories listed earlier, are of unparalleled fecundity and scope. The examples of their operations that have already been given testify to this, and it will be borne out more fully over the course of the discussion.

Recognition

These examples have also served to introduce an issue that has not been taken up explicitly so far and yet is unavoidable. The topics of recognition (*Anerkennung*), and the desire and struggle for recognition, have come to receive much attention in recent years, indeed to be at the leading edge of Hegel studies. This is a somewhat surprising development since they have not traditionally had any such status.

Thus, to take a simple but telling indication, there is no entry for *Anerkennung* in Glockner's *Hegel Lexicon*, published in the 1920s. Its more recent prominence is due above all to the work of Kojève, the most influential and arresting commentator on Hegel's philosophy of history in the twentieth century. This late arrival at centre stage is not in itself grounds for scepticism. It is after all perfectly possible that Kojève and his followers have unearthed an important theme that eluded their predecessors, or discovered a way of organising the conceptual field that, once it has been pointed out, makes compelling sense. These matters will have to be considered further.

The earlier discussion had reached the point at which phenomeno-logical movement had become 'the process of recognition'. The movement now needs to be taken forward a little, with reference both to the *Phenomenology* and the parallel account in the *Encyclopaedia* philosophy of spirit. At first it takes the crudely direct form of an attempt to prevail by sheer self-assertion, to compel the other self-consciousness to yield recognition. Since the other is driven by the same impulse, the immediate outcome is a 'life and death struggle' (PS: 113–15). Such a 'trial by death' must, however, if carried through to the bitter end it postulates, destroy the very possibility of recogni-tion, as death is 'the *natural* negation of consciousness' (PS: 114). The futility of the struggle comes eventually to be grasped by one of the combatants who registers this insight by surrendering to the other. The one who surrenders becomes the 'servant' (*Knecht*) and the other the 'master' (*Herr*) (EPW 3: 222–3; HPM: 173–4). Thus, the life and death struggle is succeeded by the relationship of master and servant, a transition which gives rise to 'human social existence' and 'a begin-ning of *states*' (EPW 3: 223; HPM: 173). It is plainly a most significant moment of the dialectic so far as the present inquiry is concerned. For with these first intimations of society and politics, the groundwork of truly historical development has been laid. Phenomenology now opens up decisively towards history and a bridge to the central concerns of our inquiry has been established.

Kojève wishes, however, to claim much more for these early episodes. The relationship of master and servant, or, as it is often but less happily rendered, of master and 'slave', is taken by him to be not merely the harbinger of history but its central motif. Indeed, his entire reading of Hegel's philosophy of history is a kind of heroic generalisation of this relationship. Neither party to it is able, for reasons that will appear later, to obtain the recognition that is the object of their deepest, most human, desire, and so it is inherently restless and unstable. History is, for Kojève's Hegel, the product and expression of this situation, 'the history of the interaction between warlike Masters and working Slaves' (Kojève 1980: 43). It is not possible here to do full justice to Kojève's merits as an interpreter of Hegel, though important aspects of his interpretation will emerge in the course of the discussion. This would in any case be a far from straightforward task, not least because of his disdain for matters of mere exegesis. He believed that in his time Hegel's philosophy was less the revelation of a reality than a project to be realised, and so any serious interpretation of it must be 'political propaganda' (Kojève 1993: 380). It seems wholly in keeping with this belief that he should hold that 'the question of knowing if Hegel truly said what I have him say would seem to be puerile' (cit. in Roth 1985: 299n). In these circumstances prolonged attempts to gauge the scholarly worth of his reading are liable to seem flat-footed and beside the point. At the very least one should bear in mind that whatever brilliant insights or transforming perspectives he may provide, they are unlikely to come with a panoply of textual references. Nevertheless, it should be helpful to show how slight and unreliable is the textual basis for the claims now in question. For our interest is in understanding what makes Hegelian history go, and that purpose will be served by seeing how little warrant Hegel himself gives for casting recognition in the role.

The stage of the *Phenomenology* that may most plausibly be said to be driven by a desire for recognition, even though the expression itself does not occur there, is the life and death struggle. Once it is out of the way, the notion of recognition itself scarcely figures in the work, apart from the much later section on 'Conscience'. It is true, however, that it does have an important status in that section, and this would be enough in itself to vindicate Kojève as an interpreter who draws attention to truths that others have missed. Yet it will not vindicate him so far as the claims now being considered are concerned. To show this, one should cite the main propositions in which recognition appears in 'Conscience'. The 'being' of the *'person'* is said to be 'the *state of being recognised'* (*das Anerkanntsein*) (PG: 465; PS: 384). A little later the common element of distinct self-consciousnesses, and the substance in which activity has existence and reality, is said to be 'the moment of *being recognised* (*des Anerkanntwerdens*) by others' (PG: 470; PS: 388). In still more exalted language the 'reconciliation' of existent spirit with its opposite is described as 'a reciprocal recognition (*Anerkennen*) which is *absolute* spirit' (PG: 493; PS: 408).

These are, indeed, large claims. What is significant for present purposes, however, is that they employ 'recognition' and its variants in a context of achieved conditions or states of affairs, not of ongoing tasks or striving. These terms are used to signify not the motive force of a process but the character of the product that crowns it. This formula will also cover their only occurrence in the *Introduction* which is of theoretical interest. It is the previously cited assertion that we are free in so far as we 'recognise' the rational as law, and, thereby, the objective and the subjective will are 'reconciled'. The implication that recognition is an essential moment of realised freedom is most important. It does not follow, however, that this moment should be conceived as the fruit of a struggle, driven by the desire, to bring it about.

The view that it should not be so conceived seems in any case to be wise on general grounds. For there is a conceptual oddity about the notion of a struggle for recognition, and it is reasonable to suppose that Hegel would have been aware of it. The difficulty is one of seeing how such a consciously pursued struggle could be successful. In this respect, recognition belongs within a class of which the same is true to a greater or lesser extent of all its members, a class that includes such items as spontaneity, innocence, sincerity, ingenuousness, happiness and forgetting a traumatic event. There are differences between these cases which would be important in some contexts. What matters at present is what they have in common; that they are not, for one reason or another, appropriate objects of intentional striving. Anyone who grasps this must, in so far as they are rational, cease to struggle for them, and anyone who persists in that struggle must have an inadequate awareness of what they are doing. In the case of recognition it is not hard to see how the oddity in question arises. It does so from the tension between the goal being satisfied and its being exacted. The two are, as it were, inversely related, in that recognition must be devalued just to the extent that it is perceived to be enforced through struggle. It is not the least of the deep links between recognition and freedom that true recognition must be freely bestowed, a spontaneous benefaction. There are, of course, numerous intentional projects in this area that are not at all misconceived. Thus, one might strive to make oneself worthy of recognition as an artist by creating works of art. In such a case the recognition is not the direct object of the will, but comes, one might say, as a by-product of the object that is, in a way often supposed to be true also of happiness in particular. It remains the case that the injunction to struggle for recognition is in itself wholly empty and pointless.

The textual evidence suggests that Hegel is well aware of all this. The view that any struggle for recognition is doomed to fail may surely be taken as one of the lessons of the trial by death and master–servant episodes. It is, moreover, a lesson that is, one may assume, absorbed by the various consciousnesses implicated in the phenomenological movement. At any rate it should be recalled that these episodes occupy but a few pages of text at a very early stage of the movement, and that nothing that could be characterised as a desire for recognition emerges as a motive force thereafter. Against this background, the heroic character of Kojève's reading, its generalisation of a brief, superseded moment to be the whole of human history, stands out sharply. That Hegel sets his face directly against any such development is shown even more clearly by the discussion in the *Encyclopaedia* philosophy of spirit, a source which Kojève resolutely neglects.

Hegel remarks there that the life and death struggle for recognition can occur only in the natural state 'where human beings exist as single individuals'. It is, however, absent in civil society and the state because that recognition is 'already present' (EPW 3: 221; HPM: 172). This reasoning would seem to relegate the struggle for recognition as such to a primitive stage of human development. Moreover, it is relegated to prehistory, for history, as will emerge fully later, is essentially the realm of the state. What Hegel supposes the individual citizens of the state can properly seek to do, in full accord with this line of thought and with our preceding discussion, is to make themselves 'worthy' of the recognition they receive. Significantly, too, worthiness is achieved 'through the post he fills, through the trade he follows and through other working activity'. The citizen thereby escapes the 'empty subjectivity' that characterises the natural state where individuals 'want to compel their recognition' (EPW 3: 221–2; HPM: 172–3). The reference to 'empty subjectivity' may surely be taken as a Hegelian acknowledgement of the kind of conceptual oddity described earlier. This is a subjectivity that can never gain content, a union with the objective, in the way it wishes through its own sheer self-assertion. For the objective cannot be commanded in the way such an enterprise assumes. It appears that there are textual grounds, backed by theoretical considerations, for concluding that the struggle for recognition cannot, for Hegel, be the driving force of history.

It is still true that the notion of recognition is of strategic importance in his scheme, and that we are greatly in Kojève's debt for forcing it on our attention. The recognition in question is that mutual recognition which Hegel had genially assured us *is* absolute spirit. The *Encyclopaedia* account puts the basic case succinctly. Since '*true* freedom' consists in my identity with the other, 'I am truly free only when the other is also free and is recognised by me as free' (EPW 3: 220; HPM: 171). As the argument can be reiterated for any individual 'I', it follows that for the other to be truly free she must also recognise me as free. Hence, true freedom necessarily involves a system of mutual recognition. Indeed, a number of Hegelian trains of thought converge on this central point. It may be approached in an especially effective way through the images of reconciliation and being at home. For the world can truly be my home only if I know myself to be welcome here, and the basic expression of welcome is to be accepted and esteemed by the other inhabitants. I can identify with, and be fully reconciled to, the structures of intersubjectivity that comprise the 'I' that is 'We' only if my own status as a pillar of those structures is reflected back to me by being intersubjectively recognised. Then my sense of the rightness of my place is endlessly re-enacted and reaffirmed in my experience of social life. This is to attain the condition referred to in the *Introduction* account of the bond of freedom and recognition, the reconciliation of objective and subjective will in 'one and the same untroubled whole'. The futile struggles of empty subjectivity are now left far behind, wholly sublated in the objectivity of the ethical life of the state. To see the significance of recognition for the philosophy of history in these terms, in terms of the product rather than the process, is to answer some questions and to generate others. For if one takes the struggle for recognition out of the process, out of the story of what makes history go, there is a responsibility to fill the gap that is created. The next chapter will begin the attempt to fulfil this responsibility.

Actual and rational

In any discussion of the connection between history and system in Hegel a certain principle is almost bound to surface at some stage. Yet it is curiously difficult to interpret in a fully satisfactory way. The principle is formulated in the Preface to the *Philosophy of Right* as follows: 'What is rational is actual (*wirklich*); and what is actual is rational' (GPR: 24; EPR: 20). This formulation attracted a good deal of attention from the outset, and Hegel had to return to it in the second edition of the *Encyclopaedia* in order to warn against misunderstandings. The chief misunderstanding his warning is addressed to is the assumption that he was giving generalised approval as rational to everything that exists. In political and social terms this would seem to imply a rigid conservatism that would allow no reform, still less revolution, in any existing institution or practice. Hegel's main line of rebuttal is to point out that 'actuality' (*Wirklichkeit*) has a status which distinguishes it from mere 'appearance' (*Erscheinung*), 'contingent existence' (*zufällige Existenz*) and from such other ontological levels as 'determinate being' (*Dasein*) (EPW 1: 47–8; EL: 29–30). In support of the point he draws attention to the account of actuality he had given in the *Science of Logic* (SL: 541–3; cf. EPW 1: 213–25). The rebuttal is satisfactory so far as it goes. It is certainly true that Hegel is in principle committed to a complex, layered ontology which admits, in addition to those just mentioned, such other determinations as 'being' (*Sein*), 'reality' (*Realität*) and 'objectivity' (*Objectivität*) (Royce 1901: 461–3). Its invocation in the present case suffices to discredit the claim that he is offering a blanket approval, in the name of reason, to whatever exists. What he says here is, nevertheless, not wholly convincing, and its deficiencies are worth exploring a little. The question of the actual and the rational is one of considerable difficulty on both textual and theoretical grounds, and it will be possible to deal only with the aspects that are relevant to our immediate purposes.

The problem with the invocation of Hegel's layered ontology in the present context is that nowhere does he offer a way of demarcating the layers that is not a variation on the theme of the extent to which they embody or express rationality. As the accounts in the logical works make clear, these layers should be understood as stages in the self-making and self-manifestation of the Idea, that is, of reason. Thus, to come to our immediate concerns, it is significant that, in the *Encyclopaedia* rebuttal of the critics, Hegel provides no independent criterion for distinguishing the actual from, say, mere existence. That is to say, he provides no criterion other than the one that hovers in the background of the discussion, the presence or degree of presence of reason. The implication is simply that the actual is the existent infused with, or infused to some particular degree with, the rational. Now, however, the assertion that 'what is actual is rational' will have to be taken as making a conceptual point. It is that nothing that exists will count as actual except in so far as it is rational. In a less sympathetic vein, one may interpret Hegel as asserting tautologically that rational existence is rational. It will still be possible to give a substantive meaning to the other half of the *Philosophy of Right* principle. What 'the rational is actual' tells us is that there is rational existence, an existential, and not conceptual, claim. It is, of course, a wholly familiar doctrine by now, a version of the central thesis of Hegel's metaphysics. The *Encyclopaedia* rebuttal goes on almost at once to offer another version by reminding us that the Idea 'is not so impotent that it merely ought to be, and is not actual' (EL: 30). It is difficult now to think that this truth is best conveyed by being made to serve as one half of the *Philosophy of Right* formula. Hence, it is natural to look for some other way of getting the basic relationship of actual and rational into a nutshell.

An obvious pointer is provided by the statement in the epigraph to the present work that 'all that is rational must be' (Heine 1948: 254–5). It is true that Heine is not the most reliable of witnesses, and that he may in fact, as has been suggested, have caught this version not at first hand from Hegel but indirectly through one of his pupils (LNR: 9). Nevertheless, the statement itself is, as we now know, solidly grounded in lectures Hegel gave in Heidelberg before the publication of the *Philosophy of Right*. These assure us, in terms virtually identical to those reported by Heine, that 'what is rational must be' (LNR: 242, 247). If one wished to expand these claims into a full-blown alternative to the *Philosophy of Right* version, one could turn to another series of lectures delivered in Berlin a couple of academic sessions later. There Hegel's audience learned that 'what is rational becomes actual, and the actual becomes rational' (PRV: 51). This seems an improved formulation in that the central role it gives to becoming brings out more adequately the dynamic and dialectical character of Hegel's thought.

In the light of our preceding discussion, however, the second part of it will hardly do just as it stands. For one who maintains that the actual becomes rational is not naturally to be taken as making a conceptual point, to be simply expounding what it means to be actual. If, on the other hand, it is read as a substantive claim, one can scarcely profess to be assuming the layered ontology referred to earlier. 'The actual' ceases to be a term of art in the context of that ontology, and reverts to being a way of making a quite general or neutral existential claim, abstracting from the question of grades of existence. The second part of the statement will then simply mean that 'all that exists becomes rational'. This can itself be read as sound Hegelian doctrine, but still something of value has been lost. What is lost are the ontological discriminations that normally lurk in the background of Hegel's references to the actual and are indispensable for doing justice to his general position. Hence, it may be best to sacrifice symmetry here by taking elements from each of the alternatives so far offered. This would be to settle for saying: 'the actual is rational and the rational becomes actual'. Admittedly, it does not have the aphoristic neatness of either of the originals. Nevertheless, it has the advantage of managing to combine a conceptual and a substantive point in a way that allows for both the complexity and the dynamism of Hegel's ontological vision.

It should not be thought that we have moved far in substance from the doctrine of the *Philosophy of Right*, or even of its Preface. That portion of text has traditionally been the chief source of suspicions concerning Hegel's opportunism, and his reputation as the philosopher of absolutism and reaction. It might with more justice be seen as the main repository in the *Philosophy of Right* of his hopes of placating or deceiving the Prussian censorship. Yet even here there are, for readers more careful than the censor need be assumed to be, clear indications of the true bearing of his thought. The most remarkable of them is, perhaps, the fact that the proposition about the rational and the actual is introduced precisely in the context of a 'world revolution' (EPR: 20). The revolution in question is that wrought by the emergence of the principle of subjective freedom in Greek ethical life. According to Hegel the principle encapsulated a rationality implicit in the existent forms of that life, and its becoming explicit was a factor making for revolutionary upheaval. This analysis is fully in keeping with our revised version of the rational–actual formula. If the rational *becomes* actual, what is rational is most naturally to be identified with constant change, not with the unchanging persistence of the existing order. A more eligible philosophical grounding for political and social radicalism seems hard to conceive. This is, however, a suggestion whose full import and basis will become clear only gradually in the course of the inquiry.

The main body of the text of the *Philosophy of Right* offers various formulations that accord well with the revised statement of the rational–actual relationship. Most strikingly, perhaps, there is the assertion that 'it is the absolute end of reason that freedom should be actual' (EPR: 279; cf. LNR: 221). Here the rational and the actual are, one might say, mediated by freedom. It is through the process of achieving freedom that reason manifests its inherent dynamism, its impulse to actuality. This form of mediation takes one directly to the sphere of history, for it is there that freedom has to become actual. If one bears the ontological background in mind, it is evident that history is now being accorded the largest possible significance and responsibility. It is the indispensable medium in which the higher reaches of the central ontological drama of the concept becoming the Idea are enacted. The discussion should turn to consider the details of this process.

PART 2

THE COURSE OF HISTORY

Chapter 7

Passion and conquest

The question to be discussed in this and the following chapter is presented in the *Introduction* as one of 'means'; the means 'whereby freedom develops itself into a world' (H, 78: 68; M, 33: 20, 25, 23). In the most general terms the answer Hegel gives is plain enough. The only possible means of such development is 'the activity of human beings in the world at large' (H, 81: 69–70; cf. M, 36: 22, 28, 25). To begin with, Hegel's attention is fixed on individual human beings, though this will turn out not to be in the end his deepest and most characteristic concern. The springs of their activity are variously said to consist in 'need', 'drive', 'inclination', 'passion' (*Leidenschaft*) and 'interests' (H, 81–2: 70; M, 36–7: 22, 28, 25). The chief organisational notion in this list, or at any rate the one generally used to represent it, is 'passion'. Thus, Hegel declares that the Idea and human passion comprise 'the warp and the weft of the fabric of world history' (H, 83: 71; cf. M, 38: 23, 29, 26). In slightly less picturesque language we learn that 'The Idea as such is the reality: the passions are the arm with which it extends itself (*sich erstreckt*)' (H, 83: 71). The problem is how this self-extension is to be conceived in detail, how precisely it is that the warp and the weft combine to weave the historical fabric.

Interests

Hegel's depiction of the springs of historical activity is decked out in some of his most exuberant rhetoric. This has to be set aside to reach the definite and defensible thesis beneath. The rhetoric strikes a curiously Nietzschean note, hymning imperious self-assertion and defiance of convention. Its impact depends on a contrast with such influences as 'goodness', 'worthy patriotic sentiments', 'love of one's family or friends', 'rectitude in general'; in short, 'all virtues'. The virtues have a relatively limited scope compared to that of 'passions, the ends of particular interests, the satisfaction of selfishness'. What makes these forces powerful is precisely the fact that

> They do not heed any of the restraints which right and morality seek to impose upon them, and the elemental power of passion has a more immediate hold over human beings than the artificial and wearisome discipline of order and moderation, right and morality.
> (H, 79: 68; M, 33–4: 20, 26, 23)

From passages of this kind it is easy to form the impression that, for Hegel, history is largely a theatre of blind, violent, egotistical forces.

The attempt to uncover his true position may start from a standard item in his listings of 'motive forces'. Its indispensability is not in doubt: 'if I put something into practice and give it existence ... it must be an interest of mine' (H, 81–2: 70). Hegel seeks to avoid misunderstanding here by distinguishing two ways of invoking interests. It is, he notes, a distinction which language 'correctly expresses', and no less so, one might add, in English, than in German, usage. A justified form of censure, he remarks, is to say of someone 'that he has an interest (*interessiert überhaupt*) – in other words, that he is merely seeking some personal advantage'. By way of contrast, Hegel reminds us that 'anyone who is active for a cause does not just have an interest but is interested in it' (H, 82: 70; M, 37: 22–3, 28, 25). The distinction is, it may be said, between objects that are in one's interest and those in which one takes an interest, or between those that serve one's interests and those that engage them. The two kinds of interest are, of course, linked in that the welfare of whatever arouses one's interest will, usually or typically, come to be seen as part of one's interest in the sense, crudely speaking, of 'personal advantage'. Nevertheless, the distinction is sound so far as it goes, and has the merit of suggesting the complexity of talk of interest as a motive force. It is fully in line with this complexity that, as Hegel goes on to observe, those who are active for a cause demand that 'they should be able to enter into it with their own opinions and convictions regarding its goodness, right, utility, advantage for themselves and so on' (H, 83: 70–1; M, 37: 23, 28, 26).

The general point is later developed with explicit reference to motivation in history:

> The agents pursue finite ends and particular interests in their activities; but they are also knowing and thinking beings. For this reason, the content of their ends is interwoven with universal and essential determinations of right, goodness, duty etc. For mere desire, the barbarity and crudeness of the will, falls outside the theatre and sphere of world history.
>
> (H, 95: 81; M, 44: 28, 36, 31)

The distinction within desires and volitions implied here is not so clear as one would wish. Nevertheless, the implication seems to be that the historically significant items are those that are interwoven with general normative considerations. This might well be thought to exemplify a tendency to over-refine the historical. If so, however, it is plainly not in the direction of any form of crude egotism. Knowing and thinking beings in history are, one might now suppose, essentially self-justifying agents who need a sense that what they do has some kind of legitimacy. Hence it is that their desires and volitions are mediated by considerations of goodness, right and duty alongside expectations of 'advantage for themselves'. A persuasively complex picture of historical motivation seems to be emerging. It allows for the interweaving of particular interests and universal determinations, and for both to contribute to the forms of satisfaction to which, as was noted earlier, Hegel insists that the agent has an 'infinite right'. This is a long way from thinking of history as an arena of naked self-seeking, of wholly unregenerate means which can be connected to universal ends only by feats of prestidigitation.

The case for Hegel's historical immoralism has not by any means been disposed of at this point. It may even be suggested that its strongest card has still to be played. Before considering that possibility, the account of interests should be related to what was earlier said to be the key notion of the passions. In making the link Hegel admits that 'passion' is not entirely the right word for what he is trying to express (H, 85: 72; M, 38: 23, 29, 26). Nevertheless, he proceeds in a way that seems reasonably in keeping with the normal usage, at least as a heightened version of it. The conclusion which has so far been reached is that 'nothing at all has come to pass without the interest of those whose activity is involved in it'. The next step is to note that 'we call an interest "passion" ' in so far as

the whole individuality, to the neglect of all the many other actual or possible interests and aims, applies itself to an object with every fibre of the will, and concentrates all its needs and powers on attaining its end

(H, 85: 73; M, 37–8: 23, 29, 26)

Thus, the language of the passions is the language of intense and total commitment, of the condition in which human beings dedicate 'the entire energy of their will and character' to their goals (H, 85: 72; M, 38: 23–4, 29, 26). Indeed, passion in a certain sense *is* energy, 'the subjective and thereby formal aspect of energy, of will and activity' (H, 85–6: 73; M, 38–9: 24, 30, 27). Bearing in mind the conclusion of the discussion of interests stated above, the inference to be drawn is that 'nothing great has been accomplished in the world without passion' (H, 85: 73; M, 38: 23, 29, 26).

The status thus established for passion is later brought to bear on the specific issue of morality: 'Passion is the prerequisite of all human excellence, and there is accordingly nothing immoral about it'. The point, one may suppose, is that passion is not as such, or intrinsically, immoral. It is just as indispensable, and as available, for noble and virtuous actions as for any others, and, hence, is itself morally neutral. Hegel goes on at once to shed a more favourable light on passion from another direction. When its 'zeal' is of a genuine nature, he declares, it remains 'cool' and the theoretical faculty has 'a clear view of the means by which its true ends can be realised' (H, 101: 86). Thus, passion is not to be regarded as a blind, unreflecting force. On the contrary, its very authenticity is bound up with a capacity for calculation. Here, as elsewhere, Hegel seems to blend what are often taken to be antithetical elements of the rational and the irrational, a tendency whose other aspects will come into view as the discussion proceeds. For the present what should be noted is that his conception of the sources of historical action seems to have come a long way from its rhetorical starting point. In particular, that conception now allows historical actors to be interested in good and just causes, and to pursue them with the entire force of their will and character. It is time to play what was earlier described as the strongest card on the side of his alleged historical immoralism, that which introduces the activities of those he terms 'world historical individuals'.

States of mind

These individuals are not simply to be credited with great achievements in any conventional sense. What they do is truly revolutionary in being destructive of old worlds and in laying foundations for the new. The examples Hegel gives of Alexander, Julius Caesar and Napoleon, the conquerors of Asia, Gaul and Europe, show the very exalted nature of his conception. It must be admitted, however, that the little he offers by way of discursive presentation seems rather at odds with its evident importance in his scheme. Moreover, the clues he does provide have to be fitted together carefully if they are to yield a coherent picture. This is true not least as regards their implications for the authority of morality and ethical life. It is also true of another large issue which is best taken first by way of preliminary. The issue is that of the level of consciousness and cognitive grasp which the world historical individuals manage to achieve of their situation.

The first step is to set out the main indications we have of the truth of the matter. It may be well to cite the relevant passages from both of our editions of the *Introduction*, without repetition of what they have in common. For they differ in points of striking detail, even if not in substance.

> Such individuals did not have in their aims the consciousness of the Idea as such, but were practical and political human beings. Yet at the same time they were thinking beings with insight into what is needed and what is *timely*. That is the very truth of their time and their world, the next species, so to speak, which was already present within (*im Innern*). It was theirs to know this universal, the necessary next stage of their world, to make it their aim and to put their energy into it. The world historical human beings, the heroes of an era, are therefore to be recognised as the insightful ones; their deeds and words are the best of their time.
>
> (M, 46: 30, 40, 33)

> world historical individuals are those who have willed and accomplished not something imagined and intended but something correct and necessary, those who know what has revealed itself to their inner vision (*in deren Innerem*), and what is timely and necessary.
>
> One can distinguish here the realisation that even such forms are only moments of the universal Idea. This realisation is the prerogative of philosophy. World historical individuals do not need it, as they are practical beings ... they know what is the truth of their world and their time, what the concept is, the next universal to emerge ...
>
> (H, 97–8: 83)

With a little care, and minimal interpretative charity, the indications given in these passages will fit together to yield a consistent, if schematic, account of the state of consciousness of world historical individuals. What they primarily offer is a set of limits within which the consciousness of particular individuals may be supposed to range. To fill in a detailed content is then a matter for further inquiry in each case. It is just to be expected, on the one hand, that world historical individuals should fail to grasp the historical forms of their time as moments of the universal Idea and, indeed, that they should lack any awareness of the Idea as such. These achievements are, after all, the prerogative not simply of philosophy but of a philosophy that comes on the scene at a comparatively late stage of historical development. On the other hand, the individuals in question are thoughtful people who are distinguished from their contemporaries precisely by their deeper insight into the needs and potentialities of the age. More specifically, they have a sense of the nature of the 'truth' that is maturing within the existing order and will succeed it. To that extent, they may properly be said to apprehend the next stage in the progress of spirit, 'the next universal to emerge'.

The world historical individual we hear most about is Julius Caesar. Hegel attributes to Caesar a relatively high level of understanding of the situation in which he had to act. He had, according to Hegel, 'a most correct picture (*Vorstellung*) of the so-called Roman Republic', and, indeed knew that it was 'a lie'. Moreover, he knew that 'another structure must be put in the place of this hollow one', and that what was necessary was 'the structure he himself created' (H, 104–5: 89). This kind of knowledge fits comfortably within, and lends substance to, the general description of the world historical individuals. There is no suggestion that Caesar had the kind of insight into the significance of his own historical period that would involve a consciousness of the Idea as such. What he saw vividly and concretely was that the old republican order could not be sustained and must give way to the rule of one person over the Roman world. This may legitimately be described in Hegelian language as a grasp of the next universal to emerge, and, hence, of what the concept required at that historical moment. Such a grasp need not be supposed to be speculative in character, or even fully discursive. It shows itself in a complex blend of explicit understanding and semi-conscious awareness, precipitating together into a deep instinct for what in practice needs to be done. This seems by no means an unrealistic picture of the condition of effective historical actors in general. Those actors do not lack an intelligent, conscious grasp of their situation, and yet, of course, their intelligence is necessarily limited and their consciousness not fully reflexive. They inhabit, and act in, a world that is neither wholly transparent to their vision, nor blankly opaque. Even world historical figures such as Caesar see, one seems almost irresistibly drawn to say, through a glass darkly. Yet they may be assumed to stand significantly closer to the clearer portions than do the contemporaries who comprise their opponents and followers.

Hegel does not attempt any detailed inquiry into the state of mind of those he deems world historical individuals, but is content to set its terms and boundaries. His chief concern is to make clear that their role is intelligible only in the light of the development of spirit. A series of pronouncements bears on this point. The great world historical individuals, he declares, are those who 'realise the end appropriate to the higher concept of spirit' and whose inspiration is drawn from 'that hidden spirit which knocks on the present but still lies beneath the surface' (H, 97: 82–3; cf. M, 45–6: 30, 40, 32–3) They arrive on the scene when spirit 'has outgrown the world', but has not yet discovered what it wants. In this situation their task is to make that discovery on behalf of spirit, and 'first say to human beings' what the wants in question are (H, 99: 84). Thus, the significance of such individuals is to be grasped through the central propelling image of Hegel's historical dialectic, the progressive disclosure of what is concealed, the emergence of spirit from an underground existence into the sun of self-consciousness. Hence, what underlies the conception is the philosophy of history as a whole and, beneath that, the ontological ground. It is only to be expected that it should in turn serve to sharpen and vivify the general scheme. This is achieved by exhibiting the explanatory power of that scheme, as a particular instance will demonstrate.

The issue is one of explaining the grip that the great individuals of history exert on their contemporaries. This is, of course, the factor that enables them, often from unpromising beginnings, to sweep all before them in carrying out their historical mission. According to Hegel, their 'true power' resides in the content which is the substance not merely of their own particular ends but also of 'the will of the world spirit'. As such, it is present in the 'universal unconscious instinct of humanity'. Hence, it is that human beings are incapable of resisting the individual who makes this instinct conscious through the ends he pursues. On the contrary, the peoples 'flock to his standard, for he reveals to them and carries out what is their own immanent impulse' (H, 90: 76). It is this coming together of inner and outer, of subjective, hidden motives and objective, public forms, in the person of the world historical individuals that is the secret of their success. It would be hard to exceed Hegel's estimate of the force that is thereby generated:

> For the advanced spirit is the inner soul of all individuals, although it is an unconscious interiority (*Innerlichkeit*) until great men bring it to consciousness. It is that which they themselves truly want, and therefore it exerts a power over them to which they surrender even in contradiction with their conscious will; hence they follow these leaders of souls because they feel the irresistible power of their own inner spirit which confronts them.
>
> (H, 99: 84–5; M, 46: 30–1, 40–1, 33)

The contemporaries of the world historical individual find his voice compelling because they recognise it as the true voice of their inner selves, speaking to them the secrets of their own hearts. That this should be so is itself to be explained in terms of the evolution of spirit as the soul of all individuals, great ones and followers alike. Thus, the relationship of leader and led may be comprehended within the framework of Hegelian philosophy of spirit, and it reveals in an important specific case the explanatory potential of that framework. It should be added that the underlying question of how to account for the careers of a Caesar or a Napoleon is one that any serious engagement with history has to address. Hegel's answer has definite advantages over its obvious rivals, for instance, over opportunist and theoretically vacant talk about 'charisma'. Indeed, it can serve to give such talk a grounding and a substance by linking it to a general scheme of intellectual order, a scheme at once parsimonious and comprehensive in the highest degree. This is true also of Hegel's own example of explanatory nullity, a form of 'psychological' approach popular in his time and still familiar in ours. Such an approach does not, in his view, introduce a genuinely independent causal factor but simply gives a circular re-description of what is to be explained. Thus, the 'proof' that Alexander acted from 'a lust for fame and conquest' is that 'he did that which brought him fame' (H, 102: 87; M, 47–8: 31–2, 42, 34). Hegel deals sharply with the envy and meanness of spirit he detects in the 'psychologists', citing the saying that 'no man is a hero to his valet' and crediting himself with the addition, taken up by Goethe, that this is 'not because the former is not a hero, but because the latter is a valet' (H, 103: 87–8; M, 48: 32, 42–3, 34).

A factor that may need some further emphasis is the extent to which the world historical individuals are simply instruments. The source of their power is not sheer genius imposing its vision on a recalcitrant world but a precocious gift of interpretation which reveals that world's own emergent vision to itself. What matters is not the ability to swim against the tide but the ability to catch it early and use it to the full. The great historical figures are servants of a larger purpose, not autonomous creators and masters of events. So much is this the case that their individuality seems wholly absorbed in their mission: 'What they are is just their deed; their passion comprises the range of their nature, their character'. Moreover, their lives are utterly consumed in its pursuit: 'When their end is attained they fall aside like empty husks ... they die early like Alexander, are murdered like Caesar, or deported like Napoleon' (H, 100: 85; M, 47: 31, 41, 33).

The general point emerges most vividly in the thesis that world historical individuals are replaceable and that nothing of significance hangs on their being the particular persons they are. Thus, if the ends they set themselves had not been those of the inner will of humanity, they would, Hegel assures us, 'have remained within the ordinary channels of humanity, and another would have accomplished what spirit willed' (H, 104: 88). The issue of contingency and necessity arises once more at this point. In terms of it the moral to be drawn is the characteristically Hegelian one that the development of spirit indispensably requires a sphere of contingency, and the existence of such a sphere is thereby necessary. It is necessary that there be some individual mediators and catalysts of great events, for someone must be the first to interpret spirit to itself. That this was done by the specific individuals known to history is, however, merely a contingent fact. Had they not done it, others would have appeared to do the work of spirit. This view is very far from suspending the entire weight of historical interpretation on the unique, personal qualities of individuals. Indeed, it might be thought to go too far in the opposite direction, to allow individual identity to be assimilated too fully into the working out of the universal. It may seem to concede too little, and nothing essential, to the fact that it was, after all, Cleopatra whom Caesar and Antony encountered as Queen of Egypt, or that it was Lenin who stepped from the train at the Finland Station. This suggestion raises complex, general issues about historical causation that cannot be resolved here. It suffices for present purposes to conclude that while Hegel is no valet and can recognise true heroism, he does not place heroes and hero worship at, or near, the centre of his understanding of history.

The world's court of judgement

It is time to turn to the other large issue raised by Hegel's account of the world historical individuals, its implications for the status of morality and ethical life. They are problematic because of two prominent features of that account. On the one hand it is plain that the individuals in question disregard or violate at will all moral and ethical norms. On the other, Hegel evidently regards their doing so as in some sense justifiable. The prospect that opens up is that his philosophy of history will serve to condone acts of wickedness and barbarism, and, indeed, the more monstrously effective such acts are, the more eligible to have it called in their defence. In order to get to grips with this problem one should describe and document the features that give rise to it.

There can be no doubt that world historical individuals do not consider themselves to be bound by ordinary standards of conduct. Their exclusive concern with 'their own momentous interests' leads them to 'treat other intrinsically admirable interests and sacred rights light-heartedly, cursorily, hastily and heedlessly, a way of behaving that is exposed to moral censure'. Nevertheless, Hegel seems content at this point just to issue the brutal warning that 'A mighty figure tramples, as it proceeds, many an innocent flower underfoot, and must destroy many things in its path' (H, 105: 89; cf. M, 49: 32, 43, 35). The implication that it may be the opponents of these mighty figures who have ethics and morality on their side is also explicitly drawn:

Those who, on ethical grounds, and hence with nobler feeling, have resisted what the progress of the Idea of spirit made necessary, stand higher in moral worth than those whose crimes had been transformed within a higher order into means of accomplishing the will of this order.

(H, 171: 141; M, 91: 67, 82, 71)

The air of heroic immorality that attends the great criminals is enhanced when one recalls the special role of passion in their case: 'they were people of passions, i.e., they held to their goal with passion and put their whole character, genius and nature into it' (H, 101: 86). The worst are indeed, it seems, full of passionate intensity.

The second point that is evident from Hegel's account is that the actions of world historical individuals are nevertheless, in some sense, justified. They have, he assures us, 'right on their side', and, in truth, 'whatever they do is right'. This is so, of course, only when they are, as it were, acting in their world historical capacity. It is 'only in so far as their ends are compatible with that of spirit which has being in and for itself' that they have 'absolute right' on their side, a right that is, however, of a 'wholly peculiar' kind (H, 98: 83–4). It is the right of the world which 'rises above all particular claims' (H,109: 92; M, 54:37, 48,40). Thus, 'whatever is required and accomplished by the ultimate end of spirit' stands above all that attaches to individuality 'in regard to its ethical life'. Moreover, world history, as the accomplishment of this end, 'moves on a higher level than that on which morality has its proper place', the level of 'private sentiment' and 'the conscience of individuals'. Hence it is that those who champion the cause of morality and ethical life against the depredations of world historical individuals defend only 'a formal right, abandoned by the living spirit and by God' (H, 171: 141; M, 90–1: 66–7, 82, 70–1).

This line of thought should be taken a stage further to find its true ground. It will then emerge that the notion used to express the superior claims of the world historical individuals, that of 'right', derives its own importance from the notion which is truly fundamental in this area, that of 'freedom'. Right is, Hegel explains, 'in general, freedom as Idea' (EPR: 58). That is to say, it is the 'determinate existence' of the 'self-conscious freedom' which is 'the highest thing on earth' (LNR: 329). The peculiar right of world historical individuals is grounded in their function as instruments by means of which the highest thing on earth is achieved. This process is itself, of course, the ultimate source of meaning and value in world history, the dialectic through which

> the *universal* spirit, *the spirit of the world*, produces itself as unlimited and exercises its right – which is the highest right of all – over [finite spirits] in *world history* as the *world's court of judgement* (*Weltgericht*)
>
> (GPR: 503; EPR: 371)

An attempt to vindicate whatever world historical individuals do will, it seems, have to invoke the fundamentals of Hegel's philosophy of history. To point this out is not, however, likely to appease his critics. It will not of itself allay their central concerns over the apparent exoneration of foul deeds, of what Hegel himself calls 'crimes', or, in a treacherous metaphor, the trampling underfoot of innocent flowers. There have been, it may be thought, too many massacres of innocents, not least in the blood-soaked twentieth century, for us to find this tolerable. It remains the case that Hegel seems to have developed a systematically immoral, or at any rate amoral, view of history in which large-scale evil is approved or condoned. This is a most serious charge which has still to be properly addressed. Hegel has, it will now be argued, an adequate defence to the substance of it, even if one will never be able to eliminate a characteristic bleakness of vision that cannot be congenial to everyone.

Might and right

The first element of the defence is to note that Hegel is far from holding in any straightforward way the doctrine that might is right. Indeed he seeks to distance himself from it on every suitable occasion. This is so not least when he explains what is involved in regarding world history as a court of judgement. He insists that world history is not 'the mere judgement of might', and adds a reminder of the underlying theory. Since spirit in and for itself is reason, world history is the necessary development 'of the *moments* of reason and hence of spirit's self-consciousness and freedom' (GPR: 504; EPR: 372). These formulations point once more, to state their direction in rough but serviceable terms, towards Hegel's deep and principled optimism, an optimism that is the true expression of his philosophy of history as a whole. Characteristically it takes the form of the conviction that the forces opposed to reason do not have the strength to hold out against it indefinitely, and that what is right comes in the long run to be armoured in might. It is from this conviction that the authority of history, as the court which judges the long run, derives. Its authority is ultimately that of reason, while mere might as such cannot be a source of legitimation in any sense.

There is another form of limited reassurance which is worth offering at this point. It may be introduced by remarking that Hegel is well aware that, among those who deviate from the 'established order', there will be false prophets and ordinary criminals whose actions express no higher end of spirit but merely their own vast egos and wicked hearts. Such individuals have no world historical significance, whatever ideals they may profess: 'Adventurers of all kinds have such ideals. ... But the fact that all such attitudes (*Vorstellungen*), sound reasons, or general principles differ from existing ones does not justify them' (H, 97: 83). Thus, we are not in principle simply helpless in the face of just any repudiation of conventional values. Its significance may belong to individual biography or pathology rather than to world history. The contrast is taken up immediately in Hegel's restatement of his position:

> The only true ends are those whose content has been produced by the absolute might of the inner spirit itself, and world historical individuals are those who have willed and accomplished not something imagined and projected but something correct and necessary.
> (H, 97: 83; cf. M, 47: 31, 34)

It is, no doubt, salutary to bear in mind that, for Hegel, a rebel against the existing order may not be a harbinger of the new but a mere adventurer. To do so does not of itself, it must be admitted, go very far towards resolving present anxieties. It is, nevertheless, helpful in that it takes one to the point where it becomes fruitful to ask what is still missing from Hegel's position. To see what that is should reveal the real source of these anxieties. The suggestion that presents itself is that what his position so far lacks is a practical dimension, the ability to yield criteria for deciding in particular cases the courses of action to initiate or support. Yet these are surely what historical actors, whether would-be leaders or potential followers, need most of all. Hence, their absence leaves the defence of Hegel in a state of disabling uncertainty at a critical point. His theory allows in principle for the possibility that ordinary moral and ethical standards may be disregarded with justification. It does not seem unreasonable to ask that it provide some means of determining when these situations arise. What response can Hegel make to the demand for relevant criteria of practical judgement?

It may be well to begin by recalling some familiar aspects of his thought. He is not, to put it mildly, in any obvious sense a radical or iconoclast so far as ethics and morality are concerned. He shows no desire to subvert conventional beliefs in those areas, or to go systematically beyond the conceptions of good and evil they employ. So far from being a revaluer of values, he is pre-eminently the upholder of established norms and practices, and, as was seen earlier, takes them to be the primary recourse in all questions of conduct. Neither, as was also shown, is he indifferent, still less hostile, to the morality of private convictions and the 'sanctuary' of individual conscience.

Moreover, the ethical life of the rational state is the sublation of the various spheres of practical judgement only, as will appear later, in virtue of incorporating a respect both for conscience and for custom. These familiar Hegelian doctrines throw into sharp relief the specificity, indeed uniqueness, of the capacity of world historical individuals to transcend ethics and morality. Theirs is indeed a wholly peculiar right. Its peculiarity lies not least, it should now be said, in the nature of the tribunal that alone can affirm and uphold it, the court of judgement that is world history. For the verdict of that court is precisely the verdict *of* history, and as such cannot be available to those, whether they are adventurers or world historical figures, who struggle *within* history in pursuit of their goals. This point is crucial here.

It is not at all surprising that world historical individuals themselves are in no position to anticipate the conclusions of the world court of judgement. They have, after all, no understanding of the Idea as such, and see only the next link in the historical chain, not the pattern of the whole. It is not, however, their lack of speculative insight that is decisive. For nothing would be gained by looking to the philosophers who have that insight. 'The philosopher', as Hegel sharply warns in the *Introduction*, 'has nothing to do with prophecy' (H, 210: 171; cf. M, 114: 87, 90). It is a position he consistently maintains: since philosophy is the comprehension of its own time in thoughts, its face is turned resolutely away from the future (EPR: 21). Thus, there can be no one who can be entitled to prejudge the verdict of history. Nor do things change if one turns to the entity which, as will later emerge, should be seen as a higher embodiment of reason and freedom than any individual human being; that is, to the state. Hegel reminds us at one point in the *Introduction* that in world history the sole authority is 'the right of absolute spirit', and goes on to declare flatly that 'this is a right to which no state can appeal' (H, 147: 124). It seems that the judgement of history cannot legitimately be appealed to in the midst of events by any of the forms of historical spirit.

It follows that there can be no alternative in practice to the authority of ethics and morality. Those who in their name oppose the trampling down of innocent flowers have the support of all operative and effective right. This is so even in the extraordinary case where the trampler is in truth, and will ultimately be seen to be, a world historical figure. No one can know this truth in advance, or properly assume it. Thus, the ultimate peculiarity of the right of such figures is that it is wholly without practical force or significance for its legitimate invocation never arrives in time to be a guide to action. It follows also that anyone who claims to be justified in violating ethical and moral norms in pursuit of their goals should be regarded as a charlatan and, where their actions fit their words, as an unredeemed villain. More generally, the conclusion to be drawn is that the philosophy of history cannot be a mode or instrument of practical reasoning, and that this is in the end the substance of Hegel's dusty answer to the demand that it yield criteria of conduct. Hence, there is no room in his thought for any 'teleological suspension of the ethical', a feat of which he has sometimes been accused (Kierkegaard 1941: 67–77, cf. Wood 1990: 232–4).

It is true that the teleological, the domain of world history, is in a fundamental sense superior to the ethical. Yet the ethical can never be suspended within history. Its claims may be seen to have been superseded only when the events in question have run their course, too late to have any practical bearing on the outcome.

It should be emphasised, to complete this discussion, that not only are world historical individuals not entitled to appeal to the court of world history, they have no need to do so. For they have, as Hegel depicts them, other resources at their disposal. These are resources that are in principle available to any of their contemporaries but from which they, with their deeper insight, are the first to draw strength and legitimacy. The point is once again best illustrated by Julius Caesar. In preparing the ground for the assertion that he knew the Roman Republic to be a lie, Hegel tells us that he realised 'that the supposed laws of *auctoritas* and *dignitas* had fallen into abeyance and that it was proper to put an end to the latter as particularly arbitrary'. He 'was able to accomplish this', Hegel adds, because 'it was correct' (H, 104: 89). The implication is, as before, that the support needed for success was obtained because others could grasp the truth once it was brought home to them, at least to the extent of being drawn to follow the person who represented it. Here one recalls once more the nub of Hegel's account, his understanding of the phenomenon of the world historical individuals in terms of their lifeline to the hidden spirit. This is what enables them to express the unconscious, rational impulse of their time. It is a truth that may easily be obscured amid all the attention to the drama of their roles as the great criminals of history.

Chapter 8

The cunning of reason

This discussion of historical means has still some way to go in answering the question with which it began, that of how to conceive of their service of the Idea. Indeed, that question now seems to arise even more pressingly. For one might well wonder how precisely it could be that world historical individuals, with their limited understanding and limitless passions, manage to advance the cause of the universal. The problem is one that arises in the case of their followers too and, in truth, of all historical actors. Hence, Hegel poses the issues in suitably general terms. Having given his standard list of the items of which we have taken 'passion' to be representative, he comments as follows: 'This immeasurable mass of wills, interests and activities constitutes the instruments and means of the world spirit for achieving its end, to raise it to consciousness and to realise it'. He goes on to narrow the focus a little by declaring that those very life-forms of individuals and peoples are, in seeking and satisfying their own ends, 'at the same time the means and instruments of something higher and broader of which they know nothing, and which they unconsciously fulfil' (H, 87: 74; M, 40: 25, 31, 28). There is plainly a theoretical space here between finite instruments and infinite ends which has to be filled. Hegel's primary recourse is to the device, prefigured in these remarks, of the 'cunning of reason' (*List der Vernunft*).

It is a device that gives rise to an even sharper sense of incongruity between Hegel and his interpreters than is the case with the world historical individuals. A mountain of commentary rests on relatively brief portions of text, themselves given over in large part to a vigorous rhetoric. Once again, however, it should prove possible to identify a literal and defensible thesis. It will turn out to be both firmly grounded in Hegel's thought and of value in addressing questions that also have a life outside it, questions that arise for any theoretical engagement with history. Indeed, the very rootedness of the cunning of reason may itself go some way to account for Hegel's lack of explicitness. The place for it is so decisively preordained, and its function so firmly delimited, by systemic considerations that the need for it to be worked out discursively may not have seemed compelling to him. It is not a device with a rich internal structure demanding elaboration but one in the service of larger factors by which its use is determined and, one might say, over-determined. Thus, it might be assumed that anyone with a sense of the architecture of Hegel's thought could readily acquire a grasp of its role.

These remarks may be filled out in a preliminary way so as to motivate the introduction of the cunning of reason theme. In very general terms the need for it is obvious enough. That need must arise in some form for any speculative philosopher of history, at least for any who views the overall story as in some sense, however vague or attenuated, one of progress. He or she will have the challenge of explaining how impure, insensible or base forces can yield results that transcend their own aspirations. It seems inevitable that the progressive movement will have to be seen as occurring in large measure 'behind the back' of the consciousness of the human participants (PS: 56). The term 'cunning' is bound to have a certain appeal in this context in view of the elements of indirection, complexity of mediation and surprise that the process involves. Such elements capture, at any rate, one aspect of the usual associations of the term. Thus, for instance, Kant's writings on the philosophy of history may, as has already been noted, be said to postulate a cunning of nature or providence. This works through the '*unsocial sociability* of men', the warring inclinations of living in society and as isolated individuals. It is the dialectical interplay of the two which, in Kant's conception, sets human beings on the path leading 'from barbarism to culture', an outcome wholly unintended by the barbarians who bring it about (Kant 1991: 44). With Hegel the pressure of strategic requirements is even more direct. History may be characterised for him as essentially the development over the long run of progressively higher levels of consciousness and self-consciousness. It is inescapably part of this conception that the levels of awareness which crown any particular phase are not those that animate the individuals struggling within it. These toilers of the deep 'unconsciously fulfil' what is only to be apprehended fully in retrospect by others nearer the surface. Some means of conceptualising the emergence of the consciously rational through successive layers of the unconsciously or less consciously rational is a necessity of the scheme. The device of the cunning of reason is designed to meet this requirement.

Types of purpose

The manner in which the cunning of reason comes on the scene in the *Introduction* is as follows:

> it is not the universal Idea which involves itself in opposition, struggle and danger; it keeps itself in the background, untouched and unharmed. ... This may be called the *cunning of reason* that it allows (*lässt*) the passions to work for it, whereby that through which it gives itself existence pays the penalty and suffers the harm ... The Idea pays the tribute of existence and of the past not out of itself, but out of the passions of individuals.
>
> (H, 105: 89; M, 49: 33, 43–4, 35)

The cunning of reason is presented in this passage as the chief mediator of human passions and the Idea, that is to say, as the basic answer to the question of how the warp and the weft combine in the historical fabric. When one tries to conceive its role in concrete terms, however, difficulties begin to arise.

They arise in large part from the fact that the passage seems, in a familiar manner, to be pointing in two directions at once. To open up the issues, one may start with a matter of detail, the interpretation of the central claim that reason in its cunning 'allows' the passions to work for it. This rendering appears in only one of our standard translations, while the others tell us that reason 'sets' the passions to work for it. The difference reflects an ambiguity in the normal usage of *lassen*, as meaning either to let or allow to happen on the one hand or to cause or make to happen on the other. The choice of translations is, however, theoretically significant in that they seem to assign different kinds of roles to reason. To bring this out more concretely, and obtain some guidance as to which reading is to be preferred, one should look elsewhere in Hegel's dealings with the cunning of reason.

The *Encyclopaedia Logic* assures us that reason is 'as cunning as it is mighty', and that 'with regard to the world and its process, divine Providence behaves with absolute cunning'. For God 'lets human beings, who have their particular passions and interests, do as they please (*lässt ... gewähren*), and what results is the accomplishment of *his* intentions which are something other than those whom he employs were directly concerned about' (EPW 1: 365; EL: 284). On the surely warranted assumption that Hegel is concerned here with the same basic relationship of reason or the Idea or God and human passions as in the *Introduction* passage, the reading of 'allows' in that passage also now seems vindicated. The theoretical implications of this conclusion are obvious. A God who really does let human beings do as they please is no superhuman Iago, manipulating the unwitting instruments of his purposes. Indeed, it is hard to see how he can have any effective role at all in the process through which the universal ends are accomplished. An explanatory gap now seems to open up in the story and, in particular, there is the need to ground the expectation that these ends really will be accomplished by letting human beings do as they please. Thus, it seems that if God has to be envisaged as an autonomous personal subject, he is simply redundant and may as well be left out of the picture. It, however, God could be identified with a reason immanent in the world and its process, religious language would be available once more to represent speculative truth. The ambiguity of the *Introduction* passage is, however, such that this immanent interpretation can also claim support there. In particular, there is the reference to reason giving itself existence through its cunning. This seems to postulate not independent pre-existence but the immanent subject and its self-making in and through history.

It should be conceded, however, that the main weight of the passage, whatever that amounts to, falls on the transcendent side. This is no less the case if one accepts that reason 'allows', rather than 'gets', the passions to work for it. If anything, a God who holds aloof from human affairs may be more straightforwardly conceived transcendently than one who actively intervenes in them. Thus, for all the explanatory nullity, at least where the philosophy of history is concerned, of the spectator God conception, it can never be wholly deprived of its links with the texts. In such circumstances the strategy must always be to set these links against other, more numerous and weighty, indications on the opposing side. Attempts have been made to carry out that strategy at various points in the present inquiry. It may be worthwhile to show how the indications in questions readily arise with specific reference to teleology.

In the *Science of Logic* Hegel criticises the tendency to link 'the teleological principle' with 'the concept of an *extramundane* intelligence'. It is, he notes, a link which leads to this principle being 'favoured by piety' (WL 2: 438; SL: 735). What piety envisages, one may suppose, is the identification of the extramundane intelligence with a divine providence shaping human events to its own premeditated ends. That Hegel does not wish to make use of any such conception of purpose is suggested by his disavowal of the link that piety favours. It is further borne out by the assertion in the *Introduction* that 'world history does not begin with any conscious end'. Instead, it begins with 'its universal end, that the concept of spirit should be realised'. This is at first, however, only 'the inner, the innermost, unconscious drive', and the entire business of world history is 'the labour of bringing it to consciousness' (H, 86–7: 73–4; M, 39–40: 25, 30, 27). It is hard to see how the rejection of a purpose formulated in advance, or a purposer to formulate it, could be firmer, or how it could be more plainly attested that historical development depends on a *telos* inherent in its material.

The notion of such a *telos* may be developed by considering some further difficulties to which the account of the cunning of reason in the *Introduction* gives rise. They arise from the fact that the account seems intended to cover a certain familiar kind of situation. This is the situation exemplified by the building of a house, using the elements of fire, air and water and such materials as iron, wood and stone. The elements are, of course, used in accordance with 'the universal laws of nature' and as their own natures permit (H, 84: 71). Yet the result is a human dwelling that shuts them out and restricts their activities. In Hegel's view of the matter they are, as it were, turned against themselves. It is in a similar way, he goes on, that the passions satisfy themselves: 'they fulfil themselves and their ends in accordance with their determinate nature and produce the edifice of human society in which they provide right and order with power against themselves' (H, 84: 72; M, 42: 27, 35, 30). The passions serve, just as the elements do, to raise a structure that limits their own operation. Both may, it seems, be taken to exemplify the cunning of reason, the process by which the universal emerges unscathed from the curbing and buffeting that particulars have to endure.

To draw an activity such as house-building within the scope of the cunning of reason is to create, initially at least, as much darkness as light. This is so in part because it reinforces the suggestion of an independent, purposive and, in relation to history, transcendent subject. It is also because the building of a house seems a straightforward, indeed paradigmatic, case of instrumental reasoning, the intelligent adaptation of means to ends. As such, it has nothing of the humanly unforeseen and unforeseeable character which, in a historical setting, lends colour to the supposition that achieving the ends of reason involves a form of cunning. Moreover, if building a house is drawn in, it becomes hard to see how any exercise of instrumental reason could be excluded. The notion of cunning then begins to lose any serviceable, determinate shape. It may help with these difficulties if one turns to consider the way in which the cunning of reason is presented in the *Science of Logic*.

At first sight this serves only to confirm what has so far been gleaned from the *Introduction*:

> that the end posits itself in a *mediate* relation with the object and *interposes* another object *between* itself and it may be regarded as the *cunning* of reason ... It puts forward an object as a means, allows it to wear itself out in its stead, exposes it to attrition and shields itself behind it from mechanical violence.
>
> (SL: 746–7)

This passage offers the now familiar picture of what is essential safe-guarding itself through a kind of surrogacy, the displacing of all risk elsewhere. Moreover, it reinforces the suspicion of the peculiar kind of inflation to which the figure of the cunning of reason seems liable. For, it appears, one may indeed speak of cunning wherever there is mediation, the interposition of an object between the purposer and the goal. This would seem to incorporate the entire sphere of reason in its practical dealings with the world. A final point of correspon-dence with the *Introduction* is that Hegel goes on to take human labour as the model of what he has in mind, citing the example of the use of a plough. Where the discussion goes substantially and helpfully beyond the *Introduction* is in the fresh perspective it provides. The plough, as a tool through which 'the human being possesses power over external nature', is now seen as exemplifying '*external* purposive-ness' (*aüssere Zweckmässigkeit*) (WL 2: 453; SL: 747). This should be taken as an invitation to set our difficulties in the context of the distinction between 'external' and 'internal' (*innere*) purposiveness, a distinction central to Hegel's account of teleology in the writings on logic.

Kant's conception

The distinction is described by Hegel as one of Kant's 'great services to philosophy' (SL: 737). The external kind is, as the *Encyclopaedia* explains, what people usually have in mind when they speak of 'purpose'. From this point of view, things 'count merely as *means*, which are used and used up in the realisation of a purpose that lies outside them' (EL: 282). It is a matter of what Kant explains as the

'adaptability of a thing for other things'. The obvious source of illustrations is human productive labour, and so he cites the use of 'the ox
or, as in Minorca, even the ass or pig for ploughing' (Kant 1922: 231;
Kant 1952: 15). This is all familiar territory. It is Kant's 'internal
purposiveness' that, as Hegel sees it, breaks new ground in that it
opens up 'the concept of life' (SL: 737). For the paradigms of such
purposiveness are what Kant refers to as 'things considered as physical ends'; that is to say, organisms. Their peculiarity is that their
component parts, the skin, bones and hair of animals and the leaves
of trees, are not to be understood as means to anything external to the
organism itself. Instead, each part exists '*for the sake of the others* and
of the whole' (Kant 1952: 21). Moreover, in contrast to works of art
which are in other respects analogous, each is active in producing the
other parts and so is 'reciprocally both end and means' (Kant 1952:
21–2, 24).

This is, in Hegel's eyes, a higher form of purposiveness than that
which applies reason instrumentally to the object from outside.
Indeed, it 'stands infinitely far above the concept of modern teleology
which had only *finite*, or *external*, purposiveness, in view' (EL: 280).
The language of finite and infinite puts one in direct touch with
Hegel's chief specific complaint against external purposiveness. This
is its conjuring up of the spectre of an '*infinite progress of mediation*'
(SL: 749). For every end may, once achieved, be viewed as a means to
something beyond itself. The spectre thus conjured up is what Hegel
refers to as the 'bad infinite' of indefinitely prolonged linear sequence
(SL: 149). However far such a sequence is extended, it can never, in his
view, attain to true infinity. Hence, the association with it of external
purposiveness is part of what is signified by labelling the latter merely
'finite'. For a better image of the infinite one should turn from the
straight line to the circle (SL: 149). This is the image that is made flesh
in the organism, a whole made up, as Kant recognises, of reciprocally
interacting parts. Moreover, each part is specifically adapted to its role
as means and could play no other, nor could the end be served in a
different way. By contrast, the means which happens to be employed
in a case of external purposiveness is, in principle, only one of potentially many which differ at most in technical suitability but are alike in
having no intrinsic relation to the end. They are to that extent arbi-

trary, and so in another sense, for Hegel, merely 'finite'. The organism, on the other hand, is the living circularity, an entity which is, in Kant's phrase, 'an *organised* and *self-organised being*' (Kant 1952: 22).

The inference seems obvious that the teleology appropriate to spirit will be that of the infinitely higher, internal form. Hence, this will be the teleology on which the interpretation of history will essentially have to rely. It will, moreover, be relied on in a crucial role, for purposiveness of some kind is, one might suppose, the standard way in which reason shows itself to be at work in a process (PS: 12). Thus, the search for it will in practice be the form that the search for signs of reason must take. It may therefore be concluded that internal purposiveness is the appropriate model for understanding the cunning of reason in history, and that the cunning in question will be that of a reason which manifests itself as such purposiveness. Hence, the passages in which Hegel seems to extend the scope of cunning to include the external purposiveness of labour will have to be taken as simply inflationary, at best offering a partial analogy based on the common factor of mediation. This conclusion fits precisely, one should note, with the immanent reading of Hegel's ontology. The significance of internal purposiveness, the great service rendered by Kant's elaboration of the notion, is that it promises to flesh out the postulate of an immanent subjectivity at work in history. Before taking up this promise, however, it may be well to look more closely at what has so far served as the chief model of the internal form, the physical end or organism. To do so is to raise once again a larger question of great importance for the present inquiry, that of the general relationship between spirit and history on the one hand and nature on the other.

Principles of development

The frequency with which organic metaphors and analogies recur in Hegel's dealings with spirit is truly striking. The central case of the 'life' of spirit has often been cited in the present discussion. In the *Introduction* there are many other instances, as when it tells us that 'just as the seed bears within it the whole nature of the tree and the taste and form of its fruits, so also do the first traces of spirit contain virtually the whole of history' (H, 61: 53; M, 31: 18, 23, 21). The natural organism itself is important for Hegel, as for Kant, in constituting a simple, concrete alternative to having to think of ends as merely externally related to means. By its very existence it shows that other models are conceivable and viable. Hence, it encourages one to suppose that human history too may be intelligible as, in some sense, a self-determining whole that does not derive its *telos* from outside, a realm of 'the passion and the life whose fountains are within'.

In spite of these affinities Hegel has also a sharp sense of the limits of the language of organic wholes as applied to history. He never allows us to lose sight of the basic truth that 'world history arises from the soil of the spirit, not of nature, and so its ultimate end can only be deduced from the nature of spirit' (H, 262: 212). The distinction is worked out in detail in terms of the 'principle of *development*' on each side. This is done in a passage which starts by specifically acknowledging the analogy of spirit and 'organic natural objects'. Thus, it is true of spirit, whose 'theatre, property and sphere of realisation is the history of the world' that it is 'in itself (*an sich*) the absolute determinant'. The existence which belongs to organic entities also has its source within itself, in 'an immutable inner principle'. The heart of the analogy, the theme of self-making, is then presented explicitly: 'Thus, the organic individual produces itself: it makes itself into what it implicitly (*an sich*) is; and spirit too is only what it makes itself, and it makes itself into what it implicitly is' (H, 151: 126; M, 75: 54–5, 68–9, 58).

It is at this point that the different principles of development begin to assert themselves. The development of natural organisms takes place, Hegel declares, in an 'immediate, unopposed, and unhindered way' in which 'nothing can intrude between the concept and its realisation'. It is 'different with spirit'. There the process by which the inner determination is translated into reality is 'mediated through consciousness and will', giving rise to a dialectic of opposition and hindrance. What in the natural world is a 'peaceful growth' is in the spiritual 'at once a hard and unending struggle with itself'. The fact that development in nature lacks the dynamic of internal conflict ensures that it is essentially an endless repetition, a 'continuous process of change' turning continuously into 'the opposite' of change (H, 151: 126–7; M, 75–6: 54–5, 68–9, 58–9). As a matter of intellectual temperament, it is plain that Hegel finds such senseless spectacles antipathetic: 'The reawakening of nature is merely the repetition of one and the same process; it is a tedious chronicle (*Geschichte*) with always the same cycle. There is nothing new under the sun' (H, 70: 61; cf. M, 74: 54, 68, 57).

It is a relief for him to turn instead to 'the sun of spirit', under which movement is 'essentially progress' (H, 70: 61). So strong is Hegel's sense of this contrast that when he finds the cyclical pattern in a human society he is inclined to qualify its claim to belong to history. Thus, he attributes to the ancient Orient an awareness of the principle of individuality that is as yet 'powerless, unconscious and natural'. This ensures that its history is still predominantly 'historyless' (*geschichtlos*), 'the repetition of the same majestic decline'. In such circumstances, 'no progress occurs' and all the restless movement amounts to merely 'an unhistorical (*ungeschichtliche*) history' (H, 245: 199; cf. M, 137: 106, 94). The circle is ultimately not, it appears, the most fitting emblem of spirit's development in time.

Hegel's picture of the contrast between unchanging nature and progressive spirit may seem overdrawn in the light of the now general acceptance of the theory of evolution. However regrettable it may seem, one must recognise that in this matter he is a faithful Aristotelian, wholly committed to the hierarchy and fixity of species (H, 153–4: 128; M, 96–7: 72, 87, 75). Indeed, in expounding his philosophy of nature he explicitly opposes the evolutionary thinking of his own time, a form of thinking which, he declares 'explains nothing' (HPN: 213). It should, of course, be remembered that he was writing well before Darwin, before the scattered intimations of an evolutionary past were drawn together in a comprehensive theory. It is hard to suppose, given the respect he consistently shows for scientific achievement in its own sphere, that he would have maintained his anti-evolutionary stance if confronted with the authority of that theory. There certainly seems to be nothing in the logic of his own thought that would require him to do so, and one might well postulate a deep affinity that should induce rather an attitude of welcome. This is so not least because natural selection is, after all, the most successful

attempt ever made to flesh out and demonstrate the notion of purposiveness without a purposer. The issues involved are, however,
complex, and their investigation would lead well beyond the scope of
the present inquiry. Instead, it is necessary to return to the question of
the light that the distinction between external and internal purposiveness can shed within the philosophy of history, and, more especially,
on the cunning of historical reason.

Literal truths

It was suggested earlier that internal purposiveness is both the intrinsically more spiritual form and the one specifically suited to the needs
of Hegel's ontology as it has been interpreted here. The two features
are closely related and mutually supportive. If one accepts them in
combination, the assumption of God's teleological influence on
history becomes the assumption of a deep rational bent in the historical material itself. It seems clear from the *Introduction* where this
assumption is to be grounded. Hegel refers to 'the means which the
world spirit employs in order to realise its concept', and explains that,
'simply and abstractly', this is 'the activity of subjects in whom reason
is present as their inherent (*an sich seiendes*) substantial essence' (H,
109–10: 92–3; M, 54: 37, 48, 40). The entire scheme has, it appears, an
ontological ground in the essence of individual human beings, and
that essence is the ultimate source of all teleological energy in history.
It is what makes it intelligible to postulate a general inclination of
humankind to pursue whatever is experienced, however dimly and
inarticulately, as a higher expression of spirit. This may, in virtue of
its ground, be thought of as an inherent tendency, an impulse of
normality, however numerous its failures and exceptions. The teleological energy in question may be understood as an energy that, so to
speak, pushes history from behind and from within, rather than
pulling it from the front and from outside. Such a means of propul-
sion will, it may be assumed, suffice to give a shaping influence, a
purposive inclination, to the succession of events. This assumption is
wholly compatible with accepting that the cause of reason in history
must endure many setbacks and episodes of stagnation. Since,
however, the pressure behind it can never, in virtue of its ontological

status, wholly remit or be removed, it will, Hegel is entitled to assume, sooner or later reassert itself in the form of renewed development, and must, in the long run of history, prevail.

The use of the term 'cunning' in connection with this process is in some respects, one must admit, unfortunate. It is so most of all because it tends almost inevitably to hypostatise, in the manner indicated above, what the cunning is attributed to, that is to say, 'reason'. This tendency is, however, incompatible, as we have seen, with other decisive features of Hegel's presentation, and is impossible on general grounds to sustain or justify. It should, perhaps, be recalled that he seems to introduce the term in question in a self-consciously distancing or cautionary way in both the *Science of Logic* and the *Introduction*. The phenomena he has in mind involve what 'may be regarded' or 'may be called' the cunning of reason. What this way of seeing and naming has to offer is a striking metaphor with its rewards as well as limitations. It serves very well to suggest the deviousness and lack of transparency of the historical process, the depths from which it springs and the extent to which it goes on behind the backs of the individuals caught up in it. If all these circumstances are borne in mind, the metaphor of cunning cannot seriously mislead.

There are, moreover, a number of ways in which one may try to grasp the truth behind it in literal terms. The underlying conception may be determined negatively, set off by contrast with what it is not. In addition, one may seek to understand the process captured in the metaphor positively and concretely, under what might be called, in terms to be explained below, its specific modalities. The chief point to make by way of negation is that we are not dealing with a theory of unconscious motivation, at least if that implies that consciously held motives are mere proxies for something hidden. Hegel is not, so to speak, the discoverer of the rational unconscious who manages in advance to stand Freud on his head. He is in general content to accept the effectivity of the motives by which historical actors are consciously led, the complex mixture of self-interest and loftier considerations discussed earlier. He does not seek to undercut this level of explanation by locating the true springs of action elsewhere. His conception is rather that the effective motives of which actors are aware are themselves partially formed, or at any rate inflected, by their rational essence. It is true that the contribution of reason may be more or less well understood by the actors themselves. Individuals vary in this respect, and in any case, viewing the matter in very general terms, one may expect to see a pattern of development across historical time with the progress of spirit. Thus, after making the remark about the presence of reason as the subjects' inherent substantial essence, Hegel adds that it is 'as yet (*zunächst*) a ground which is obscure and concealed from them' (H, 110: 92–3; M, 54: 37, 48, 40). The precise temporal reference of the 'as yet' is by no means clear. Yet it seems safe to assume that some movement in the course of historical time from concealment to disclosure is being envisaged. What changes, however, is not so much the ability of historical actors to know their own motives as their knowledge of the ground, of what determines their motives to be what they are. The overall historical movement is, of course, towards self-conscious determination by reason; that is, towards freedom.

To note this is to be brought directly into contact with the two chief modalities through which to conceive concretely of the process in which reason exercises its cunning. That process is at once, and in ways that will by now be familiar, a development of self-consciousness and of freedom. These are indeed just aspects of a single totality, but it may focus the issues to think for particular purposes of reason as expressing itself through the one or the other. To think of the process under the first aspect is to be recalled to the immanent logic of consciousness and self-consciousness, the dialectical movement towards ever greater reflexivity, generality, concreteness and richness of intersubjectivity. Under this aspect, the path leads from reason as a 'universal unconscious instinct' of humanity to the consciousness of the philosopher who grasps the Idea. To think in terms of freedom is equally to be in touch with the central Hegelian conception of a historical ascent through multiple layers of being and knowing. Since the motif is freedom the constant factor is the resolve to be determined by nothing that is merely external to the self. This serves to unify the primitive impulse to annihilate the other at one extreme and the conscious identification of the citizen with the state at its opposite pole.

Ancients and moderns

Within the modality of freedom, there is a qualitative shift that has particular implications for the cunning of reason. It is the shift from the ancient to the modern world, from the situation in which, at best, some were entitled to be free to one in which freedom is known to be the birthright of all human beings as such. In view of Hegel's general failure to deal discursively with the cunning of reason, the fact that he does not relate it explicitly to this contrast is scarcely surprising. The metaphor of cunning seems, nevertheless, to be accommodating enough to fit both halves. That this is true of ancient freedom is scarcely open to doubt: the metaphor applies there if it applies anywhere. The historical action characteristic of modernity will also, however, fall within its range. It may, that is to say, be applied to the self-conscious pursuit of freedom, the project of making the objective forms of social life embody the awareness that freedom belongs to our nature as human beings. This is, of course, a relatively high level of consciousness and self-consciousness. Nevertheless, it need not involve more than the intuitive, pre-philosophical grasp of the notion of freedom that was previously said to be the hallmark of the modern world. It will be still further removed from any speculative understanding of reason as the Idea. Hence, it leaves us still in the mode of cunning, where reason has to be conceived as working through imperfectly conscious instruments.

To think of the cunning of reason under the aspect of freedom is, as will already be evident, to think politically. The striking precedent set in this matter by Kant should be recalled. For him the hidden plan of nature, its 'cunning', so to speak, is directed to bringing about through history a 'perfect political constitution as the only possible state within which all natural capacities of mankind can be developed completely' (Kant 1991: 50). For Hegel, as was noted above, a key illustration of the workings of the cunning of reason is the way in which the passions in fulfilling themselves 'produce the edifice of human society', a specifically political society in which right and order prevail. It should also be observed that Kant finds an analogy with the internal purposiveness of natural organisms in the 'complete transformation' of 'a great people into a state', a whole in which 'no member should be a mere means but should also be an end' (Kant 1952: 23). The thesis of the sublation of ordinary notions of means and ends in the state is expressed by Hegel in a way that differs only verbally. The citizens of the state are, he tells us, 'moments like those of organic life, in which no member is an end and none is a means' (H, 112: 95). At this point in the *Introduction* the discussion has moved on from the means of history to its 'material' (*Material*). It is now a question of the 'material cause'; that is, of whatever may be said to play the part in history that iron, wood and stone play in the building of a house. Hegel's consideration of the question leads him to peoples and beyond them, and decisively, to states. The solution to the riddle of history must for him, no less than for Kant, be political.

Chapter 9

Peoples

When Hegel turns from the means of the realisation of spirit to its material, the character of his discussion changes. The obvious way to conceive of this is as a shift in orientation from individual to social. The focus had been on the significance for history of the passions of individuals, with world historical individuals as egregious cases in point. It now shifts to such collective entities as peoples and states. To ease the transition, one should note that the contrast is not so sharp as it might at first appear. The individual historical actors who had earlier been the object of concern are essentially social beings whose very individuality is owed to membership of their community. The closeness of the relationship is emphatically conveyed in such passages as these:

> the individual finds the existence of the people as a ready-made, stable world, into which he must fit himself. He has to appropriate this substantial existence to himself in order that he may be something himself.
>
> (H, 67: 58; cf. M, 99: 74, 90, 77)

Each individual is the son of his people at a determinate stage in this people's development ... The individual does not invent his content, but merely activates the substantial content within him.

(H, 95: 81)

These passages show that what underlies and enables the transition in Hegel's argument is the commonality of individual and social substance or content. The common substance is, of course, spirit, the 'spiritual content' that forms the 'essence' of the individual just as much as it is 'the spirit of the people' (*der Geist des Volkes*) (H, 115: 97). It is the latter manifestation, spirit as crystallised in the spirits of peoples, that is now our prime concern. For it is in this guise that the material of history is encountered: 'The spirits of peoples (*Volksgeister*) are the elements of the process whereby spirit comes to free knowledge of itself' (H, 64: 55). Hence, in world history, 'the spirit we are concerned with is the spirit of the people', and it may be conceived as the temporal array of such spirits (H, 59: 51).

The spirits of peoples have a variety of tasks to perform in Hegel's scheme. Most obviously, they permeate and animate all aspects of their peoples' existence, thereby constituting them as the peoples they are:

[Spirit] ... alone propels itself forward in all the deeds and aims of the people. Religion, science, the arts, destinies and events are all forms of its development. This, not the natural determinacy of the people ... gives the people its character.

(H, 64–5:5 6; cf. M, 99: 74, 89–90, 77)

The identity of each individual as a social being, a 'son' of his people, is derived from the same source. Hence it is that 'he can distinguish himself from other single individuals, but not from the spirit of the people'. This is just as true of the 'great ones of the people' as it is of all others. Indeed, their greatness consists precisely in their grasp of the spirit of their people and ability to shape their actions in accordance with it. They are the ones who 'translate into reality what the spirit of the people wills' (H, 60: 52). The conclusion to be drawn is quite general: 'No one can escape from the spirit of his people, any more than he can escape from the earth itself' (H, 95: 81). Neither, of course, is there any escape from the spirits of peoples for the philosopher of history or philosophical historian. To turn from the overt array of these spirits in history to the spiritual content that is the essence of individuals is not to effect it. For that content is drawn from the common stock of the people, the indispensable source and matrix of spiritual existence to which the individual is indissolubly bound.

In a general way spirit seems well fitted to ground the identity of a social group since it is, as we have seen, by nature intersubjective and public, an 'I' that is 'We'. The shift from individual to social in Hegel's account may be eased still further by approaching it from, as it were, the opposite side. This would be to emphasise the second half of the formula, the 'We' that is 'I', the individuality of the social rather than the sociality of the individual. The crucial claim is that 'we apprehend a people as a spiritual individual' (H, 114: 96; M, 73: 53, 67, 56). This serves to indicate that individual human beings are not, for Hegel, the sole or, in the end, the most significant, 'individuals' in history. 'Individual' (*Individuum*) has to be taken as a term of art in the sense it bears in Hegelian logic. There it partakes of the character both of 'the particular' (*das Besondere*) and of 'the universal' (*das Allgemeine*), and signifies that they have been dialectically combined and sublated (EL: 239–43). This pattern is repeated in the philosophy of history. Thus, the spirit of a people is 'essentially particular and at the same time nothing other than the absolute universal spirit'. It is 'the universal spirit in a particular form' (H, 60: 52–3).

These terms should be clarified further. The particular may simply be identified with whatever can be regarded as a specific thing, a single determinate object of reference. Such entities as human beings and peoples meet this condition without difficulty. The technical sense of 'universal' that is most relevant is that of being a 'receptacle' for all the determinations to be found in a given conceptual space, and, thus, 'whole', '(all-)encompassing', 'comprehensive' (Inwood 1992: 303). In so far as whatever is 'individual' partakes of this character, it will come close to what Hegel calls a 'concrete universal'. Such a universal has to be thought of as the growing together, the 'concretion', of a plurality of moments, and so as 'concrete' in the sense, roughly speaking, of being dynamically complex, not an abstract, isolated, static, simple. Individual human beings and peoples seem readily intelligible as universals in this sense. It will raise no theoretical difficulties if these universals are themselves seen in their turn as grown together into a single universal at another level of conceptualisation. The language of whole and parts easily allows that a whole such as an individual person may be part of a larger whole such as a people or state. Thus, history may be conceived in terms of a nested structure of concrete universals; human individuals, peoples and states, the world spirit. It is the middle section of this structure that needs attention at present.

Ethnic diversity

So far as peoples are concerned the best way to proceed is, as so often, that of negation. As was hinted earlier, what Hegel is most anxious to negate is any suggestion that a people is essentially, or primarily, a natural entity. A human community cannot, of course, simply dissociate itself from nature: it must, as he puts it, have a 'natural existence' (H, 64: 55). When he is concerned with this dimension in the *Introduction* he tends, however, to use the term 'nation' (*Nation*). Thus, he remarks that in so far as peoples are nations 'their principle is a natural one' (H, 64: 55). This procedure is influenced by one of those facts of etymology on which he so often relies, 'the derivation of the word *natio* from *nasci*' [to be born] (H, 65: 56). Hence, he takes 'nation' to indicate a group united by common descent, a natural determinant. He is dismissive of any claims for the significance of such groups for world history. Thus, for instance, he ridicules the first stirrings in his own time of the idea of an Aryan race, an *Urvolk*, to which modern Germans belonged and from which 'all science and art has simply been handed down to us' (H, 158: 132: cf. M, 78–81: 57–9, 72–4, 61–3). These are, for Hegel, hard-won achievements of spirit, not automatic deliverances of nature. What constitutes the unity of a people as a spiritual, and not natural, individual is its distinctive forms of consciousness, 'its self-consciousness in relation to its own truth, its essence', or what, in a broad sense, might be called its culture (H, 114: 96). In being a spiritual individual, a people is essentially a cultural individual, an individual whose identity is formed from such elements as language, religion, customs and artistic traditions.

There is an aspect of the way of negation that deserves to be considered further. It is the implication that world historical peoples are not to be thought of as ethnic groups, a point on which Hegel is unequivocally firm. Thus, he pours scorn on claims for the significance of racial purity, and insists instead on that of racial impurity, in spiritual development. He declares, for instance, that it is 'superficial folly' to suppose that the 'beautiful and truly free life' of the Greek spirit could arise from 'the simple development of a race (*Geschlecht*) keeping within the limits of blood relationship and friendship'. On the contrary, the Greeks, like the Romans and every world historical people outside of Asia, developed themselves from 'a *colluvies*, a conflux of the most various nations'. Heterogeneity or foreignness (*Fremdartigkeit*) is 'an element of the Greek spirit', and the beginnings of Greek 'cultural development' (*Bildung*) are connected with the advent of foreigners in Greece (M, 278–80: 226–7). This line of thought is fully sustained when Hegel comes to deal with the Germanic world. The development of the Germanic peoples was, he asserts, 'kindled by a foreign culture, a foreign religion, polity and legislation'. The process consisted precisely in 'taking up and over-coming' foreign elements, and Germanic history is the 'internalising' and 'self-relating' of such elements (M, 413: 341–2). It is hard to see how Hegel could show himself to be more truly innocent of racist attitudes or less inclined to view world historical development in racist terms.

Hegel's enthusiasm for ethnic diversity may be seen as theoretically motivated in a number of ways. There is the familiar idea that opposition, and, hence, diversity, are preconditions of dialectical development. The idea figures prominently in his discussion of the origins of Greek civilisation. This reminds us that spirit requires a spiritual 'antithesis', that is to say its own 'inherent heterogeneity', if it is to 'gain the power to be spirit' (M, 278: 226). Moreover, historical progress, for Hegel, is itself in one important aspect a breaking free of the bonds of nature. From this standpoint the significance of the Greeks is that it was among them that for the first time 'submersion in nature' was sublated (M, 277: 225). From the very beginning they were not 'patriarchally united by a bond of nature' but combined 'in another medium, in law and spiritual custom' (M, 277–8: 225–6). In general, Hegel consistently evaluates the stage of development of peoples in terms of the extent to which they have risen above a merely natural condition. Thus, it is an alleged failure in this respect that forms the burden of his strictures on the peoples of Africa (H, 218–24: 177–82; M, 121–9: 93–9). In this context, ethnic homogeneity appears as the direct expression of continued submersion in nature, of the still unchallenged grip of natural forces. As such, it stands condemned in the perspective of Hegel's philosophy of history.

Non-European peoples

The explanatory value of spirit's struggle with nature is not yet exhausted. This is fortunate for, even with the theoretical background sketched above in place, there is still something to be explained. The extent of the problem may be gauged by considering further the character of Hegel's aspersions on the non-European peoples of his own time. These are many and various, but include a good deal that is bound to seem obnoxious and shocking. They range from coarse defamation of a straightforward kind to more studiedly offensive remarks such as the claim that slavery, with its inducement to sell, rather than kill, captured enemies 'has awakened more humanity among the Negroes' (H, 225: 183; M, 128–9: 98). The prize for absurdity must, however, go to the story, retailed by Hegel, that Catholic clergy had to ring a bell at midnight to remind Paraguayan Indians of their matrimonial duties (H, 202: 165; M, 108: 82, 85–6). It would be pointless to try to exonerate him from all blame in respect of this material, but some remarks may be made in his defence.

To begin with, the paucity and poverty of Hegel's anthropological sources, especially with regard to Africa, should be noted. He had for the most part to rely on the tales of travellers, officials and missionaries eager to highlight the primitive and exotic, not least in order to cast a glow over their own civilising presence. It was to be nearly a century before the results of the scientific study of African traditional societies, and, hence, a proper appreciation of their cultural achievements, were to be widely available to Europeans. This will not, however, explain why Hegel seems to delight in selecting the most lurid and blood-curdling of the tales available to him. Something may be due here to the histrionic temptations of the lecture theatre, a source of corruption to which he may not have been altogether immune. In place of such speculations, however, it may be more useful simply to point out that his picture, in the case of Africa as elsewhere, is by no means unrelievedly bleak.

Thus, he acknowledges that the peoples there 'are not just slaves, but assert their own will (*Willkür*) too' (H, 230: 187). Moreover, he is aware that individual 'Negroes' had become skilled ministers and physicians and that, for instance, it was one of these who first discovered the use of quinine (H, 202: 165; M, 109: 82, 86). At another, and much more significant, level of discourse, one should note his recognition that Egypt was a source of conceptions that were important for the development of Greek art and religion, together with the earlier observation that 'Egypt probably received its culture from Ethiopia' (M, 291–2: 237; M, 248: 201). The effect is to incorporate Africa directly within the main line of the genealogy of spirit. These are, apart from the last, relatively modest concessions on Hegel's part, and yet for all their modesty, they are difficult to make from a racist standpoint. At least they are incompatible with the view that biology is destiny, a fate that ineluctably attends a people and is indelibly inscribed in every individual son and daughter of it. Such comments serve at best, however, to draw attention to mitigating factors on Hegel's side. For a more substantive defence one has to turn elsewhere and, in particular, to the question of spirit's relationship with nature.

The case of Africa is, once again, instructive. Hegel's discussion is indeed dominated by the belief that nature is triumphant there over spirit, but the triumph is, it appears, one of geography rather than biology. There is an irony here in that expert opinion in our own time seems quite generally agreed that humanity in fact originated in equatorial Africa. Our distinctive characteristics as a species, from relative hairlessness to upright posture and a large and complex brain, are seen precisely as evolutionary responses to the challenges and opportunities of its physical environment. Hence, if one had to say where it actually was that the stones first cried out and raised themselves up to spirit, it would be there. Moreover, the next great advance by spirit, its turning against and beginning to master, nature seems all too literally encapsulated in the appearance of manufactured stone tools in East Africa around three million years ago. Hegel did not, of course, have access to the empirical evidence on which such views rest, nor to the body of evolutionary theory that gives the evidence its significance. Nevertheless, he would, as has already been indicated, have had no difficulty in principle in accommodating them. There is nothing in his theoretical position which, given a more enlightened scientific outlook, could have prevented him from recognising Africa as the birthplace of spirit and its only home for all but a tiny proportion of its time on earth. Indeed, it is hard not to suppose that such a recognition would have been congenial to him, as setting the drama of nature and spirit, both temporally and spatially, in a perspective of appropriate sweep and grandeur.

In Hegel's actual situation, however, he was impressed rather by what he saw as the inhospitable character of the African terrain, its deserts, swamps, high mountains, narrow coastal regions, lack of navigable rivers and so on (H, 213–17: 173–6; M, 106: 80, 84). The main geographical influence is, however, climate. In this respect Africa's problems have their counterpart, with, as it were, the signs reversed, in the most northerly regions of the globe. Taken together they ensure that 'neither the *torrid* nor the *frigid zone* are the basis for human freedom or for world historical peoples (H, 189: 154; M, 106: 80, 84). In those zones, the conflict of spirit with nature is too unequal, and spiritual strivings are constantly overborne by natural powers. At the most basic level the struggle to wrest from nature the necessities of life leaves no scope for 'higher spiritual interests'. Thus it is that 'the frost that grips the Laplanders and the fiery heat of Africa are forces too powerful for human beings, for spirit to achieve free movement'. It is, therefore, the temperate zone which 'must provide the theatre for the drama of world history' (H, 190–1: 155; cf. M, 106: 80, 84).

This is so categorical and comprehensive a thesis that one seems entitled to attribute to Hegel a general deterministic doctrine, a species of geographical materialism. Its role at present, however, will be just to explain spiritual backwardness in what he takes to be its severest forms, without having to assume any inherent natural, and, hence, any racial, inadequacy. There is no suggestion in Hegel's account that Africans, or Laplanders, are of inferior stock. It is rather that any people would be overwhelmed in their situation: climatic forces are simply 'too powerful for human beings'. A final point to note at this stage of the discussion is that racist assumptions are not merely otiose in Hegel's argument and lacking in textual warrant. They would also directly contradict the universalism of his philosophy of spirit with its central themes of freedom as the birthright of all human beings as bearers of spirit and of history as the process by which it is won for them. It is true, and only to be expected, that different peoples will at different times exhibit differences in the degree to which they embody and advance these themes. There is, however, no room in Hegel's vision for such radical and elemental divisions between human groups as racists characteristically propose. Indeed, a firmer theoretical basis for the fundamental equality of human beings than Hegelian spirit provides can scarcely be conceived.

Eurocentricity

At this point the case against Hegel may shift its ground. Abandoning the suggestion that his explanation of cultural backwardness is infected with racism, it may seek instead to deny that there is any backwardness to be explained. The appearance of it is, it may be said, a function of the flawed and tendentious criteria of judgement being employed. It may be argued that in this respect Hegel's position reflects a certain Eurocentricity, an attempt to impose specifically European values and standards on the rest of humanity (Walsh 1971: 181–98). These are European both in the sense that they are the products of the distinctive historical experience of European peoples and that these peoples tend to do relatively well when judged by them. Putting the point more strongly, it is that their use by Hegel signifies a kind of cultural imperialism that goes all too easily with, and serves to legitimate, imperialism in the ordinary sense. In this connection one might cite his approval of French interventions in North Africa as tending to draw that region towards Europe (H, 214: 174; M, 121: 93). His stance is, it may be concluded, an unwarranted universalising of what is in truth culturally relative and serves to add lustre to injustice and oppression. It is important to see what response might be available to him against this charge.

It will be helpful, even beyond the needs of the immediate occasion, to bring the accusation of Eurocentricity into sharper focus. There is the obvious truth to be recalled that, for Hegel, the terms 'Europe' and 'world history' are far from being referentially equivalent. World history did not begin in Europe and, at least if some striking formulations bearing on the point are to be trusted, does not end there. The best known of these is the reference in the *Introduction* to 'America' as 'the land of the future' whose world historical importance 'has yet to be revealed in the ages which lie ahead' (H, 209: 170; M, 114: 86, 90). If it is to be taken seriously the accusation needs to be qualified in another way, not just temporally, as it were, but also spatially. For talk of 'Eurocentricity' fails to capture the specific character of Hegel's preferences. He is certainly no 'good European', no champion of a pan-European ideal or of Europe itself as a cultural entity. His vision is centred rather on the 'Germanic' (*germanisch*) peoples who are in effect those of Germany (*Deutschland*) proper, Scandinavia and England (M, 421: 349). These are the peoples 'on which the world spirit has conferred its true principle', and so are the first to develop 'a realm of the real spirit' (H, 254: 206). Somewhat less elevated in this perspective are the 'Romanic' peoples of Italy, Spain, Portugal and France (M, 421: 349). Lower still, indeed 'excluded from our consideration', are the Slavic peoples who have not hitherto appeared as an 'independent moment in the series of phases that reason has assumed in the world'. Nevertheless, in another piece of testimony to the openness of the future, Hegel seems to concede in the next breath that they may do so 'hereafter' (M, 422: 350). In a letter from the same late phase of his life as the philosophy of history lectures, he sharpens this prospect in a way that makes a curious parallel to the remark about America. There he refers to the 'higher destiny' in world history which 'no doubt' is in store for Russia and to the 'immense possibility for development of her intensive nature' she may well 'bear within her womb' (HL: 569).

Hegel characterises the Germanic peoples at one point as 'more or less *German speaking*' (M, 421: 349). It is plain, however, that his conception of them is essentially religious, not linguistic. They are above all the peoples of Protestant Northern Europe, the peoples of the Reformation. It is relevant at this point to acknowledge what is truly one of the most consistent forms of partiality he displays, his low opinion of Roman Catholicism. It is, the *Introduction* assures us in his characteristic vein, a religion that 'does not permit the inner righteousness and ethical life of the state which lies in the inwardness of the Protestant principle' (H, 123: 103–4; M, 71–2: 52, 65, 54). Thus, the Catholic Middle Ages were, for Hegel, a dark night of the spirit from which humanity was rescued by the Reformation, that 'all-enlightening *Sun*' (M, 491: 412). It is an event of the greatest importance in a Hegelian perspective for its essential content is that 'humanity is through itself determined to be free', and its practical achievement is to realise this destiny in the life of the Church (M, 497: 417). This great revolution arose out of 'the ancient and strongly cherished *inwardness of the German (deutschen) people*', and, most immediately, from the strivings of a 'simple *monk*' of that people (M, 494: 414). Having originated in Germany proper (*Deutschland*), it took hold, according to Hegel, only among the Germanic peoples, and so, outside of Germany itself, only in Scandinavia and England. The Romanic and Slavic nations in contrast 'kept themselves aloof from it' (M, 499–500: 419), Hence, it was the Germanic peoples who at this crucial juncture bore the entire responsibility for the cause of spiritual freedom. It is values first realised specifically by them, and in the light of which they appear relatively favourably, that Hegel can legitimately be accused of seeking to universalise and to use in judging the progress of all peoples. The question is how far this procedure can be justified.

The answer must in large part simply consist in pointing to the logic of Hegel's philosophy of history as a whole. That logic inevitably yields a criterion for judging human communities, the extent of their progress in grasping and realising the principle of freedom. It is a criterion that turns out to be complex and ramified in use. For Hegel holds that freedom can be realised only as a system of rights grounded in a constitutional order, the 'inner righteousness' of the state. Hence, it will be important to assess how far individual peoples have succeeded in creating such an order. Moreover, the distinctive form of self-consciousness that religion represents has, for Hegel, a special significance in facilitating, or impeding, the growth of a free constitution. He is therefore led to assess the historical development of peoples also in terms of their particular version of religious self-consciousness. The entire structure of judgement pivots on the principle of freedom, the element on which all else in Hegel's philosophy of history depends.

Against the background of this structure it becomes clear how far his predilections, and his Germanic-Protestant vision in general, may be said to be theoretically motivated. The basic theory is itself wholly free of ethnic, national or other forms of collective bias, and, indeed, as a theory of the universal human spirit, cannot be reconciled with the existence of such bias. The core of Hegel's procedure is an impartial working out of the implications of this position, giving more or less persuasive reasons for the conclusions he reaches. It can hardly be doubted that his true and deep attachment is to the freedom of spirit itself, not to any particular historical setting in which it is best realised. It would, nevertheless, be bad faith on his part not to follow the argument wherever, by the best light available to him, it leads. He has, one might say, both the duty and the right to do so, even where it is towards the elevation of his own world of Protestant Europe.

Imperialism

Hegel's situation needs to be seen in a wider context. It is surely true of anyone who wishes to understand the modern world that they will have to accord a central place to developments that were given a powerful impetus in Europe and spread globally under the auspices of European imperialism. The obvious candidates are science and technology and the capitalist market economy. Hegel's distinctive addition to the list is the modern constitutional state, conceived as the indispensable setting of human freedom. It may be instructive at this point to consider some thinkers, self-proclaimed pupils of Hegel, whose life work is centred on the other candidates. For Marx too, history is a dialectic of human emancipation, leading to the condition he calls 'the true realm of freedom' (Marx 1974: 820). Like Hegel, he has to enlist base and blind forces in the service of the cause, indeed to employ a version of the cunning of reason. 'England', he declares, 'was actuated only by the vilest interests' in India, and 'was stupid in her manner of enforcing them'. Nevertheless, whatever her 'crimes' may have been, she was 'the unconscious tool of history' in bringing about the social revolution in Asia without which humanity cannot 'fulfil its destiny' (Marx 1973: 306–7). For an even more direct parallel with Hegel, one may cite Engels' judgement on a later phase of the European expansion into North Africa referred to above: 'The conquest of Algeria is an important and fortunate fact for the progress of civilisation' (Marx 1969: 47).

To complete this circle of affinities, one should take account of the theory of colonial expansion sketched in the *Philosophy of Right*. Hegel's chief interest there is in the way in which countries are driven to found colonies by internal economic pressures. Since the colonies are deprived of rights enjoyed by the inhabitants of the mother country, 'this situation has resulted in wars and eventual independence'. The liberation of the colonies proves, however, to be, in Hegel's view, 'of the greatest advantage to the mother state' (EPR: 269). As the advantages to the colonies in terms of gaining rights and, thereby, freedom, are not in question, it follows that their liberation is comprehensively beneficial. Hegel is thinking particularly of the recent history of the British colonies in North America and the Spanish colonies in South America. Since the logic of the argument holds, however, for every similar situation, it is plain that he envisages, and welcomes, the downfall of the entire colonial system. Hence any approval he seems to give to particular colonial adventures will be in the provisional, double-edged, cunning of reason mode. His support for the French in North Africa is of essentially the same kind as that of Engels, or Marx's support for the British in India. The one is as much or as little of an imperialist as the others; that is to say, not in truth an imperialist at all.

At this point it must, of course, remain the case that Hegel's position is open to many legitimate kinds of theoretically and empirically based criticism. They cannot be explored in detail here, nor is it possible to do justice to the general question of cultural imperialism versus cultural relativism under which discussion of these matters is often subsumed. Something may, nevertheless, be done to suggest the limits within which criticism of Hegel must keep if it is to be well-directed. There are, after all, some familiar pitfalls to bear in mind. Thus, the complaint may be that Hegel uses normative ideas in an absolute fashion that is intolerant of the traditions of many human societies. It will be preferable on grounds of consistency if this complaint does not itself rely on an ideal of tolerance conceived as an absolute, or at least cross-cultural, standard. Yet if it does not appeal to some such larger authority, it becomes hard to see why Hegel or, indeed, anyone not already committed, should take any notice. No reasons that need count as reasons for them, no considerations capable of determining their intellects, will have been advanced. It is, moreover, not always clear that the critics truly mean what they say in holding or implying that there is nothing to choose between social arrangements that differ significantly in their respect for individual freedom and rights. It may not be obvious that, for instance, they are seriously committed to regarding wage labour and the slavery still widespread in our contemporary world as, so far as all non-economic normative considerations are concerned, equally eligible modes of production.

With those who do maintain a resolute and self-conscious neutrality in such matters the situation is, of course, quite different. Yet theirs is a difficult path to follow, not least because of being liable to a kind of dialectical reversal. Thus, the implication may be that values such as individual rights and freedom are alien and inappropriate to some non-Western societies that should, therefore, not be expected to have to realise them, or even to move in the direction of doing so. This stance is surely in danger of patronising the objects of its concern, even of denigrating their humanity and human capacities. It may also dishonour the many indigenous movements of rational criticism and practical protest within the societies in question. Moreover, if one asks what could underlie and motivate it, the obvious suggestion is that some deep-seated, though perhaps repressed, assumptions of inherent, and thus ethnic, inferiority are at work. At this point extremes seems to meet: liberalism turns into racism before our eyes. Hegel's philosophy of universal spirit has at least the merit of being free from the risk of such varieties of cant and self-deception.

As an individual human being, Hegel does not himself always live up to the standards and demands of that philosophy. It yields him, as we have seen, a conception of freedom, and thereby of justice and rights and of religious awareness, which he uses as the criterion of historical development. His procedure is principled and defensible in so far as he relies on this standard and applies it impartially. He is, as it were, entitled to the hard-earned fruits of his theoretical labours in using it, and it would be a failure of integrity, or an affectation of diffidence, were he not to do so. The *Lectures*, as we have also seen, contains elements that cannot be redeemed in such terms, a residue of cultural prejudice, complacency and arrogance which has to be plainly acknowledged. All one can do is to show that it can claim no ground in, and, indeed, is directly at odds with, the inner logic of Hegel's thought. It should, perhaps, be added that as a result of scientific advances and political struggles, the opinions he ingenuously expresses, especially with regard to Africa and India, would be possible today only for the truly insensible or vicious. What could then be said without exciting special comment by an eminent professor lecturing in a major European university would surely now have the character of hotel bar rantings. In may be possible to see in these circumstances a modest Hegelian message about the progress of spirit.

Chapter 10

States

The decisive step in the transition from individual to social in Hegel's philosophy of history has still to be taken. For the truly historical collectivity is not the people but the state, 'the more narrowly determined object of world history in general' (H, 115: 97; M, 57: 39, 53, 42). The closeness of the relationship between peoples and states is evident in Hegel's nearest approach to a definition: 'The spiritual individual, the people, in so far as it is internally articulated, an organic whole, is what we call the state' (H, 114: 96). A state is, it appears, a people which has achieved a certain level of organisation and unity, or it is a people conceived under the aspect of an organised, unified entity. Every such state is, for Hegel, an 'individual totality', a form of description which, as we have seen, he applies with equal readiness to peoples. Moreover, the actual state is 'animated' by the spirit of the people that is its 'fully developed (*an und für sich seiende*) content' (H, 125: 105; cf. M, 69: 50, 63, 52).

The way in which world history relates to this pattern seems easy to specify. The basic idea would be that when a people succeed in developing into a state it thereby moves from the prehistorical to the historical phase of its existence: 'world history takes account only of peoples that form a state' (H, 113: 95–6; M, 56: 39, 51, 41). Hegel recognises that peoples may have had a 'long life' without the state, and may even have achieved 'a significant development in certain directions' (H, 163: 134; M, 82: 59–60, 74, 63). They may also, it emerges a little later, have experienced many 'complications, wars, revolutions, declines' without giving rise to history (H, 166: 137; M, 85: 62, 77, 66). This 'prehistory' does not concern Hegel's inquiry, however, regardless of 'whether a real history followed or the peoples never arrived at the formation of a state' (H, 163: 134–5; M, 82: 60, 74, 63). The general picture now seems reasonably clear. A state is a developed form of organisation of a people. World history begins with the emergence of such forms and their activities comprise its 'true object'.

This scheme may be retained throughout what follows as capturing the main outlines of Hegel's conception. Nevertheless, it will have to be qualified in some important respects if it is to fit the complexities of his practice. Thus, his work in philosophical history is far from insisting on any one-to-one correspondence of peoples and states. The Greeks are, as we have seen, regarded by him as a truly world historical people. Yet they were in their greatest period organised politically in a plurality of cities. These are, for Hegel, not just authentic states but also, in certain respects, lasting exemplars of political organisation. The Roman Empire, by contrast, incorporated a wide variety of peoples into a single state that for centuries successfully bore the chief responsibility for the development of spirit. Where the modern world is concerned, Hegel recognises that a state may be substantially based on a particular people and obtain its leading impulse from the spirit of that people. Indeed, this may be said to be the working model of people–state relations that he tends to assume for much of the time. Yet the manner of his recognition, its suggestion of being a matter of what holds in general or for the most part, already serves to distance it from the neat correlations of the original scheme. Moreover, Hegel was convinced throughout his career that the peculiar strength of the modern state is bound up with its ability to accommodate cultural diversity. Since a people is essentially, as was shown earlier, a cultural individual, this suffices of itself to establish that such a state cannot draw its strength exclusively from the life of a single people.

Hegel's view of these matters remains in essentials what it was in his early essay on the German constitution. There he declares that 'In our day the tie between members [of a state] in respect of customs, education (*Bildung*), language may be loose or even non-existent'. While differences in these respects were overcome in the Roman Empire by 'the preponderating weight of power', the same result is produced in modern states by 'the spirit and art of political institutions'. Indeed, these differences are 'a necessary product as well as a necessary condition' of the stability of modern states. It is even the case that identity in religion, that 'wherein humanity's innermost being is expressed', is something that these states 'have found that they can do without' (FS: 477–8; HPW: 158). A common political spirit, the commitment to and involvement in specifically political forms of consciousness and action, is all the unity the modern state requires. If this is present, it can readily accommodate, indeed make a stabilising virtue of, the greatest cultural, and by implication ethnic, diversity. It is ironic that the constitution essay should mark the high point of Hegel's enthusiasm, admittedly still tentative and unfocused, for German unification. For its underlying political theory is far removed from that of modern nationalism with its demand that nations should form states and that the international order be a system of nation states.

This is no less true of Hegel's mature theory of the state, as presented in the *Philosophy of Right*. The state described there has no difficulty in accommodating diversity, and specifically the diversity of groups which cannot be thought of as sharing a single *Volksgeist*, a cultural identity. In that state, '*A human being counts as such because he is a human being*, not because he is a Jew, Catholic, Protestant, German, Italian, etc.' (EPR: 240). The position of Jews is particularly significant, for there was a movement in Hegel's time to deny them civil rights on the grounds, as he puts it, that they 'should be regarded not just as a particular religious group but also as members of a foreign people'. In opposition to this, Hegel insists, as one would expect, that 'the Jews are primarily *human beings*', and in virtue of that status are entitled to full civil rights. He adds that the demand for their exclusion 'has proved in practice to be the height of folly', while the way in which governments have acted in including them has proved 'wise and honourable' (EPR: 295–6). In taking this view, Hegel was setting himself directly against the most powerful form of racism of his time and place. Moreover, in proclaiming the state's embrace of all kinds of heterogeneous groups, he is at odds, just as in the constitution essay, with the mind-set of modern nationalism. This theoretical bent is fully in line with what is known of his personal opinions. They are marked by an absence of national feeling which is most strikingly shown in his support for the French during the Napoleonic campaigns in Germany (HL: 114–15, 122–3). His personal and intellectual antipathy to the claims of nationalism was evident to his contemporaries and immediate successors. Among them it was, unsurprisingly, a source of scandal to the nationalists for whom he was 'the fellow without a fatherland' (cit. in Ottmann 1996: 61). The myth of Hegel as the philosopher of German nationalism is wholly the creation of a later period (ibid.: 53–69). As the achievement and embodiment of spirit, the Hegelian state is not to be viewed along nationalist, tribal or any other naturalistic lines.

Forms of state

There is another way in which the original scheme needs to be qualified or, at any rate, relaxed. It arises from noting how varied are Hegel's uses of the term 'state' by the usual standards of his time, or ours. Two of these uses are particularly important for the argument of the *Introduction*, and are picked out in following passages:

> with the state and constitutional law, as distinct from religion, science and art, one usually signifies only the political aspect. Here, however, 'state' is used in a more comprehensive sense, just as we use the expression 'realm' when we mean the appearance of the spiritual.
>
> (H, 114: 96)

The word 'state' is often applied only to the political and legal framework; in another sense religion can also be ranked with it.

(H, 264: 214)

It seems that one may speak of a less and a more comprehensive sense of the term. In the narrower sense, the state is 'the political and legal framework'. It is in this sense that the *Philosophy of Right* refers to 'the political state and its constitution' (EPR: 288). In a wider, more amorphous, sense, the state incorporates a range of spiritual phenomena, including religion and, it seems, science and art too. This sense is never clearly defined or delimited by Hegel, and it may be pointless to seek for it a sharper outline than he provides. The state in the wider sense may well be one of those useful, but inherently vague, notions that are distorted in being made more precise. The effort is all the less required, since, as will soon be apparent, this sense is not the one that bears the main burden in Hegel's philosophy of history. He does, nevertheless, offer some clues as to what he has specifically in mind in invoking it. These should be followed up, for they also point in the right direction for the topic which is now of central concern, the political state.

The initial clue is to be gleaned from the immediate setting of the first of the passages quoted above. What precedes it is the remark, also previously cited, about a people being a state in so far as it is internally articulated as organic whole. The suggestion is that, even in the more comprehensive sense, a state must be more organised and unified than is required of a people. This will be true all the more of the narrower, political sense. The second clue, or perhaps just the first spelled out more usefully, is offered a little later. Hegel goes on to link the state, still apparently in the wider sense, with a higher level of conscious awareness than belongs to a people or nation as such. 'The universal which brings itself forward and becomes known in the state' is, he observes, in a passage in which 'people' and 'nation' are used interchangeably, 'in general the same as that which comprises the cultural development (*Bildung*) of a nation' (H, 114: 96–7). This development is, it appears, crystallised as an object of knowledge to itself in the comprehensive state, the state which embraces science, art and religion. Hence, one might say, that state is a self-conscious cultural entity. For the state in the narrower sense, the association with a level of self-consciousness beyond what is characteristic of a nation or a people is even more important for Hegel's thinking. The political state is, as will soon be evident, the most self-conscious of all the forms of collective life, and it is just in virtue of this that it comprises the true object of history.

It is, of course, necessary not to lose sight of the ambiguity of Hegel's usage. Nevertheless, it remains the case that the political state is the indispensable core of his conception. It is what he normally has in mind, as the context will make clear, in referring to the state without qualification, and what he says is not properly intelligible except on that assumption. Hence it is, unless otherwise indicated, the narrower sense that is at issue in what follows. To adopt this convention is, of course, to enjoy the benefits of conforming to the standard usage of the modern world. The centrality of the political for Hegel should also be seen, however, as theoretically motivated. The significance of the state in his philosophy of history, as of everything else there, directly or indirectly, stems from its connection with freedom. This is as strong as is possible to conceive: the state is quite simply, 'the realisation of freedom' (H, 116: 98; M, 58: 40, 54, 43). It has that status primarily because, as our earlier discussion has shown, Hegelian freedom has to be realised as a structure of rights and justice, a constitutional order such as only the political state can provide. This is the basic reason for holding that Hegel's sense of the meaning of history has a specifically political character.

Since the constitutional state is the indispensable setting of freedom, it is perhaps to be expected that so much space should be taken up in the *Introduction* with a quasi-Aristotelian survey of types of constitution (H, 138–48: 116–24; M, 61–74: 43–54, 56–67, 45–56). What may be more surprising is how little of substance is added to what Aristotle had to say on the subject. Elsewhere Hegel holds quite closely to the view that 'the detailed development [of the concept of] the state is for the philosophy of right to provide' and is not the concern of the philosophy of history (M, 57: 40, 53, 42). Some details of its development will have to be taken up in the course of the present argument, but in general this demarcation line will be respected. There is, however, one matter on which the *Introduction* is so insistent that it cannot be ignored.

The issue is the relationship between the state and the ethical. In one formulation the state is said to be 'the present, actual ethical life' (*sittliche Leben*) (H, 112: 94; M, 56: 38, 50, 41). In others, ethical life (*sittliche Lebendigkeit* or *Sittlichkeit*) is identified as its 'essence' (H, 112: 95), and its 'living reality in individuals' (H, 112: 5; M, 72: 52, 66, 55). The notion of ethical life is, it was suggested earlier, best understood as having been developed polemically by Hegel in opposition to the individualism of Kantian morality. It refers to norms of conduct that are socially conceived and embodied or, one might also say, to the institution of practical judgement and action guidance in its social dimension. The state is by no means the only major form of ethical life. It may be helpful to follow the *Introduction* in tracing the contrast with another of these forms. The family too is an 'ethical whole', but its spirit typically expresses itself through 'love and emotion', not through 'consciousness, volition and knowledge' as in the state. The individual knows that 'his freedom consists' in obedience to the laws of the state. Hence his relationship to it is not, as it is with the family, a matter of 'natural impulse' but of 'willed and conscious unity' involving a 'moment of rationality' (H, 119–20: 100–1; cf. M, 60–1: 42–3, 55–6, 44–5). The state inhabits a higher region of spirit than the family, the region in which freedom is realised as conscious identification with the rational substance.

At this point some threads of the discussion may be drawn together by considering the relationship between, on the one hand, the state and its ethical life and, on the other, the people and its *Volksgeist*. This relationship too may be conceived in terms of different positions on the ladder leading to spirit from nature. The observation that a people has a natural existence does not find any answering echo in Hegel's dealings with the state. Thus, while every individual is the 'son of his people', no such natural metaphor can capture the position of the citizen. This is a matter not of birthright but of conscious acceptance of the values, and willed participation in the practices, that enable the laws and institutions to function. Some further light may be shed by returning to the issue of minority groups. There is no difficulty in accommodating Jews within the Hegelian state, even on the assumption that they represent a foreign people. That places no obstacle on their being loyal and active citizens with equal rights. Neither is it, of course, an obstacle to their contributing to the religious, scientific and artistic life of the state in its more comprehensive sense. Hegel deals in a significantly different way, however, in the same passage of the *Philosophy of Right*, with such religious groups as the Quakers and Anabaptists.

The emphasis now is not on the inclusion of equals as of right but on the state's magnanimous toleration of anomalies of self-exclusion. Members of these groups do not swear oaths, will not defend the state against its enemies, and, in general, according to Hegel, fulfil their direct duties to the state only in a 'passive manner'. It follows that they are 'private persons' rather than citizens, with no right of belonging to the state since they do not recognise their duties towards it. The state's willingness not to enforce its own rights strictly against them is a tribute to 'the strength of its ethical character and the inner rationality of its institutions' (GPR: 421; EPR: 295). The ability to forbear is itself enough to place it at a higher level of self-consciousness and self-movement than entities that have been stamped with a determining inheritance, whether this is primarily natural, as with the family, or primarily cultural, as with the people. It is in this capacity for spiritual freedom that the significance of the state for world history has ultimately to be found.

Beginnings of history

A reader of the *Introduction* is likely, however, to be more immediately struck by the state's role in defining the scope of world history; that is, in marking out that portion of the human past Hegel regards as truly historical. Most immediately of all, there is its use in determining when history may properly be said to have begun. The simple answer, as we have seen, is that it is contemporaneous with the arrival on the scene of states. That answer represents, however, another respect in which the original scheme has to become more complicated. The first step in the process is to relate the function of the state to that of another criterion Hegel offers to guide our thinking in this area. To do so the distinction between 'history' as events, or *res gestae*, and as narrative, or *historia rerum gestarum*, must be explicitly invoked once more. It was earlier suggested that, for Hegel, the two meanings are inextricably tied together in virtue of having an 'inner common ground'. This ground is, it should now be added, the state.

Hegel suggests a number of reasons why the public power should be especially interested in having a record of events. An important factor is that 'a community that is raising itself up to be a state requires rules, laws, universal and universally binding directives'. Hence, it produces 'a record of, and interest in, intelligent, definite, and in their effects lasting, actions and events' to which Mnemosyne, the goddess of memory, is then 'impelled to add duration by remembrance' (H, 164: 136; M, 83: 61, 76, 64–5). A merely instrumental, bureaucratic explanation of the origins of *historia* is not, however, what Hegel really wishes to propound. Historical narrative is a deeply inherent need of the state, an integral moment of its development, in a way that goes well beyond what would be mundanely required for the legal system to function. It is the state's vocation of self-consciousness that is the real heart of the matter. Thus, Hegel goes on to point out that the 'external existence' of the state, despite its 'rational laws and customs', is only an 'incomplete present' which, for the integration of its consciousness, requires an understanding of the past (H, 164: 136; M, 83–4: 61, 76, 65). The state must be enveloped in the kind of awareness that only *historia* can provide if it is to achieve full self-consciousness, and thereby realise its concept. *Historia* and the state are locked in a relationship of mutual implication and dependence, and it is only when this relationship is functioning properly that there can be history as *res gestae* in the true sense.

The consistency with which Hegel maintains this position should be illustrated. It is best done by a topic on which, unfortunately, he brings to bear, as we have seen, an uncharacteristic weight of bias and insensibility. There cannot, he declares, be a 'true state' in India, and Indian political existence is merely that of a people, not a state. With such a people, 'what we call in a double sense "history" is not to be looked for'. They are 'incapable of writing history', and since they have no '*historia*' they have 'no history as deeds (*res gestae*); that is, no development towards a truly political condition' (M, 201–4: 161–3). Setting aside the content of these claims, their logic is still of immediate interest. That rests directly upon, and reaffirms, the interrelatedness of historiography and the state as the essential precondition of genuinely historical action.

It seems fair to conclude that Hegel offers what might be called a 'statist' conception of history, one that ties the historical indissolubly to a certain form of political organisation. That such a verdict has a core of truth cannot be denied. If, however, one continues to qualify his position as it deserves, it will emerge in a form which is both more precise and more persuasive. An obvious step is suggested by some recently cited passages. On the one hand, it should be noted that it is not states as such but communities raising themselves to that position which initiate record-keeping and set Mnemosyne to work. On the other, one should take account of the casual gloss on history, in the sense of *res gestae*, as being a matter of a 'development towards a truly political condition'. The immediate context of this claim, together with the entire weight of Hegel's political theory, warrant the inference that the condition in question is precisely the condition of being a state. Thus, history in its double sense finds its material not merely in the actual existence of states but also in their coming to be. This interpretation of Hegel's statism can draw textual support from elsewhere in the *Introduction*. A striking example runs as follows: 'the state first provides a subject matter that is not only appropriate for the prose of history but creates it together with itself' (H, 164: 136; M, 83: 61, 76, 64). The state, it seems, creates a historical subject matter, the material for *historia*, in the course of its self-creation. To put the moral another way, it is that the field of reference of 'history', in both of its senses, takes in not just the fully formed state but also the process of its formation.

This moral accords well with Hegel's familiar tendency to conceive of a result as incorporating the movement through which it was obtained, so that, as it were, it casts its denotative aura backwards over its own origins. Moreover, it brings him much closer than he may have seemed at first to ordinary conceptions and usage. It rescues him, for instance, from the awkward and counter-intuitive implication that what are standardly termed struggles of national liberation, the struggles of subject peoples to form their own states, do not belong to history. More generally, it accords with our everyday sense of the scope of history if one allows historical time to expand and prehistorical time to contract by not insisting on having fully developed states as the material. Hegel's conception may still be described as statist, but at least it now takes in the history of the origins of states as well as the history of their subsequent adventures. It allows, as he puts it himself, for 'concrete' – that is, in this context, 'historical' – reason to find significance and interest in such matters as the growth of language and the fortunes of nations in connection not merely with states as such but also with the 'beginnings of state formation' (H, 166–7: 138; M, 86: 63, 78, 67). This outcome is in keeping both with ordinary ways of thinking and with the natural bent of Hegel's own thought.

Role of memory

With the character of Hegel's statism more clearly established, it is time to place it in a larger setting and to ask how it can be theoretically grounded. This is all the more pressing since it is perhaps the most familiar criticism of his philosophy of history that it gives too large a place to the state (Collingwood 1946: 120–2). It is a criticism which loses only some of its force on our present understanding of his position. In order to come to grips with it one has to return to basics, and, in particular, to the thesis that world history is 'the progress of the consciousness of freedom'. What now has to be emphasised particularly is the element of progress, an emphasis that Hegel immediately goes on to supply himself by referring to it as 'a progress that we must come to know in its necessity' (H, 63: 54; M, 32: 19, 24, 22). To do so would be to achieve in a particular field what he had earlier declared to be the sole aim of philosophical inquiry: 'to eliminate the contingent'. There he had identified contingency with the external necessity that 'originates in causes which themselves are only external circumstances' (H, 29: 28). History has, it appears, to be comprehended in terms of an internal necessity, one which originates in causes inherent in the material itself, in some immanent power binding its successive moments. This is the necessity that belongs to what Hegel standardly refers to elsewhere as dialectical movement. The suggestion to be pursued is that the central significance of the state derives from its role in ensuring that history may be conceived as an internally necessary, dialectical progress.

An indication of how this role may be conceived more concretely is to be found in Hegel's references to Mnemosyne, the goddess of memory and mother of the Muses, including, of course, the Muse of history. The community, as it develops, creates, we had been told, a record of events to which Mnemosyne is impelled to add 'duration by remembrance'. It is an impulse which, as Hegel had earlier made clear, the goddess cannot satisfactorily obtain from merely tribal or family sources (H, 164: 135–6; M, 83: 60–1, 75–6, 64), nor, as he later explains, from the developed, but stateless, societies of India (M, 201–4: 161–3). The peculiar responsibility of the state in this situation is to be the prompter and sponsor of Mnemosyne, a responsibility it must discharge if it is to complete its self-understanding. This basic idea appears in another aspect a little later, and, curiously, still under the auspices of Greek mythology.

The passage in question begins with a reminder that a people is world historical only in so far as the product of its spirit is an 'ethical, political organisation'. The impulses that prompt its deeds otherwise 'pass away without trace'. Thus, the Greeks, Hegel remarks, speak of the rule of Cronos or Time, the devourer of 'his own children, the deeds he has produced', as a golden age, but one without any 'ethical work'. It was Zeus, the 'political god', who first subdued time by creating 'a conscious ethical work', that is 'the state' (H, 176–7: 145; cf. M, 101: 75–6, 91–2, 79). This organisation overcomes time, or, as Hegel puts it less extravagantly later, sets limits to its devouring action, by rescuing human achievements it would consign to oblivion (H, 178: 147; M, 102–3: 77, 93, 80). The developing state's need to keep records, reflecting its deeper need to integrate its own consciousness, leads, in the ways sketched earlier, to historical narrative. This serves in turn to mark out a region of enduring human value and meaning amid the vast wastes of temporal happenings, so generating historical *res gestae* in step with the state's self-generation. From this standpoint, one might say, history emerges as the systematic embodiment of the urge to memorialise which shows itself at so many levels of human achievement from obituaries in the parish magazine to such peaks of art as Shakespeare's sonnets. Thus, history in its double sense is, to continue to speak metaphorically, the daughter of memory and the enemy of time. The essential means it employs to lay hold of its inheritance and confound its enemy are political, the creation of the self-consciously ethical institution that is the state.

To move away from metaphor, this account has to be related to the theoretical function of memory in Hegelian dialectic. The classic source is the final pages of the *Phenomenology*, a source whose significance for present concerns was indicated earlier. The context is explicitly one of philosophical concern with history, of concern, that is, with history conceived as 'spirit emptied out into time'. This 'becoming' presents 'a slow movement and succession of spirits' in which the specific task of memory or recollection (*Er-innerung*), the 'making inward' of experience, is to preserve the spiritual achievement of each individual phase. Thus, each phase is enabled to start at a 'higher level' than the one before, and the whole can constitute an internally linked sequence of rising steps, a progress of consciousness. The overall picture that emerges is of a 'realm of spirits' constituting 'a succession in which one relieved the other and each took over the empire of the world from its predecessor' (PG: 590–1; PS: 492–3). All that the *Phenomenology* can offer at this point is an abstract, programmatic sketch. The achievement of Hegel's philosophy of history is to fill it with a detailed content.

By the light of that philosophy it becomes apparent that the spirits who conduct the great relay race of the 'empire of the world' have, as a first approximation, to be identified with the *Volksgeister*. The earlier discussion has, however, shown that, as vehicles of spirit, peoples in themselves are, for Hegel, too unfocused and unarticulated, too immediate and undeveloped, to bear the main burden. Popular memory as such will be too haphazard in its workings, and too prone to distortion and discontinuity, to guarantee an extended temporal dialectic. The power of memory has to be entrusted to some more organised and self-aware institution, and this can only be the state. The role of guardian of Mnemosyne is, in any case, one for which it seems pre-eminently suited. It is, as we have seen, driven by the needs of its own nature to keep records and sponsor narratives. Its sovereign authority, executive drive and scope, and stability and endurance in time, combine to leave it well placed to take responsibility for the transmission of spiritual achievements across generations. Moreover, its high level of self-consciousness, and correspondingly developed sense of self-interest, enable it to appreciate and assimilate the spiritual achievements of other states and peoples. This is turn helps to ensure that such achievements are not lost and that the baton continues to be passed on in the sequence of world history. It seems clear that Hegel's focus on the state is not an irrational fixation or simple power worship but an intelligible and coherent response to deep needs of his own thought. These needs deserve to be explored a little further.

Hegel's philosophy of history is ultimately founded, as was shown earlier, on a general logic or dialectic of consciousness. All determinate vehicles of spirit, from individual human beings to whatever collective centres of human consciousness there may be, participate in this logic. A crucial role is played by memory in ensuring that whatever is of value in the successive moments is taken forward and sublated. This is essential to maintain momentum and enable the process as a whole to be conceived in terms of dialectical movement. In the individual human being, memory may be thought of readily enough as residing in, and partly constitutive of, the self. For a historical dialectic to be intelligible, some collective analogue of the individual self as the bearer of memory has to be found. There must be some institutional locus of memory that is itself an individual self-moving entity persisting through significant stretches of historical time. Once again, the state is the only possible candidate, the only sufficiently close correlative of the self of memory in the social world.

It follows that if the state's claim to a central position is rejected, Hegel's philosophy of history must fail to yield a coherent story. The issue marks, as it were, the site of a strategic crux in his thinking, a crux predetermined by the requirement of exhibiting history as necessary progress. It could only be resolved by a bold theoretical stroke, and just such a stroke as Hegel attempts in invoking the state. His critics may still hold that its burdens are excessive, that, for instance, the political cannot be so vital for spiritual development as he proposes. All that has been attempted here is to show his deep grounds for proposing it; that is to say, to bring out the systematic character of his thought in its bearing on the matter. It will not do, as sympathetic critics have sometimes supposed, to wish away the centrality of the state with everything else remaining as before

(Collingwood 1946: 122). The structure stands or falls as a whole. To put the point in another way, one might suggest that anyone who is sympathetic to the Hegelian project in general should allow the case for his qualified, historical statism some significant weight. This discussion has tried to present that case so as to reveal his position to be less wilful or paradoxical, more capable of being soberly maintained, than it may appear at first. A considered verdict on it is not, however, possible without taking account of an issue that has at various times hovered on the fringes of the inquiry. A sense of its importance may be borne upon one in a variety of ways by central features of that position. It will suffice for present purposes to note how natural it seems, since we have discussed the role of the state in getting history started, to raise the possibility of its having a role in bringing it to a close. The issue now in question is that, much-canvassed in recent years, of the end of history, and an attempt to engage seriously with it can no longer be postponed.

Chapter 11

The end of history

The question of the end of history is a complicated one for the student of Hegel, and its curious status is attested by even the briefest survey of the debate. In spite of the natural way it has now arisen, it received little attention for a century or so after his death. A couple of striking contributions to the topic in the nineteenth century should, however, be acknowledged. The first was made by Friedrich Nietzsche in one of his 'Untimely Meditations'. Having complained of the Hegelian elevation of history and historical consciousness, he goes on:

> This history, understood in a Hegelian way, has contemptuously been called the sojourn of God on earth, which God, however, is himself first produced by history. But this God became transparent and intelligible to himself inside the Hegelian craniums and has already ascended all possible dialectical steps of his becoming up to that self-revelation: so that for Hegel the apex (*Höhepunkt*) and terminus (*Endpunkt*) of world history coincided in his own Berlin existence. He should even have said that all things after him are

properly judged to be only a musical coda of the world-historical rondo, more properly yet, to be redundant. He did not say that ...

(Nietzsche 1964: 167; 1980: 47)

It seems that Hegel should, in accordance with the logic of his thought, have proclaimed that history had ended in his own time, but failed to do so. This judgement is the more to be respected, in spite of its satirical trappings, for the deep insight from which it derives. The insight is that Hegel's God is the product of human history in the sense of being a God who comes to self-knowledge, and thereby the fullness of existence, only in and through the historical process, a process comprising the dialectical steps of the divine becoming. That such an interpretation of Hegel is essentially correct has been a central thesis of this discussion.

The second contribution to be acknowledged is that of Engels. He argues that Hegel 'was compelled to make a system', and, hence, to accord with traditional requirements, had to conclude with 'some sort of absolute truth'. So far as the historical process is concerned, this implied an 'end' (*das Ende der Geschichte*) that involves, on the one hand, humanity's arrival at 'the cognition of the absolute Idea', and, on the other, its carrying out of the Idea in reality. The realisation of the Idea takes the form of 'the monarchy based on social estates', described in the *Philosophy of Right* and promised, but never delivered, by Friedrich Wilhelm III of Prussia to his subjects (Engels 1958: 363–4; 1962: 268–9). Various fertile and important issues are sketched in these remarks. The first involves the belief, shared with Nietzsche, though arrived at by a different route, that Hegel is committed to postulating an end of history for general theoretical reasons. The second is the suggestion that history ends in the specific arrangements depicted in the *Philosophy of Right*, themselves an idealised version of the conditions obtaining in the Prussia of Hegel's own time. Finally, there is an issue which has already come into view at various points and has been described as 'the Hegelian problem', that of 'the relation between Truth and Existence' (Hyppolite 1969: 167). In Engels' version it is the problem of the relationship between cognition of the absolute Idea and social reality. This in turn seems an echo of the form in which it appeared most pressingly to the Young Hegelians among Hegel's early followers, that of how to conceive of the 'realisa-tion' (*Verwirklichung*) of philosophy (Marx 1975: 257). All of these issues have now to be pursued to a conclusion.

Kojève

For all the vigour with which Nietzsche and Engels present the end of history motif, its later prominence in discussions of Hegel is owed much more to a twentieth century source. As with 'recognition', it is owed largely to the work of Kojève, a thinker who combines Marxist and Nietzschean elements in a remarkable blend of his own. According to his reading of Hegel, history is, as we have seen, the history of the interaction of 'Masters' and 'Slaves', with both sides vainly seeking the recognition that is the object of their deepest, most human, desire. Hence, it is just to be expected that it 'stops at the moment when the difference, the opposition, between Master and Slave disappears'. Kojève's contention is that 'according to Hegel, it is in and by the wars of Napoleon, and, in particular, the Battle of Jena', the battle which was supposedly sounding in Hegel's ears as he finished writing the *Phenomenology*, 'that this completion of History is realised through the dialectical overcoming (*Aufheben*) of both the Master and the Slave' (Kojève 1980: 43–4). They are dialectically over-come in what Kojève calls 'the universal and homogeneous State', which, he asserts, 'for Hegel, was the Empire of Napoleon', and is more generally the modern state in its various manifestations (Kojève 1980: 237). Here every individual 'is *universally* recognised: recognised by the State as a citizen enjoying all political rights and as a "juridical person" of the civil law' (Kojève 1980: 237). The achievement of this fully satisfying form of recognition brings history to an end by, as it were, switching off the motor of its movement.

It was argued earlier that Kojève's account of the motor cannot be accepted as faithful exegesis. The general merits of his conception of the end state in that respect will emerge in the course of the discussion that follows. Something should be said initially, however, about a particular issue that is of the greatest importance for this inquiry.

For Kojève, freedom is 'ontologically Negativity' because it 'can *be* and *exist* only as *negation*'. In slightly more expansive terms, it must be understood as 'the *negation* of the given' (Kojève 1980: 222). Such negation is the hallmark of our humanity: 'Man properly so-called' is 'Action negating the given' (Kojève 1980: 158–9n). What is more specifically characteristic of human action is the negation of the given in the service of desire, and this, as we have seen, constitutes the substance of history. Thus, freedom is inseparably bound up with historicity: 'Man is a *historical free Individual*' (Kojève 1980: 235). The stage has now been set for a series of identities, and Kojève presents them in the starkest terms: 'Freedom = Negativity = Action = History' (Kojève 1980: 209). It is not too much to say that this serves to leave Hegel's view of the relationship between freedom and history standing on its head. For Hegel, history is the movement from various degrees of 'unfreedom' to fully realised freedom, while, for Kojève, freedom belongs exclusively within, and is co-extensive with, the historical realm. At the end of history, in a condition of satisfied desire, there is no action to negate the given, indeed no human action as such at all (Kojève 1980: 209). It is, therefore, impossible to charac- terise the individuals living in this condition as being 'free'. The conditions for the application of the term have disappeared from the scene, and history is, one has to say, a movement out of freedom. The contrast with Hegel serves to emphasise how far Kojève is from being a sober and reliable guide to his thought. It may, of course, still be the case that Kojève has important insights to offer, and one of them may well consist in his focusing on the unduly neglected topic of the end of history. He has, at any rate, succeeded in forcing it into the limelight. Almost every commentator since his time has felt obliged to take a stance on it, an obligation that cannot be evaded here.

Before turning to the textual evidence for Hegel's views, there is a conceptual matter to consider. It is necessary to be clear about what it might mean to affirm or deny that history has an end, or that it has ended. The essential point is captured in the phrase from Nietzsche rendered above as 'apex or terminus'. It is that there are two main strands of meaning in the English word 'end', as in the German '*Ende*'. The first is the sense of an ending as terminus or closure, of a form of existence or activity ceasing to be or coming to a stop. The second embraces whatever may be conceived as the apex or crown of a process, as realising the potential for development it contained. Thus, to vary the formula, one may speak of an end either as 'cessation' or as 'fulfilment'. It will also be convenient to have a term of art that requires both strands of meaning to be present, and, for this, 'consummation' seems a suitable choice. While they are analytically distinct there is bound to be much referential overlap, as well as separation, in practice. It is, however, their joint satisfaction that is standardly envisaged in talk of the end of history. This could not be merely a closure brought about by, for instance, the extinction of human life through nuclear or environmental catastrophe, for history must be fulfilled in being concluded. Neither is it the case, one should add, that the posthistorical condition has to be thought of, as Kojève seems to do, in terms of more or less complete stasis. It is just that whatever changes do occur in it, they will not be of the kind properly designated as historical. The conclusion to be drawn is that cessation and fulfilment are individually necessary and jointly sufficient conditions of the end of history. That end must be a consummation.

The last stage

It is time to consider the evidence of the texts for Hegel's views. To begin with, it should be said that the *Introduction* offers little or no direct support for attributing any kind of end of history thesis to him. The body of the *Lectures*, on the other hand, is perhaps the richest source of indications pointing in that direction. The main ones are as follows:

> World history travels from East to West, for Europe is absolutely (*schlechthin*) the end of world history, Asia the beginning.
>
> (M, 134: 103)

> the Christian world is the world of completion (*Vollendung*); the principle is fulfilled and thereby the end of days is fully come.
>
> (M, 414: 342)

> With this formally absolute principle [of reason] we come to the *last stage of history, to our world, to our time.*
>
> (M, 524: 442)

The first two of these statements seem immediately subject to a kind of reservation which limits their value and impact. Yet, if one looks further, their credibility can be largely restored, and they will be found to bear in a solid and dependable way on our concerns. The third is, as will appear, wholly reliable as it stands, and indeed may be taken to represent Hegel's best brief statement of his position.

The setting of the first assertion serves to give it an adventitious air. For it seems to have been arrived at because Hegel had become locked into a spatial metaphor for representing historical time and, on the terrestrial globe, had, as it were, run out of space. The metaphor is one of the course of world history as 'the great day's work of spirit', and since the historical sun rose in the East, it plainly has to set in the West when the day's work is done. Hegel is in the grip, it might be suggested, of a crude kind of pictorial thinking which constrains his expression. Whatever the merits of this suggestion, it has to be said that he goes on almost at once to present what seems to be the substance of the original claim in a less problematic way. The means of doing so is the familiar litany which assures us that 'The East knew and knows only that *one* is free; the Greek and Roman world, that *some* are free; the Germanic world knows that *all* are free' (M, 134: 104). The point to note for present purposes is the impossibility of surpassing the finality of 'all are free' in its own terms. The proposition does indeed represent a terminus beyond which there can be no progress in that particular line. Hegel's attachment to it will have to be given its due weight in reaching a verdict on the issues.

The second statement has the disadvantage that it would prove too much. Taking it seriously in the present context might seem to imply that the end of history coincides with the birth of Christianity, that the central human drama really was 'completed' on the cross. Alternatively, one might suppose that the end came with its being established as the official religion of the Roman Empire, or as the principle of unity of medieval Europe, or, perhaps, with the reconstitution of the Christian Church at the Reformation. All of these suggestions seem, however, to push the end of history too far back in time to accord with the rather numerous observations Hegel has to make about modern history, still less to be independently plausible. There is, nevertheless, a nugget of substance contained in the formulation being considered. It may be brought out by noting how decisively Hegel takes Christianity to be the 'absolute' or 'complete' (*vollendet*) religion, and, as such, a non-transcendable limit of religious development. This aspect, too, will have to find its place in any final reckoning.

The third statement is at once narrower and wider than the others in its focus of the topic of the end of history. It is narrower in that it ties the topic to an object of reference, Hegel's own world and time, which is less vast than 'Europe' or 'Christianity'. The context suggests that it is the post-Enlightenment world he has specifically in mind. For it was, it appears, the Enlightenment that definitively established the 'formally absolute principle' in question, the principle that everything is subject to rational explanation and questioning (M, 524: 442). Hegel is not altogether consistent in identifying the great inaugural event of what he thinks of as distinctively his world and time. Elsewhere the Reformation or the French Revolution seem to figure in rather different ways in the role. This variety arises largely, however, from the argumentative needs of particular occasions and does not much matter at present. What does matter is the crucial importance of the modern world, the world in which Hegel believed himself and his audience to be centrally and securely placed.

The sense in which the statement being discussed is wider than the others emerges when one observes that it does not straightforwardly assert or imply that the end of history has already arrived. It is rather that we are living in the final act before the curtain comes down; not, as it were, in the 'completed world' but in the 'world of completion'. This is still an episode within history, and one that, presumably, may be filled with historical actions and events of great importance. Moreover, we are given no indication of its likely duration. This statement seems more modest and persuasive than its two predecessors, and in addition, offers a simple framework with which it should be possible to accommodate their rational kernel. The special status of modern Christian Europe consists, one might suggest, in the fact that, while it belongs squarely to history, it is the harbinger of a new form of human existence, the prelude to posthistory. This serves to shift attention from claims that since the Battle of Jena, or some other unlikely event, we have actually been living in the posthistorical world, claims that could be sustained only with the self-assurance and blinkered intensity of a Kojève. Yet it also offers the prospect of doing justice to the air of finality that attends so many of Hegel's pronouncements on his own world and time.

The framework suggested above seems to have the merit of being able to cover not only the textual appearances favouring an end of history view, but also those that seem to belong on the other side. They include, as was hinted earlier, virtually everything the *Introduction* has to contribute to the question. There is, for instance, the remark that 'work still remains to be done' in history, a 'further work' that is required for spirit to 'attain its reality and become conscious of itself in actuality' (H, 257: 209). A reference has already been made to the prospects held out of a leading historical role for America, and to the similar prospects held out elsewhere for Russia and the Slavic peoples in general. This further work and future prospects might readily enough be assigned to a final phase of history that is itself of indeterminate length. A similar point may be made of the conclusion of the *Lectures*:

> This is the point to which consciousness has attained, and these are the chief moments of the form in which the principle of freedom has realised itself, for world history is nothing but the development of the concept of freedom.
>
> (M, 539–40: 456)

There is no suggestion here that the point which consciousness has attained is the terminus of its historical development. If that had been Hegel's view it would have been natural for him to have revealed it on such an occasion and downright misleading not to have done so. The suggestion is rather that the present is but a temporary anchorage of spirit within historical time. It is true that there is no hint either of an ultimate end such as our framework postulates. What has been said is, nevertheless, wholly compatible with that postulate. All that it strictly entitles one to infer is that consciousness and freedom will continue to develop beyond the present into a historical future. This still accords with the assumption of a fixed horizon towards which the development is taking us and which is itself the outer limit of the historical realm. Thus, the proposed framework seems to reconcile in a loose but coherent way the main items of textual evidence bearing on the end of history theme, and it is hard to see how else that might be achieved. This is itself an important consideration in its favour.

Two forms of development

Whatever sense may be made of the direct evidence of the texts, its quality is not such as to allow a definitive conclusion to be drawn. This is almost inevitably so in view of Hegel's failure to address the central issues in a self-conscious, systematic way. Hence, the direct evidence has to be supplemented by more theoretical considerations of what he is committed to in virtue of his general position, the approach taken by Nietzsche and Engels. For that purpose one need scarcely look further than the canonical description of history as the progress of the consciousness of freedom and of its realisation. What has now to be emphasised is Hegel's determination not to allow this progress to be conceived as merely a perpetual striving, the interminable succession of a 'bad infinite'. There are, as has been observed, deep features of his thought which rule out such a conception. These are as strongly marked in the *Introduction* as they are elsewhere: 'progress', he asserts, 'is not an indeterminate advance ad infinitum', for 'it has a definite aim (*ein Zweck da*)'; that is to say, spirit's achievement of self-consciousness (H, 181: 149). There is other textual evidence, as straightforward as one could wish, bearing on the matter. Thus, Hegel assures us that the expression 'the ultimate end (*Endzweck*) of the world' itself implies that the end is destined 'to be realised, made actual' (H, 50: 44; M, 29: 16, 20, 19). The depths from which this assurance draws in his philosophy have still to be explored in all their relevant aspects. For the present, one has only to note the implication that history, the time of the development of freedom, is something bounded by its very nature. This is Kojève's best insight, the insight which ensures that his reading survives for all the exotic additions with which he surrounds it. He has seen that 'History itself must be essentially finite', and so 'must have a definitive *end*' (Kojève 1980: 148). The conclusion to be drawn at this point is that the doctrine of the end of history is to be attributed to Hegel in virtue not simply of isolated remarks but of the inner logic of his thought. What has to be discussed further is the question, raised so dramatically by Kojève, of where the modern world, the world we share with Hegel, stands in relation to that end. In particular, the suggestion that it represents the final phase of preparation needs to be spelled out and tested more thoroughly.

In exploring these matters it seems natural to take account of the twofold character of Hegel's canonical description of history as the progress of the consciousness and the realisation of freedom. To grasp the principle of freedom is to grasp that 'the human being as such (*der Mensch als Mensch*)' is free and that 'the freedom of the spirit constitutes his very nature'. It was 'the Germanic nations in Christianity' who first achieved this consciousness, and so it may be said to have dawned 'in religion, in the innermost region of the spirit'. The awareness that humanity as such is free is from one point of view, as was remarked earlier, itself the apex and terminus of a movement of consciousness. Its attainment seems, nevertheless, to leave room for further development in a variety of ways. The most obvious is simply extensional, the continuing dispersal of the basic insight beyond its original home in Germanic Christianity. That there has been progress in this respect since Hegel's own time, as part of the overall movement of modernity, can scarcely be doubted, and would not have surprised him. That it is even now far from complete seems equally clear. It is, for one thing, still by no means the case that all ideologies and world views with significant numbers of adherents could accept the basic insight readily, or even with difficulty. On the other hand, it is very widely disseminated, and its status is such that direct, public repudiations are relatively rare. Moreover, one should bear in mind the Hegelian point that there is no dialectical path leading away from it, no conceivable immanent movement of spirit that would consign it to oblivion. Barring the most disastrous of external shocks it may therefore be accounted a secure achievement of humanity. It seems reasonable in the circumstances to suppose that some critical corner in historical development has been turned, and to express this by speaking of a final stage of such development in which, nevertheless, much 'further work' remains to be done.

A second kind of possible development is, it might be said, qualitative in character. It is wholly unsurprising that the consciousness of universal freedom should have first emerged under religious auspices, since religion is, as Hegel constantly reminds us, a form of absolute spirit of great cognitive significance. It remains the case, however, that the truth can emerge there only as representation, and for a conceptual understanding of freedom one must turn to philosophy. At this point there arises once more the question of how, in a Hegelian perspective, philosophy may be conceived of as having been 'realised'. What may now be suggested is that its realisation is indissolubly bound up with that of freedom, and must consist essentially in the conceptual understanding of freedom obtaining in society at the end of history.

Morning prayer

If, in accordance with the plan outlined earlier, one turns from the consciousness of freedom to its realisation, the way ahead seems plain. As the discussion has shown, the entire burden of what Hegel has to say on the subject is that freedom can be realised only in and through the state. Hence, it will be necessary to inquire how far in his view the existing states of his time meet the requirements of realised freedom, and so embody, or portend, the end of history. In this inquiry it is natural to take one's cue from Engels and allow the *Philosophy of Right* a special importance. It is Hegel's treatise on the state, his systematic attempt to exhibit the rational features of the most advanced states of his time. Moreover, it is, as was noted earlier, the textbook he recommended to his philosophy of history students. Any other available evidence will also, of course, have to be considered, with particular reference to the conclusions he arrived at in Berlin in the last period of his life, the period of the *Philosophy of Right* and of the philosophy of history lectures.

A rather lowly form of evidence may be cited by way of background, that of his immediate responses to the events of the day. The following remarks occur in correspondence near the start of the period now in question:

I am about to be fifty years old, and I have spent thirty of these fifty years in these ever-unrestful times of hope and fear. I had hoped that for once we might be done with it. Now I must confess that things continue as ever. Indeed, in one's darker hours it seems they are getting ever worse.

(HL: 451)

Shortly before Hegel's death, in the aftermath of the July Revolution in France, he advises his sister: 'We are presently and – we hope – forever safe from all the [current] unrest. But these are still anxious times, in which everything that previously was taken to be solid and secure seems to totter' (HL: 422).

It hardly needs saying that these passages seem quite at odds with a belief that the consummation of history is nigh, much less that it has already arrived. Moreover, they suffice to dispel any suggestion of a thinker serenely contemplating the fulfilment of his theories in the world. This is the image of the later Hegel that underlies and gives an edge to Nietzsche's reference to his 'Berlin existence'. The passages also run counter to the alternative image of Hegel as an Olympian figure weaving his *a priori* patterns in indifference to the actual course of events. They suggest rather a marked sensitivity to their course, an almost excessive absorption in current affairs, perhaps an inability to be detached from the lessons of that newspaper reading which he had declared many years earlier to be 'a kind of realistic morning prayer' (JS: 547; AW: 2). It might be thought, however, that the very imme-diacy of these reactions somewhat lessens their value as evidence of a considered position. For that one should in any case look beyond the *Letters*.

In order to deal with the large amount of material that now comes into view, it may be well to focus on Hegel's response to some specific problems of the modern world. The problems are connected in their source and in their practical implications, not least in their ominous bearing on the prospects for realising freedom. Hegel's response to them displays a striking pattern, one quite untypical of his work in general but prefigured, however dimly, in the extracts given above from his correspondence. The response is one of resignation, of a relinquishing of intellectual grip and the consigning of their solution to the workings of time. The problems in question are the existence of large-scale poverty, the erosion of the autonomy of the state and the decline of religion. Their character, and that of Hegel's response, should be briefly documented.

Poverty, politics and religion

The setting for the discussion of poverty in the *Philosophy of Right* is Hegel's understanding of the dynamics of what he calls 'civil society' (*bürgerliche Gesellschaft*). At the heart of civil society there is the 'system of needs', the sphere in which individuals strive for the material requirements of life and of the good life. It is not, however, simply to be identified with the economic dimension of society as such, for its creation 'belongs to the modern world' (EPR: 220). In essence, civil society is the modern market economy; that is to say, capitalism. Hegel grasps this system as, in one vital aspect, a machine for generating inequality. It is a competitive system that functions by sorting its participants into winners and losers, and then by its inherent logic driving the two groups ever farther apart. Hence, it gives rise in the normal course of its operations to 'a spectacle of extravagance and misery', the creation of a 'rabble' at one extreme and 'disproportionate wealth' at the other (EPR: 222, 266). The poor are:

> more or less deprived of all the advantages of society, such as the ability to acquire skills and education in general, as well as of the administration of justice (*Rechtspflege*), health care, and often even of the consolation of religion.
>
> (GPR: 388; EPR: 265)

The creation of a rabble occurs, however, only when to this objective deprivation is added the disposition of 'inward rebellion against the rich, against society, the government etc.'. Hegel is in no doubt that those who seethe in this manner are justified in doing so. For in society, as opposed to nature, hardship instantly assumes, he declares, 'the form of a wrong (*Unrecht*) inflicted on this or that class (*Klasse*)' (GPR: 389–90; EPR: 266–7).

In the light of the earlier discussion of the need for freedom to be objectified as a system of rights and justice, the radical 'unfreedom' of those who fall outside that system will not need labouring. Hegel's own most graphic account of the connection between poverty and unfreedom is, however, given in his lectures on the philosophy of right:

> [The poor man] has the consciousness of himself as an infinite, free being, and thereby arises the demand that his external existence should correspond to this consciousness. ... The poor man feels himself to be related to arbitrariness, to human contingency ... Self-consciousness appears driven to the point where it no longer has any rights, where freedom has no existence. Because the freedom of the individual has no existence, there disappears with it the recognition of universal freedom.
>
> (PRV: 195; cf. translation in EPR: 453)

The comprehensive nature of this indictment is reflected in Hegel's failure to propose a remedy. In the *Philosophy of Right* he half-heartedly canvasses various possibilities, from charity and the founding of colonies to what he presents as the characteristically British solution, 'to leave the poor to their fate and direct them to beg from the public' (EPR: 267). These suggestions seem half-hearted because they are made against the background of a sense of the structural and endemic character of the problem, a sense that 'The emergence of poverty is in general a consequence of civil society, and on the whole arises necessarily out of it' (PRV: 193; cf. EPR: 267). It comes as no surprise here to find Hegel striking what may surely be taken as a note of resignation of just the kind referred to earlier: 'The important question of how poverty can be remedied is one which agitates and torments modern societies especially' (EPR: 267).

The second problem to be considered is the erosion of the autonomy of the state; that is to say, the invasion of the political realm by the interests, values and ways of thought of civil society. Hegel had long been aware of the danger. In one of his earliest essays he remarks on 'the bourgeois (*bürgerliche*) sense which cares only for an individual (*ein Einzelnes*) without self-sufficiency and has no regard for the whole' (FS: 516–17; HPW: 190). In the *Philosophy of Right* the threat has become a reality. Thus, Hegel analyses at length there the way in which the system of individual suffrage in geographical constituencies has brought the electoral process under the control of the 'particular and contingent' interest of a faction (GPR: 473, 481; EPR: 343–4, 350–1). In the late essay on the English Reform Bill this line of thought is developed for a specific empirical setting. 'England' constitutes in certain respects for Hegel the paradigm case in the existing world of the society of the *Philosophy of Right*. There 'the contrast between prodigious wealth and utterly helpless poverty is enormous' (BS: 121; HPW: 325). Moreover, it displays with particular clarity the tendency, deplored also in the philosophy of right lectures, to regard everything as 'purchasable' (*käuflich*), even the claims of right (BS: 85; HPW: 296–7; cf. PRV: 196). This attitude has specific and disastrous implications for the integrity of the political. Thus, in England, a significant number of parliamentary seats fall, according to Hegel, into the category of being a 'recognised marketable commodity', and, thereby, a symptom of 'a people's political corruption' (BS: 85; HPW: 296–7). His case against the Reform Bill is that it provides no remedy for these defects. It can do nothing to improve social conditions, and it fails even to extricate itself from the confusion of property rights with political representation (BS: 108–9; HPW: 315).

In the last years of Hegel's life he detects the same tendencies at work in France, the other great representative country of modernity. Thus, in the *Lectures* he presents the July Revolution as the work of a 'liberalism' that is not satisfied with 'the establishment of rational rights, freedom of the person and of property'. Instead, it sets up 'the principle of atomism, of the individual will (*der Einzelwillen*)', and insists that everything should proceed from its 'express power' and with its 'express consent'. The principle of atomism and the individual will is, of course, the distinctive principle of civil society, and there it has its proper sphere of operation. What is achieved by its introduction into politics, however, is that 'agitation and unrest are perpetuated' (M, 534–5: 452). This gloomy analysis reflects Hegel's awareness that in France, as in England, countries he could scarcely fail to acknowledge as being at the leading edge of historical development, the 'atomism' and the 'particular and contingent' interests bred in the economic sphere were coming to dominate the political. Civil society was tending, to put it crudely, to take over the state. This must render the state incapable of functioning as the autonomous realm of 'rational rights' and realised freedom. Having diagnosed the sickness, however, Hegel washes his hands of responsibility for finding a cure: 'This collision, this nodus, this problem is that with which history is occupied, and which it has to solve in future times' (M, 535: 452).

The final problem for which Hegel has no solution to offer has already been indicated in the reference in the *Philosophy of Right* to the poor being deprived of the consolation of religion. It is, as one would expect, dealt with more extensively in the philosophy of religion lectures. At the end of one course of lectures Hegel speaks of the situation in which 'the Gospel is no longer preached to the poor', and in which the people 'seem to themselves to be deserted by their teachers'. What this signifies is the 'inner bifurcation', indeed the 'passing away', of the spiritual community that is the sole repository of 'religious knowledge reached through the concept'. Hegel conceives of the problem at this point as arising from the corruption of the ministers of the Gospel by forms of thought and life that are in his work routinely and specifically associated with civil society. These ministers have elevated 'particular well-being' to an end and the pursuit of 'private right and enjoyment' becomes the order of the day. Thus, they find their satisfaction in what is 'empty and vain', a satisfaction which, however, is not possible for the 'substantial kernel of the people' (VPR: 342–3; LPR: 149–50).

The treatment of this feature of the modern world in the *Introduction* is still bleaker and more sweeping. Hegel observes that attempts to 'implant' religion often seem to be really 'a cry of fear and distress which expresses the danger that religion has already disappeared from the state or is about to disappear completely'. It is plainly a danger he takes seriously and, indeed, he goes on to argue that its seriousness is not properly appreciated even by those who raise the cry in question. For they believe in the 'implanting and inculcation' of religion as a means against the evil. This is to approach the matter as though the state were already present but religion has to be imported into it 'by the bushel or bucketful'. To try to do so is to reverse the correct order of priorities. For the proposition that the state is founded on religion really means that 'it has arisen from religion and continues to do so, now and always' (H, 128–9: 108; M, 71: 51–2, 65,

54). Hegel's insight goes deeper here than in the philosophy of religion lectures. The problem is not now one of the individual failings of the clergy, and could not be remedied by more conscientious preaching, by implanting and inculcating religion. He seems rather to be in touch with a large-scale historical development, an important aspect of the transition to modernity. This is the structural shift through which the Church lost its grip on the masses in modern market society. It would be hard to think of a development more ominous for his view of that society, for the imagery that permeates his thinking is, as been illustrated, that of foundations and their absence. Religion is variously said to be foundational not only for the state but also for the 'people' and for 'the ethical realm in general' (H, 125: 105; M, 70: 50, 64, 53; EPR: 292). Hence it is that unless the other aspects of life are grounded there, they 'will remain barren for they will not be determined by truth' (H, 132: 110–11).

The implications of all this for the prospects of realising freedom in the modern world may be drawn out in various ways. Most obviously, there is the fact that the decline of religion must undermine the foundations of the state, the only possible community of freedom. There is another route that pays particular attention to the cognitive significance of religion, a route already hinted at in the references to religious knowledge and to determination by truth. The essential points are made by Hegel in a passage that treats the 'absolute' or 'consummate' religion; that is to say, Christianity, as 'the religion of *truth* and the religion of *freedom*'. The passage rehearses the theme of freedom and reconciliation, and goes on to connect it with religion in its absolute form:

In the abstract, freedom means relating oneself to something objective without its being something alien … freedom therefore appears in the form of *reconciliation*. Reconciliation begins with differentiated entities standing opposed to each other – God who confronts a world that is estranged from him, and a world that is estranged from its essence. … Reconciliation is the negation of this separation, this division, and means that each cognizes itself in the other, find itself in its essence. Reconciliation, consequently, is

> freedom … it is posited in a religion that a representation of the
> unity of divine and human nature occurs. God has become human.
>
> (CR: 171–2)

Thus, religious knowledge, more especially the representation of the unity of divine and human nature in the Christian doctrine of incarnation, is a reconciling knowledge. It takes away the alien character of the world, enabling the believer to find herself at home there. As such it is a vehicle of realised freedom, the only possible such vehicle, as Hegel was well aware, for the broad mass of the population, its 'substantial kernel', in his time. Hence, the decay of the absolute religion must be a most serious matter for him, one that strikes at the heart of the project of revealing the emergent rationality of the modern world and of displaying that world as the true home of freedom. Yet, as his discussion of the divisions of the spiritual community makes clear, he can envisage no solution, and takes his leave of the problem in a manner that will by now be familiar: 'How the empirical present day is to find its own way out of its state of bifurcation, and what form it has to take, must be left to itself' (VPR: 343–4; LPR: 151: CR: 162n).

A vanished world

There are, it appears, certain problems of the modern world to which Hegel's final response is one of unwonted resignation, couched in similar terms in each case. The problems are important for our inquiry because each bears in a destructive way, as the discussion has shown, on the possibility of fully realising freedom, and thereby bringing history to an end, in that world. They are also connected in that they have a common source, the existence and workings of civil society. That this is so is immediately plain in the case of mass poverty and the erosion of the political, and is a less obvious, but still marked, factor in Hegel's understanding of the decline of religion. He might now be seen to be caught on the horns of a dilemma, having to choose, to put it crudely, between civil society and the goal of realised freedom. That the second of these horns has a central and immovable place in his thought will not need to be laboured further. Yet civil society has also to be seen as a formidable presence there. Much of the structure of Hegel's philosophy of right is determined by the relationship between it and the state. Such institutions as the corporations and the system of estates have their roles more or less explicitly assigned by the need to mitigate, so far as possible, its logic (EPR: 270–74, 329–30, 339–53). The hereditary monarchy for its part may be seen as a touch of nature, a victory for, so to speak, the uncompetitive principle in a world that might otherwise be dominated by the contractual engagements of particular wills. Even Hegel's curious endorsement of the value of war may be regarded as motivated in part by a wish to distract the burghers periodically from the business of getting and spending, to recall them to their sovereign master, death, and the claims of their membership in the universal community of the state (EPR: 360–65). Nevertheless, the commitment to civil society does not go quite all the way down to the foundations of his thinking in this region.

What is foundational there is his conception of private property. This is seen by him as the 'external sphere of freedom' which the person must give himself in order to exist as Idea and reason; that is, as a fully realised person: 'the personality must have existence (*Dasein*) in property' (EPR: 73, 81). Moreover, in characterising the relationship between persons, Hegel remarks that 'it is only as owners of property that the two have existence (*Dasein*) for each other' (EPR: 70; cf. HPM: 244). Thus, the recognition of each other's status as private proprietors is an essential element of mutual recognition, and the society of freedom is, one may suppose, a society of such mutually recognising proprietors. It is not enough, one should note, that the individual be recognised as having a formal right to property and, hence, as a potential owner of it. 'Everyone', Hegel insists, 'ought to have property'. It is true that he goes on to make clear that this does not imply equality of property holdings, an implication which, in its abstract flattening of particularity, he regards as 'contrary to right' (EPR: 81). Nevertheless, it is plainly a substantive thesis, one that must have implications for actual property arrangements.

The implications do not, however, have to take the form of the arrangements of civil society. Where the basic logic might be taken to point instead is towards a society of individual producers and exchangers who own and work their means of production, the economic model usually known as 'simple commodity production'. In being commodity production it gives a central place to the processes of alienation by sale, the market transactions, which are, for Hegel, a necessary expression of the fundamental right to private property, as well as a guarantee of both mutual independence and social integration (EPR: 233–9). The model allows property rights, and hence a market, only in goods and not in labour. Since no one can earn a living by participating in the labour market, economic agents must be assumed to have property holdings adequate for that purpose. This does not, of course, entail equality of property, but it does postulate a much more egalitarian society than that depicted in the *Philosophy of Right*, for it lacks the engine of wage labour that drives the unlimited accumulation of capital and unlimited pauperisation there. Indeed, since the society in question is essentially composed of individuals who have the same relation to the means of production, it may be said to be formally classless. As such, it might reasonably be expected to yield the material conditions of self-respect and eligibility for recognition by one's peers, and, in general, of the experience of finding oneself at home in the social world. It is in its main outline a familiar enough conception in the history of thought. The underlying economic model was frequently cited by the political economists who were Hegel's instructors, providing, for instance, the basis for Adam Smith's story about the 'nation of hunters' who exchange beaver and deer (Smith 1991: 41). In an expanded form the vision of a sober and sturdy property-owning citizenry may be said to haunt the political theory of private property from Aristotle to Hegel's immediate predecessor, Fichte, and on to such thinkers in our own time as John Rawls. It has, on the face of it, a better claim to express the inner connection of private property and freedom than anything the polarised world of propertied and propertyless of the *Philosophy of Right* can offer.

This vision has been presented only in the most schematic terms here, but there seems little need to do more. For all the persuasive logic and distinguished precedents that favour the society of small, independent owner-occupiers, Hegel shows no inclination whatsoever to go down that path. The reason does not seem far to seek. His reading of the political economists, and his own observation of the world, would have made clear to him that such a society must be a utopian dream without any grounding in the emergent reality of the present. These sources of insight would have tended rather to reveal the capitalist mode of production as the manifest destiny of the age, a fate not to be transcended within it. Hence, an attempt had to be made to accommodate it in such a treatise on the age as the *Philosophy of Right*, whatever the structural tensions that thereby result. Smith had himself viewed the basic economic model as typifying 'an early and rude state of society' (Smith 1991: 41). Even in sympathetic economic histories, simple commodity production routinely figures as a precarious transitional form between feudalism as a system not intrinsically dependent on market exchanges and the unrestricted commodity production of capitalism. There could not, for Hegel, be any historical dialectic running backwards to that vanished world.

Gates of hell

The immediate effect of this discussion is to deepen the sense of Hegel's dilemma. He is as much the philosopher of reality as of reason, and yet in the world he knows the two poles of his concern seem to be flying irresistibly apart. The kinds of social arrangements that might be satisfactory to reason are not in the process of being delivered by history, and what is being delivered is marked by in-built, large-scale irrationalities. It may even seem that a structural fault is now opening up in Hegel's thought, and that its main project of demonstrating the rational becoming actual is in danger of foundering. Such a conclusion needs to be averted, if that is possible. To begin with, the destructive potential of the situation should be contained by being brought under some form of intellectual control. It has to be shown that the problems it gives rise to may, for all their seriousness, be encompassed within the framework of Hegel's philosophy and cannot threaten that framework.

The essential point is made by Hegel in the very passage that deplores the 'inner bifurcation' and 'passing away' of the spiritual community:

> But ought we to speak here of *destruction* (*Untergang*) when the kingdom of God is founded eternally, when the Holy Spirit as such

lives eternally in its community, and when the gates of hell are not to prevail against the Church?

(VPR: 342; LPR: 149–50)

This rhetorical question may surely be taken, in a way familiar in Hegel, as the religious expression of a speculative truth. It conveys in its own picturesque terms the guarantee of the philosophical proposition that 'reason rules the world and world history is therefore rational in its course'. Where this fundamental thesis is concerned, Hegel never gives any sign of withdrawing or wavering in his allegiance. Such fidelity is, however, quite able to acknowledge periods, even extended ones, of stagnation, disruption and recession within the overall pattern. Hence, the problems of modern society, however large and seemingly intractable, can be given their due weight without damaging the structure of historical understanding itself. Their gravity is attested by the fact that Hegel, from his vantage point in history, can see no way to resolve them. It seems wholly appropriate in these circumstances to respond by consigning them, as he does, to the historical future, not as an admission of defeat but with a rational confidence in their ultimate solution. To do so is itself but a way of maintaining the doctrine that history is essentially finite and temporally bounded. It is also fully compatible with the view that while the present age is certainly not its end as such, it may be said to fall within the final chapter. The rational process of the development of freedom may legitimately be thought to be now so far advanced and secure as to warrant such a conclusion. Thus, it may be concluded that Hegel's historical scheme is at once loose and accommodating enough, and coherent and determinate enough, to cope with the difficulties. A further suggestion will be made in mitigation of them later in the discussion.

It appears that Hegel simply does not know in any concrete detail the character of the society of freedom at the end of history. In particular he is unable to specify the basic forms of its economic life, and has to be content to leave them to be revealed in the course of historical time. The guidance his work can offer on this question is, however, not yet exhausted. To try to draw it out further is not to engage in mere prophesying or prescribing, activities with no place in his understanding of philosophy. It is rather a matter of trying to see more deeply into a network of conceptual relationships and commitments. The question may be put by asking what, in general terms, must the society of the future be like to qualify as the home of freedom. The chief clue to be followed derives from the strongly universalist and egalitarian strain in Hegel's thinking about these matters.

Recognition and equality

The scene may be set by bringing together some of the remarkable, if still unspecific, formulations about the condition of realised freedom which the *Introduction* has to offer. The main list runs as follows:

> we know ... that *all* human beings as such (*an sich*) are free, that the human being as human being is free.
>
> (H, 63: 54–5; M, 32: 19, 24, 22)

> The substance of spirit is freedom. Its end in the historical process is hereby indicated: the freedom of the subject ... that the subject has infinite value and comes to the consciousness of its supremacy. This substance of the end of the world spirit is achieved through the freedom of each individual (*eines jeden*).
>
> (H, 64: 55)

> Conscious freedom exists only where every individuality (*jede Individualität*) is known as positive within the divine essence.
>
> (H, 63: 54–5; M, 32: 19, 24, 22)

These are very large claims, and, indeed, the first demand they make on us is that of appreciating just how extraordinary they are. For many readers of Hegel this will involve escaping from their air of familiarity, and the background noise around them, so as to respond fully to their immediacy and power. Above all it is necessary to register that they have to be taken distributively as insisting on freedom for each individual human person, each subject of infinite value. They do not license the reader to take refuge in postulating it of some vague collectivity, humanity in general. Therein lies their truly radical character. In the light they shed it becomes all the more obvious that the conditions of Hegelian freedom are not met by any existing society of his time, or of ours, or by his attempt to capture the rational elements of the modern world in the *Philosophy of Right*. Their second demand is for a thoroughgoing inner, and not merely formal, acceptance of Hegel's commitment to what they affirm. These are his ideas, and the seriousness with which he holds them is inseparable from his status as a thinker. For him, one has to appreciate, history ends only when every human being is free, and the end of history can have no other meaning in his thought.

Some further light may be shed by returning to the theme of mutual recognition. At this point one should recall the achievement of Kojève, an achievement which, as has been shown, he himself misconceived in an important respect. The essential truth is not that recognition serves as the goal of the struggle which drives the historical dialectic but that its presence is necessary for the condition of realised freedom at the end of history. Kojève's achievement, it may now be suggested, is to have forced on our attention the fact that a profoundly egalitarian notion lies at the heart of Hegel's vision of freedom. In bringing this out, one may follow Kojève's example in focusing on the master–servant relationship. It is all too obvious that the lowly position of the servant ensures that no meaningful recognition can be available to him, since the loss of humanity in his status precludes the possibility. Much more interesting is the implication that the inequality of the relationship ensures that the master's desire for recognition cannot be satisfied either. This is so for at least two related reasons, one that links quality of recognition directly to equality and another that does so through the mediation of freedom. The first reason is simply that the value of an act of recognition derives from, and cannot transcend, its source, and so recognition by a being who lacks all human worth and dignity is itself nugatory. As Hegel explains, such 'one-sided and unequal' recognition by a 'dependent' consciousness cannot suffice for 'recognition proper' (PG: 152; PS: 116–17). The second reason is that, to reiterate a point made earlier in this discussion, such recognition must be, or at least be under a fixed and vitiating suspicion of being, enforced just in virtue of the relation of dependence. As Kojève puts it in his enlightening, if strictly unHegelian, way, it is of the essence of the desire for recognition that it is 'directed toward another desire' (Kojève 1980: 40, 134). Hence, it is directed towards what cannot be commanded from without but must arise unbidden as an inner determination of the self. From the standpoint of this second reason, it appears that recognition presupposes freedom and freedom presupposes at least some significant measure of equality.

Since all of the principles at stake here admit of degrees, their realisation may be conceived in terms of a continuum. At one extreme there is the gross inequality of master and servant with a complete absence of freedom and of 'recognition proper'. At the other there is the freely self-determined mutual recognition of equals, exhibiting what are in this context the very lineaments of gratified desire. In between, the quality of recognition varies inversely with the unfreedom and inequality of the recognisers. A reasonably satisfying recognition must involve some measure of parity of status and esteem in a relationship of substantially self-dependent persons. From this standpoint also the appeal of the society of individual, petty producers seems clear. If it has to be set aside as merely utopian, there is little further help to be gained from Hegel so far as the institutional forms of realised freedom are concerned. It may be, of course, that even the most determined contemporary Hegelians will in the end have to acknowledge that we, who share the final stage of history with him, are essentially no better placed than he was in this respect. In those circumstances it would be rational for them to follow his example by consigning the solutions to history to disclose.

They may be all the more inclined to do so if some basic features of the system are kept in mind. This discussion has drawn attention throughout to the integral links between Hegel's ontological doctrines and his philosophies of history and society. What has finally to be emphasised is the sense in which his conception of realised freedom can enlist the authority and force of the ontology behind it. It is most readily shown by returning to the foundational passage of the *Introduction* that explains the 'only thought' philosophy brings to the understanding of history, 'the simple thought of reason'. In the spelling out of that thought we learn that reason is 'infinite power' and, hence, 'not so powerless as to create only an ideal, an ought beyond reality, who knows where'. The argumentative device used here is one to which Hegel is distinctly partial, and one which has already been noted in the form of the assurance that the Idea 'is not so impotent that it merely ought to be, and is not actual' (EL: 30). It is, as it were, a slight on the absolute, an insult to its majesty, whether in its character as reason or as Idea, to suppose that it is unable to develop itself into an actually existing world. That the rational is, or is becoming, actual is, of course, central to Hegel's entire metaphysical vision. Moreover, it becomes fully actual in that vision only through the society of self-conscious human freedom. Hence, the process of realising that society has an 'infinite power', the entire weight of the universe, one might say, on its side.

The point may be put still more dramatically in the figurative language of religion. In this language the power in question is identified as that of God, than which no greater power can be conceived. It is a God who, as Nietzsche so clearly and unsympathetically perceived, is produced by history, and in the course of history becomes self-transparent and self-intelligible in human craniums. This now emerges as the ultimate ontological guarantee that history ends by realising the freedom of all. It also enables a final ingredient to be added to one's grasp of the note of resignation Hegel sounds so frequently in his last years. He had often in the course of his career rebuked the 'impatience of opinion', its dissatisfaction with the slow progress of spirit (EPR: 92). This was, one might conclude, a lesson he had eventually to assimilate thoroughly and apply unsparingly in his own understanding of the world. The absolute is not in a hurry, and will not speed up, not even for the thinker who first achieved a proper conceptual grasp of its workings.

Chapter 12

The ways of God

The central thesis of Hegel's philosophy of history is that history is the progress of the consciousness of freedom and of its realisation. The process presents itself in one vital aspect as the reconciliation of spirit to the world and its coming to be at home there. When Hegel wishes to characterise his investigation in the largest terms he enlists that aspect by calling it 'a theodicy, a justification of God' (H, 48: 42; M, 28: 15, 18, 18). That this is ultimately his own favoured self-description is also suggested by the fact that it is invoked again at the end of his lecture course as the last word to his audience (M, 539: 457; cf. EL: 222). It will shed invaluable light on his philosophy of history to consider it specifically in its guise as theodicy.

Problem of evil

There is, as Hegel is well aware, a long tradition of seeking to 'justify the ways of God to man'. Indeed, whenever he self-consciously considers his own efforts in that line, he tends to do so polemically, marking them off from those of his predecessors. The chief element in the background from which he wishes to distinguish himself seems to be that represented by orthodox Christian theism. A passage that captures some of his concerns runs as follows:

> if the providence and world government of God are taken seriously, these are represented as though Christianity were, so to speak, ready made in the mind of God; then, when thrust into the world it appears to be contingent. But the rationality and thereby the necessity of this decree of God's has now to be considered and this may be called a theodicy, a justification of God, i.e., a vindication of our Idea. It is a demonstration that ... things have happened rationally in the world.
>
> (VGP 2: 497–8; LHP 3: 7–8)

Hegel's complaint is, it appears, that, given the traditional conception of the autonomous creator, even so crucial a world historical event as the arrival of Christianity appears as something merely contingent, the product, as it were, of divine caprice. To see things in that way does not, however, serve the purpose of a theodicy; that is, of rational justification. What Hegel has in mind here may be brought out more clearly by considering his view of the best-known theory of his predecessors, that of Leibniz.

Where Leibniz founders is on the issue that is central for theodicy, and the chief source of the need for it, the problem of evil. All he can offer, according to Hegel, is an optimism based on the 'wearisome thought' that God, out of infinitely many possible worlds, has chosen the best possible. This can yield, however, no 'comprehension'. It serves in effect merely to reiterate the truth that 'the world is good, but there is also evil in it', while depicting this as the outcome of 'pure choice, arbitrariness' on God's part. If one says that the evil in the world is, after all, only 'the means to a good end', Hegel's response, on the assumption that the matter is at God's discretion, is to ask why he does not employ other means (VGP 3: 248; LHP 3: 340–1). It is not possible, or necessary, to do full justice here to the merits of this criticism of Leibnizian theodicy, still less to what Leibniz might have to say in reply. What should be said, however, is that Hegel is raising familiar objections that seem liable to be incurred by any theistic approach to the problem. In resting so much on the will of a personal being, such an approach will at least be open to the suspicion of placing the contingent and arbitrary at the heart of its picture. This in turn must work against the aim of providing us with reasons for being reconciled to the way of the world. A 'true theodicy' which could exhibit that way as necessary in virtue of being rational would not be vulnerable to these charges. For a programmatic reminder of what Hegel offers by way of such a theodicy, one should turn to the *Introduction*.

> This reconciliation can be reached only through a knowledge of the affirmative, in which every negative disappears as something subordinate and transcended – through the consciousness of, on the one hand, what is in truth the ultimate purpose of the world, and, on the other, of the fact that this has been realised and that evil cannot in the end maintain itself in equality beside it.
>
> (H, 48: 43; M, 28: 15–16, 18, 18)

This statement may suffice all the more for immediate purposes since the present inquiry as a whole is, from one point of view, an attempt to show how Hegel carries through the programme it announces. It should, however, be added at once that his manner of doing so has some rather obvious advantages over that of traditional theism. What he offers is a pantheist theodicy that seeks to justify the ways of the universe as a whole to the thinking and suffering part of it. In not resting everything on personal will this greatly reduces the scope of the factors of arbitrariness and contingency which most trouble Hegel himself. In his scheme the rational and necessary are expressions of the ontological ground of the universe. They cannot be suspected of being the products of a strictly irrational and contingent, because unconditioned, choice which are injected into history from without. A second, and still more obvious, advantage is that a pantheist theodicy must avoid altogether the problem of evil in the grievous form in which it confronts theism. In this form the challenge is to explain how, in the face of the manifold evil in the world, God can be conceived of as being both all-powerful and perfectly good. Since ancient times this has presented itself as a dilemma whose resolution must require that one or other requirement be relaxed. Any such relaxation will, however, introduce finitude into the heart of one's conception of the deity. To relinquish the notion of a personal God is at least to escape this onerous inheritance, though, of course, it is not to leave all the difficulties of theodicy behind. The discussion should turn to those that remain.

Divine comedy

The burden of the case against Hegel has been maintained, with a basic consistency amid variations of detail, by many critics. It may be, and frequently is, developed in language borrowed from the accused himself. In an early essay Hegel had distinguished between tragedy and comedy in terms of their treatment of opposition, conflict and fate. The version of comedy that matters for present purposes is what he calls 'the old or divine comedy'. It seems reasonable to suppose that it is the world view of Christian theism he has in mind, the view which was given one kind of classic expression in Dante's poem. Hegel's complaint is that divine comedy presents only 'shadows of clashes' or 'mock battles with a fabricated fate and fictitious enemies'. Thus, it is

> without fate and without a genuine struggle, because absolute confidence and assurance of the reality of the absolute exist in it without opposition, and whatever opposition brings movement into this perfect security and calm is merely opposition without seriousness or inner truth.

> (JS: 496; NL: 105–6)

In this comedy 'the conflicts and the finite are shadows without substance'. Tragedy, it is implied, is the superior form since it sets forth the 'true and absolute relation' of the participants in which 'each has a living bearing on the other, and each is the other's serious fate' (JS: 499; NL: 108). The case against Hegel, it may now be said, is that in the end his own philosophy of history is a divine comedy without seriousness or inner truth. It, too, contains only mock battles between fictitious enemies in which conflict never confronts the participants as fate but rather as an appearance to be dissolved in the inevitable triumph of the absolute. The tragic element in history gives way to the teleological comedy of the ultimate purpose of the world and the vindication of the Idea (White 1973: 117–31). This is a serious charge, all the more so since it appeals to standards so plainly set out and endorsed by Hegel himself.

If one looks to the text of the *Introduction* for guidance, it offers at first sight little warrant for holding that Hegel seeks to downplay or brush aside the negative aspects of world history. On the contrary, the topic calls forth from him resources of eloquence and sensibility that seem the equal of any that have been devoted to it, and it is hard not to suppose that deeply held personal convictions and responses are at work in the passages in question. Some illustrations may serve to convey a sense of what is involved:

> The negative side of these thoughts of change moves us to sadness. What oppresses us is this, that the richest forms, the most beautiful life, perish in history, that we wander among the ruins of excellence.
>
> (H, 34–5: 32)

> It is a matter of the category of the negative ... and we cannot fail to see how in world history the noblest and most beautiful are sacrificed to it.
>
> (H, 48: 43)

> When we contemplate this display of passions and the conse-quences of their violence, of the lack of understanding which is associated not only with them but also, and especially, with good intentions and righteous aims; when we see arising from them evil, wickedness, the downfall of the most flourishing kingdoms the human spirit has produced; and when we observe with deepest sympathy the untold miseries of individuals, we can only be filled with sorrow over this transience. And since this destruction is not merely the work of nature but of human will, we might well end with moral sorrow, with a revolt of the good spirit, if such a thing is in us, over such a spectacle ... we regard history as the slaughter-bench on which the happiness of peoples, the wisdom of states and the virtue of individuals were sacrificed ...
>
> (H, 79–80: 68–9; M, 34–5: 20–1, 26–7, 23–4)

These passages are fully in keeping with, and bear out, Hegel's general sense that history is not 'the soil of happiness' and that periods of happiness are 'blank pages' in it (H, 92: 78–9; M, 42: 26–7, 33, 29). Nevertheless, it is striking how each of them is immediately followed, or preceded, by a demand for a specific justification of such manifestations of the negative in history as suffering and destruction. More generally, it is in world history, we are told, that 'the entire mass of concrete evil is laid out before our eyes', and nowhere else is there a greater need for 'reconciling knowledge' (H, 48: 42–3; cf. M, 28: 15, 18, 18). The justification, as one would expect, will have to make the role of evil comprehensible 'in the light of the absolute power of reason' (H, 48: 43). Moreover, it must, again unsurprisingly, take a teleological form in that it will be an answer to the question of 'what is the ultimate purpose for which all these monstrous sacrifices were made' (H, 80: 69; M, 35: 21, 27, 24). It would certainly be disappointing to find that the justification when it comes serves to deny the reality or seriousness of the factors that gave rise to the need for it in the first place. Indeed, such a finding might suggest a kind of incoherence in the intellectual structure of the *Introduction* as a whole. These matters will have to be examined further.

Death of God

It will be helpful to begin by looking more closely at the claim that Christianity conceives of history in terms of a 'divine comedy'. For the claim sometimes takes a superficial form which misses the true profundity of the Christian response to the problem of evil and suffering, a profundity to which Hegel is fully alive. It lies in the way in which the passion and death of Jesus Christ place the problem at the centre of our understanding of God. In grasping this achievement, Hegel takes it to the furthest limit of which it is capable within a Christian framework and even beyond that limit. He does so by means of a theme which haunts his thinking in the area now in question almost from the beginning, the theme of 'the death of God'. In an early essay the feeling that 'God himself is dead' is taken as presenting a challenge to philosophy, that of rendering the 'absolute passion' as speculative truth: 'Good Friday must be re-established in the whole truth and harshness of its God-forsakenness' (JS: 432; FK: 190–1). The theme is constantly present in the philosophy of religion lectures delivered many years later in Berlin. There Hegel insists that the death of Christ must not be represented 'merely as the death of this empirically existing individual'. What it means is rather 'that *God* has died, that *God himself is dead*', a negation that is 'a moment of the divine nature' (CR: 219). In a later lecture course he takes a reference to the death of God in a seventeenth-century Lutheran hymn as 'expressing an awareness that the human, the finite, the fragile, the weak, the negative are themselves a moment of the divine, that they are within God himself'. Thus, there is within Christian religious history 'the very presentation of the process of what humanity, what spirit is – implicitly both God and dead' (CR: 326, 125). Elsewhere the 'determination' which comes into play with the death of Christ that '*God has died, God is dead*' is said to be 'the most frightful of all thoughts, that everything eternal and true is *not*, that negation itself is found in God'. Hegel does, admittedly, go on to refer to the 'reversal' that is brought about by the Resurrection, but the idea is not developed here any more than it is elsewhere in his work (CR: 323–4). It invocation is in any case plainly not intended to undermine the philosophical significance of the 'absolute passion' by revealing as fundamentally not serious, or superseded, the reality of God's death in Christ.

That this is so is evident from Hegel's language, perhaps most of all from the insistence with which he affirms that death, the ultimate negation, pertains to the divine nature itself. It is the affirmation that leaves him outside any kind of Christian orthodoxy, for that has always sought to confine the meaning of mortality to the human nature of Christ. Seen in another way, however, Hegel is merely pushing to extremes a deep element of the Christian view. This is the conception of a God whose response to human suffering is to take it upon himself in a peculiarly gross form. Thus Christ dies, as Hegel says, 'the aggravated death of the evildoer: not merely a natural death, but rather a death of shame and humiliation on the cross' (CR: 323n). The whole conception should, perhaps, be seen not so much as an attempt at a formal solution of the problem of evil but rather as a magisterial sidestepping of it, one that, nevertheless, acknowledges its infinite weight and intractability. This is achieved, however, only at the cost of steering towards one horn of the dilemma referred to earlier. It is, as has frequently been observed, to opt to preserve the divine love and compassion even at some cost to the divine majesty and power. Whether this can ultimately be satisfactory within a theistic framework is a question that need not be pursued here. What has to be noted is the way in which Hegel has seized the essence of the Christian doctrine and turned it in a direction Christianity can scarcely countenance. In general terms his purpose in doing so is clear. It is to insist on the reality of evil, the overwhelming power of the negative, at the very heart of spirit. Hegel's treatment of the death of God theme carries another message which links with, and reinforces, central concerns of the present inquiry in a way which deserves to be remarked.

The account in the *Phenomenology* declares that the death of the 'mediator'; that is, of Jesus Christ, is the death not only of 'his *natural aspect* or of his particular being-for-self', but also of 'the *abstraction of the divine essence*'. Hegel goes on to associate this death of an abstraction with 'the painful feeling of the unhappy consciousness that *God himself is dead*' (PG: 571–2; PS: 476). The unhappy consciousness of the *Phenomenology* is an internally divided consciousness that takes itself to be variable and inessential while positing all that is unchanging and essential as radically other than itself, projecting it on to a being who dwells 'beyond'. This consciousness is unhappy because it is a living contradiction, conceiving of the eternal as unattainable while yet being filled with an 'infinite *yearning*' for unity with it (PG: 163, 169; PS: 126, 131). A conception of the divine as transcendent is clearly presupposed here, and no other presupposition will generate the same unhappiness. It is clear also that, for Hegel, such a conception always carries with it the potential for consciousness to become unhappy, even if this is, as the *Phenomenology* assumes, fully realised only in the Christian Middle Ages. Moreover, the *Phenomenology* leaves no room for doubt as to how the contradiction is to be overcome. It is through the development of God's 'individual self-consciousness', as embodied in Christ, into 'the universal, or the religious community'. Death, and specifically the death of the 'divine human being', is thereby transfigured from its immediate meaning, 'the non-existence of *this individual*', into 'the *universality* of the spirit who lives in his community, and every day dies and rises again in it' (PG: 570–1; PS: 475). The overcoming of the contradiction involves a shift from an abstract to a concrete conception of God. Thus, the death of God as an abstraction, that death of transcendence which, for Hegel, is the true message of Christianity, prepares the ground for an understanding of the immanent spirit who lives in and through the cycle of birth and death in the human community. This is the God who, in the words of the *Introduction*, 'is the spirit in his community' and who 'lives and is real in it' (H, 262: 213). The unity of Hegel's immanent ontological vision, and its ability to assimilate an unlimited wealth of material, seem to be vindicated once again here.

Consolations of immortality

The main use Hegel makes of the death of God motif is to establish the reality of radical evil within a nominally Christian framework. The motif itself can scarcely have independent significance within a pantheist one, and he does not try to give it any. He does, however, take a further, noteworthy step away from any comic vision of the world. Perhaps one should speak rather of a large absence in his thought as contrasted with orthodox Christianity. This is the absence, in any responsible, working role, of a conception of personal immortality. Hegel pays what is at best only lip-service to the notion, and that on rare occasions. The rest, in all his voluminous discussions of human destiny and divine providence, is silence, a silence that discomfits, sometimes even to mildly comic effect, those of his admirers who are most zealous on the matter (McTaggart 1918: 5–7). The fact that the doctrine of immortality has no particular significance or interest for him marks his thought off sharply from traditional Christian forms of theodicy. In them the doctrine paves the way for acceptance of this vale of tears through the prospect of rewards for the righteous and punishment for the evildoer in another world. Many generations of ordinary believers have steered their lives by this hope and expectation. Even Hegel's great predecessor, Kant, though no ordinary believer, is led by analogous considerations to regard the immortality of the soul as a demand of practical reason, even if it cannot be

203

theoretically demonstrated. For it offers a further opportunity to us to overcome the evil in our nature and move towards the perfection of holiness (Kant 1993: 128–30). All of this is quite antipathetic to Hegel. There is no suggestion in his work that the task of theodicy, or any other philosophical task for that matter, should make use of a notion of personal immortality, and no redemption of the evil and suffering of the world is to be looked for in that direction. In this respect his outlook is significantly bleaker than that which informs the standard versions of divine comedy.

Hegel offers a convenient way of pointing out the contrast. Thus, he is willing to concede that Christianity should be regarded as 'the religion of consolation and indeed of absolute consolation'. This has, admittedly, to be understood in a Hegelian sense. What the main instrument of consolation, the doctrine that 'God wills that all human beings should be saved', expresses is that 'subjectivity has an infinite value' in that here 'God himself is known as absolute subjectivity' (EPW 1: 291; EL: 223). The promise of eternal life has surely never been given a more deflating gloss. Nevertheless, it remains the case that even the 'consummate' religion may be said to function in a consolatory mode. The position of philosophy is quite different, as the *Introduction* makes clear:

> Philosophy ... is not consolation; it is more; it reconciles, and transfigures reality, which appears to be unjust, into the rational, shows it as something which is founded in the Idea itself and with which reason is to be satisfied.
>
> (H, 78: 67)

What the philosophy of history in its guise as theodicy may be expected to provide is reconciliation, not consolation. Moreover, its reconciling power exists just in virtue of its cognitive achievement, its ability to show that reality is inherently rational. All affective states stand in a merely contingent relation to this insight. They relate just as contingently to it as they do to the historical spectacle of evil and suffering that gave rise for the demand for theodicy in the first place. Thus, Hegel, as an acute moral psychologist, is all too well aware of the actual variety of responses to this spectacle. It may also, he thinks, occasion a 'lugubrious satisfaction', or a retreat into 'the selfishness which stands on the quiet shore and from there enjoys in safety the distant display of confusion and wreckage' (H, 80–1: 69; M, 35–6: 21, 27, 24). Such attitudes may indeed be thought to be a mockery of human suffering, but they are not shared by Hegel, and play no part in motivating his philosophy of history.

In a similar vein one should note that whatever psychological benefits that philosophy may confer arise adventitiously, not in virtue of the specific content of its message. Of course, it may be said that they arise, nevertheless, just in virtue of there being a message. The suggestion would be that the decipherment of meaning, the reduction of experience to order, is in itself therapeutic, even at the extreme where what the meaning and order convey is that things are as bad as they could be and there is no prospect of relief. This tells one nothing in particular about Hegel, however, and induces no relative softening of his outlook. If correct it would apply even to the fully tragic vision of the ancient world within which not only human beings but also the gods themselves are subject to the necessity of blind and inscrutable fate. Hegel admires the 'serene submission' of the ancients in this situation, but theirs is an attitude that is appropriate only for a world in which subjectivity had not yet attained its 'infinite value (EL: 223). It is a world to which human beings as essentially centres of subjectivity can never be fully reconciled as their world in which estrangement is overcome and they are truly at home in the world. Even with this limiting case in mind, it has to be said that we have by no means plumbed as yet the depths of the desolation which Hegel's own view encompasses.

To get any further one has to inquire more closely what the scope of his theodicy is, what precisely is subject to its reconciling power. Here a distinction that has recurred throughout the discussion must be invoked, that between the spheres of contingency and of necessity. Reconciliation, as Hegel conceives it, is precisely reconciliation to necessity, and is possible only within that sphere, the sphere in which reason exercises direct sway. He has a keen sense of the lines of demarcation:

> if we say that universal reason is fulfilled, this has of course nothing to do with what is empirically singular; that can fare better

or worse, for here contingency and particularity receive from the concept the power to exercise their monstrous right. In regard to particular things we may well represent to ourselves that much in the world is unjust ... But we are not concerned here with what is empirically particular; that is given over to contingency which does not concern us.

(H, 76: 66; M, 52–3: 35–6, 47, 38)

The authority of the contingent is, as the passage makes clear, a delegated one whose existence and scope are determined by the concept. Thus, it is a requirement of reason that there be a domain of contingency with determinate limits, and, one might say, contingency is, in that sense, necessary. Whatever falls within its domain is subject to the power of what may equally be called chance or 'external necessity'; that is, of merely causal forces (H, 29: 28). The lives and fortunes of ordinary individuals belong squarely within this category and outside the range of the rational and necessary. Hence it is that 'however single individuals may be injured, reason cannot stand still', and so, 'particular ends lose themselves in the universal' (H, 48–9: 43).

The attitude expressed here is, it may be worth noting, one that Hegel adopts consistently in his own life. When he writes a letter of sympathy to a friend on the death of a son, he explicitly says that he is not concerned to bring 'words of consolation', and instead urges his correspondent so to respond that 'the power of spirit to endure grief even such as this can give proof of itself' (HL: 271–2). It is not just advice he prescribed to others, for he behaved in accordance with it on the death of his own daughter (HL: 270–1, 400). The underlying stance is close to that of stoicism, a position temperamentally congenial to him. It seeks to endure what cannot be compensated for, as Hegel and his wife could not be for the loss of their child. Neither, according to his view of things, can the countless injustices and evils borne by individuals in history be compensated for or redeemed by any possible theodicy the philosophy of history has to offer.

Some conclusions on the question of comedy versus tragedy may now be drawn. It is clear that Hegel acknowledges in vivid, wholehearted terms, without attempting to mitigate or evade, the reality of evil and suffering in history. The function of theodicy is not, for him, to provide consolation in the face of it, but rather a reconciling knowledge. This knowledge locates the great events in which he is chiefly interested as necessary links in a chain that leads towards the goals of reason. Thus, it will encompass such calamities as the perishing of the richest and most beautiful forms of life, the destruction of the happiness of peoples and the wisdom of states, and the downfall of great civilisations. Where the 'untold miseries' of individuals are concerned we are, however, reduced for the most part to feelings of 'deepest sympathy'. Their fortunes are subject to the monstrous right of contingency and so fall within a class whose individual members our knowledge is helpless to redeem. This is not in any obvious way a comic vision. It is all the less so since it involves no suggestion of an afterlife in which all is made well, the element which does most to give Christianity its air of divine comedy. Neither is it tragic in the full, unreconciling and unreconcilable sense of the ancient world, that of seeing the necessity of human life as the workings of blind, and purely objective, destiny. Historical necessity is, for Hegel, the necessity of a rational and intelligible subjectivity to which we belong and in which we participate, at varying levels of consciousness, as vehicles of spirit. It should be added that what he offers will surely be quite austere and sombre enough for most people. Those whose sense of tragedy is still unsatisfied are, of course, free to devise for themselves still bleaker ways of conceiving the slaughterbench of history.

The empirical record

An exceedingly large and complex issue has yet to be considered, in however incomplete a fashion, before any verdict on Hegel's theodicy can be reached. It is the issue of how his philosophical understanding appears in the light of the overall empirical record, of our general sense of what has actually happened in history. The discussion has already noted his insistence that history is an empirical inquiry, his advocacy of the empirical study of particular phenomena and his concern to maintain a theoretical grip on the major events of his own time. The largest claim he makes for the empirical approach should be added to fill out this background. It arises in connection with the foundational thesis of his philosophy of history. The proof of the proposition that world history is governed by 'the divine, absolute reason' is declared to be 'the study of world history itself' as 'the image and enactment of reason'. It is true that Hegel goes on to say that the 'real proof' lies in 'the knowledge of reason itself' which, presumably, has to be provided by philosophy. World history is, it appears, merely the 'manifestation' of this reason, one of the 'particular forms in which it reveals itself' (H, 29–30: 28). The claim that empirical study can yield what is in any sense a proof of the central doctrine of the presence of reason in history is, nevertheless, highly significant. This significance is fully in line with the slightly later acknowledgement of the correctness of holding that 'the purpose of the world should be detectable by observation'. Admittedly, the point is immediately qualified in typical style by adding that 'to know the universal and the rational, one must be endowed with reason' (H, 31: 29–30). The effect is still to make clear that the empirical approach to history can serve not only as attesting to, and bearing out, the central doctrine but also as contributing to its derivation in the first place. It has, to use the terminology of later philosophy of science, a role not only in the context of validation but also in that of discovery. Although this cannot, for Hegel, be other than subordinate in either context to that of philosophical knowledge, it is, nevertheless, substantial and assured.

The order of priority of the philosophical and empirical approaches to history is clear from the *Introduction*, as is the character of their relationship in general. Hegel does not, it must be admitted, provide much in the way of elaboration of the matter. He may have felt the need to do so all the less since he is fully convinced that the two approaches converge on precisely the same target. That is to say, he is convinced that the main speculative theses about reason and history are wholly in accord with, and supported by, the empirical record. This is the source of the confidence with which he embarks on the outline of world history that forms the bulk of what was offered to the students on his philosophy of history course. Its very existence shows the strength of his determination to establish empirical referents and controls for his philosophy of history. This commitment has to be respected by a commentator on that philosophy, and indeed by anyone concerned with its enduring relevance. More specifically for present purposes, one should note that if it seems seriously at odds with the ways of God as they reveal themselves to observation of the world, it must lack authority as theodicy. It is not possible here to vindicate in detail its claims in this respect, but something may be said in their favour, enough to suggest that the project of such a vindication is entirely feasible and offers a worthwhile prospect of success.

World history in the twentieth century

To begin with, it should be remarked that Hegel's conception of the general course of world history is not obviously mistaken or untenable on empirical grounds. Few who accept such terms of debate will be prepared to maintain that history exhibits an overall regress in the consciousness and realisation of freedom. Neither are many likely to deny that the modern world, by contrast with all that went before, represents some actual progress in these respects. The great events Hegel appeals to in fleshing out his scheme may be more contentious. Nevertheless, such candidates as the first stirrings of subjective freedom in Ancient Greece, the emergence of Christianity, the Protestant Reformation, the Enlightenment and the French Revolution have a certain plausibility and underlying rationale. It may be most useful at present, however, to show that the story may be continued well after Hegel's death. At any rate the event of the second half of the twentieth century with the best claim to world historical significance, the collapse of Communism, seems to fit readily enough within it.

That event was, of course, determined by a multitude of factors. A place may surely be found within a complete explanation, however, for the individual's consciousness of herself as an 'infinite, free being', giving rise to the demand that 'external existence should correspond to this consciousness'. The crowds calling for 'freedom' in the streets of Prague and Leipzig in 1989 seem to illustrate, indeed, one might say, to objectify, the workings of this process all too clearly. It is not at all fanciful to see them in a Hegelian perspective as having grasped the central truth of the modern world, that freedom belongs to their nature as human beings, and as having grasped also the contradiction between that nature and their actual conditions of life. The revolutions they participated in then appear as the outcome of a struggle to resolve this basic contradiction. It is also, of course, true that the development of post-Communist societies has not been one of smooth progress in the realisation of freedom. There is, however, nothing in Hegel's conception to suggest that such a progress is at all likely. These societies may be seen in very general terms as taking the indispensable step, however halting and difficult, of embarking, or re-embarking, on the dialectic of civil society which both lies at the core of his thinking about the modern world and forms its unsurpassable horizon. That it should turn out to be a path of suffering and despair is fully consistent with the nature of historical development as he conceives it.

Various other twentieth-century instances of the apparent workings of a contradiction between the consciousness of freedom and the extent of its realisation might be cited. An event which, in view of its world historical import, one can scarcely omit to mention is the ending of apartheid. That system seemed to embody the denial of human dignity and the universality of spirit in a peculiarly gross form. Its downfall may surely be thought to have implications for the viability in the modern world of any such institutional denial. To suggest that it fits easily within, and helps to give substance to, a Hegelian perspective on history is, of course, quite compatible with acknowledging that the progress of spirit is likely to be strewn with conflict and reverses in the new South Africa. The case of apartheid points beyond itself in another way. The institutionalised racism it embodies can hardly fail to raise the spectre of the event of the twentieth century that has seemed to many the most difficult to reconcile with the workings of a providence in history, whether in the Hegelian or any other sense. This is the attempted genocide of Jews and Romany people under the Third Reich. That some of those who have personally experienced, or have laid themselves open intellectually and imaginatively to, the reality of this event should take it as eliminating the very possibility of such providential meaning is wholly understandable, and deserving only of the utmost respect. To seek to persuade them otherwise would be unwarranted, even indecent. The question will, nevertheless, have to be taken a little further, in view of the obvious seriousness of its challenge to Hegel's scheme. There is also the prospect of the light on that scheme which attempting to meet it may shed. Nothing like justice can be done to the complexity of the issues here, but some suggestions may, nevertheless, be made on the assumption that trying to continue a discourse of reason is itself something owed to the mass victims of irrational violence.

It should focus matters if one performs the thought experiment of asking how Hegel might himself respond were he, somehow, to be confronted with the realities that concern us now. In the first place he might well wish simply to point out that the attempted genocide did not, for all its horrors, succeed in its own terms, that, in a language to which he is partial, the gates of hell did not ultimately prevail even in this case. At another level he might wish to resist the assumption that the reality of suffering and death on whatever scale could strike at the heart of his conception of history. He acknowledged that reality himself, as we have seen, as fully and frankly as could be expected of anyone in his historical situation. The further revelation in a later century of what human beings are capable of could serve only to darken and deepen, not to overthrow, his perspective. It has to be admitted, however distasteful it may be to do so, that it will not make a fundamental difference in this respect if the slaughterbench is industrialised so that the corpses pile up in mountains, or are made to vanish into the air. Indeed it may be that the greatest threat posed by the Third Reich to Hegel's philosophy of history does not lie in the merciless violence it unleashed on those perceived to be outsiders and enemies. It lies rather in the prospect of the thousand years of servitude that was held out for the German *Volk* itself. That this should be so may testify to a false set of priorities on Hegel's part, but it seems, nevertheless, inescapably grounded in the logic of his thought.

It should once more be recalled that the threat was not in fact realised and that the Nazi regime vanished from history in a mere dozen years. What it represented may, nevertheless, serve to focus critical reflection on the status of Hegel's conception of history, and, specifically, on the question of its empirical vulnerability. This is not an area in which one can sensibly aim at complete certainty and precision. Its seems undeniable, however, that it would be a most serious matter for Hegel if such a regime were to succeed in establishing itself indefinitely in the country that gave birth to the Reformation, experienced the Enlightenment and was exposed to the full impact of modernity, as well as being, of course, the cradle of his own thought. This will be clearer if one picks out just the issues of most obvious and central concern to him. It was a regime that sought explicitly to devalue and deny the claims of individual freedom. Moreover, it replaced the constitutional state and its objective structure of rights with the *Führerprinzip*, the reliance on the subjective will of one individual, as the basis of law. In these respects it seems to challenge directly the confidence Hegel shows when, speaking with somewhat indefinite reference but plainly encompassing his own society, he declares:

> We know our essential being only in that personal freedom is its basic condition. Were the mere arbitrary will of the prince to be the law and were he to wish to introduce slavery we would be aware that this could not be. Everyone knows he cannot be a slave.
>
> (VGP 1: 121; LHP 1: 99–100)

To add to the tension here, one may suppose, contrary to fact, that the Third Reich had managed to impose itself as a stable and enduring entity without either the reality of serious internal dissent or the need to smother such dissent by perpetual recourse to foreign adventures and war. That achievement would seem to presuppose a general acceptance of its legitimacy on the part of the 'slaves'. This in turn would imply that among them the knowledge that freedom is our essential nature was being, or had been, lost. The general implication to be drawn is that over a significant portion of the modern world the historical dialectic was going into reverse, running backwards from freedom to unfreedom. Such a development would seem to create the weightiest of problems for Hegel's thought, problems that must shake its foundations.

It seems possible to envisage that the problems might take another form, economic rather than political. The supposition would be that all of the economically most advanced countries of the modern world were moving from systems of production based on formally free labour to ones based on formally 'unfree' labour. Civil society was, one would have to say, transposing to a slave economy. Moreover, it would have to be assumed, for the case to be truly significant, that this was not explicable as a response to external shocks such as a catastrophic decline in population caused by natural events. It demanded rather to be understood as the workings of the immanent movement of civil society, transforming itself by its own dialectic into its opposite. At some point in the process, perhaps after several generations, even the most loyal Hegelians would surely be justified in concluding that Hegel's conception of the historical dialectic was no longer tenable. It would be rational for them, one might say, to give up the central thesis of his philosophy of history that 'world history has been rational in its course'. This is, however, as the first of our key propositions showed, itself derived from the central ontological doctrine that 'reason rules the world'. Hence, by an elementary rule of inference, the founding premise itself will have to be rejected and the entire fabric of the system will be seen to be in the process of unravelling.

That this situation should be conceivable is perhaps the best indication of the crucial role of the empirical for Hegel. Seen in one way it is just the obverse of the fact, emphasised throughout the present discussion, that the philosophy of history is grounded in the ontology. The downfall of the one must then inevitably bring down the other. At another level the vulnerability of the philosophy of history to being empirically confounded is the price to be paid for its explanatory potential, and if it could wholly disengage itself from what happens in the world it would have none. This vulnerability must therefore be maintained by anyone who holds that Hegel's philosophy of history can yield a framework within which contemporary events may be situated and understood. It is also now clear why Hegel was personally so insistent on monitoring and assimilating the great events of his own time. He may at times seem over-anxious, even morbidly sensitive, in his dealings with them. In itself, however, the project merely testifies to his grasp of the structural logic of his own thought.

Responsibilities

A recognition of the empirical dimension of Hegel's thought enables one to pose more concretely the final questions to be asked about it. These are questions concerning what it might mean to see everyday

THE WAYS OF GOD

experience in a Hegelian perspective and of the practical demands that doing so might impose. They may arise the more vividly if one bears in mind that Hegel's impact on at least some readers has not been simply that of an academic philosopher in the ordinary sense. Thus, for his earliest followers becoming a Hegelian was an experience to be captured only in the religious language of conversion and salvation. They have left eloquent testimony to the 'intoxicating exhilaration of perceiving and experiencing the world as a vessel of absolute spirit' (Toews 1980: 90). It seems reasonable to suppose that there are genuine and important questions to be pursued here. Yet they are undoubtedly also questions of great complexity, and only the aspects most relevant to our discussion can be considered. That discussion has already thrown up much that has a direct bearing on present concerns, and it provides in any case a general background for them. Hence, it may suffice to add to all that has gone before some remarkable passages from the *Encyclopaedia*:

> The accomplishing of the infinite purpose consists ... only in sublating the illusion that it has not yet been accomplished. The good, the absolute good, fulfils itself eternally in the world, and the result is that it is already fulfilled in and for itself.
>
> (EPW 1: 367; EL: 286)

> the world is itself the Idea. Unsatisfied striving vanishing when we know (*erkennen*) that the final purpose of the world is just as much accomplished as it is eternally accomplishing itself ... The religious consciousness ... regards the world as governed by divine providence and hence as corresponding to what it *ought* to be. This agreement between is and ought is not rigid and unmoving, however, since the final purpose of the world, the good, only *is*, because it constantly brings itself about.
>
> (EPW 1: 387; EL: 302; cf. H, 48: 43; M, 28: 15–16, 18, 18)

These passages provide an opportunity to draw closer together, in a way that bears on everyday experience and activity, the large themes of theodicy and of the actuality of the rational. For that limited purpose their core meaning seems easy enough to state. What they do,

214

one may initially suggest, is to bring out a distinctive feature of Hegelian theodicy, of the workings of its reconciling power. They tell us that the good is already fulfilled just in virtue of the fact that it is in the process of being fulfilled. Because all shall be well; that is to say, the 'all' that is presupposed, or implied, by the achievement of freedom, all is already well here and now. The air of paradox may perhaps be lessened by putting the matter, as the second passage encourages one to do, in terms of 'is' and 'ought'. Things in general, one might say, are as they ought to be because they are on the way to being what they ought to be. Their present state is wholly appropriate to their place in the overall pattern. Thus, it is not the case that they should be any different from what they are, moments in transition to realising the 'infinite purpose'. Hence it is that the 'insight to which philosophy should lead', according to the *Introduction*, is that 'the actual world is as it ought to be, that the truly good, the universal divine reason is also the power to fulfil itself' (M, 53: 36, 47, 39; cf. H, 77: 66). All of this, viewed in one aspect, simply exemplifies Hegel's tendency, of which other instances have already been cited, to project a result back on the process of its achievement. A close parallel with present concerns may be found in the assurance in the *Phenomenology* that 'the way to science is itself already *science*' (PG: 80; PS: 56). Hegel's characteristic choice of language suggests that closer still is the idea, expressed by various religious thinkers with variations of detail, that sincerely to seek God is already to have found him. At this point it may, however, be most rewarding to restate the issues in terms of the relationship of the actual and the rational.

The obvious way to do so is to take the results of the earlier discussion of those notions and combine it with the principle of reading process as product and becoming as being which has now emerged. This would be to conclude that because the rational is in process of becoming actual it is actual already. It is a conclusion that would, in effect, agreeably reinstate the best-known formula of the entire field, the complete mutual equivalence of actual and rational proclaimed in the Preface to the *Philosophy of Right*. The formula has, admittedly, now been arrived at with some interpretative effort involving a special principle of reading. Indeed, it would not be too much to say that part of it, the part that affirms the actuality of the rational, has had to be given an esoteric meaning. This is, in general, an unnecessary and unwise proceeding where Hegel is concerned, though in view of the peculiar circumstances of the Preface referred to earlier it is there if anywhere that it might be warranted. A further point to note is that we have a new perspective on what was earlier said to be the sound Hegelian doctrine that all that is becomes rational. Here one has to recall the conceptual bond expressed in the proposition that actuality is by its very nature rational existence. To this should be added the general rule that licenses the reading of 'becoming x' as 'being x'. The result that may now be declared is that all that is, whether actual or merely existent, is rational. To take this seriously is surely to bring a transforming vision to everyday life, a vision of the infinite purpose as already fulfilled within, and by means of, its finite appearances. It is hardly surprising that Hegel's first followers should have experienced his ideas as overwhelmingly revelatory and liberating. There seems no reason in principle why their impact should be any less on whoever becomes convinced of their truth today.

The *Encyclopaedia* passages that were quoted a little earlier had referred to the good or the final purpose as 'eternally' fulfilling itself. In interpreting that reference it is essential to bear in mind that, as has already been shown, eternity is, for Hegel, not a matter of temporal duration but rather of the 'absolute present, the now'. To live in this present is, one might suggest, the experiential core of the only meaning the notion of eternal life could have for him. What that might involve cannot be explicated here in all its richness and ramifications. There is, nevertheless, an obvious way in which the notion bears on our concerns. To come to think of eternity as the now is surely to be brought insistently to terms with the immediacy of one's own life and its circumstances, to find them placed in an intense and demanding light. It is difficult not to suppose that such a vision must bring with it responsibilities, and thereby take on a practical dimension. The *Encyclopaedia* passages may seem to come as close as Hegel ever does to endorsing pure quietism and resignation in the face of the inevitable. This would, however, be a superficial lesson to draw. It is, after all, only 'unsatisfied' striving, not striving as such, that vanishes with our illusions about the world and the Idea. Moreover, the emphasis on movement and change is as sharp as it is elsewhere in

Hegel. Thus, the agreement of 'is' and 'ought' is not 'rigid and unmoving', but obtains just in virtue of being embodied in a dynamic process, that through which the final purpose of the world 'constantly brings itself about'. The entire weight of the argument of this study may now be enlisted behind the conclusion that responsibility for the process cannot belong to any superhuman subject. There is, for Hegel, no such subject to undertake it. The final purpose can accomplish itself only in and through human consciousness and action, and has no other medium of existence. With that in mind, the lesson of the *Encyclopaedia* passages may equally well be drawn in terms which are overtly closer to the distinctive concerns of our inquiry, and have already been cited in part: 'Reconciliation ... is freedom and is not something quiescent; rather it is activity, the movement which makes the estrangement disappear' (CR: 172).

This discussion had earlier raised, out of the seemingly incompatible claims of reason and reality, the spectre of a large-scale dilemma, or structural fault, in Hegel's thought. It was then suggested that even the most troubling problems that thereby arise may still be contained within, and do not threaten, its basic framework. A further point may now be made in mitigation of them. It consists in the fact that Hegelian reconciliation, the reconciliation of spirit and the existing world, is not in any case to be thought of as a condition of quiet repose but as itself activity and movement. Hence it is that the doctrine of the actual and the rational 'articulates a task for each individual rather than a legitimisation for the inactivity of us all' (Gadamer 1981: 36). To be truly at home in the world, to possess the freedom that lies in the disappearance of estrangement, is, it now appears, to be engaged in trying to change it. Individuals in history who seek to carry out the task articulated for them have no infallible guides to action to rely on, and no assurance of success, or even manifest progress, in their lifetimes. Yet the darkness in which they act is, in Hegel's conception, by no means total. Historical actors in the modern world can, as we have seen, know what the final purpose of spiritual freedom is, and know also that to fulfil it is but to realise the birthright of humanity. If this knowledge is combined with whatever empirical grasp of the world is available, they will achieve all that can be expected in their situation. It should be remembered also that each individual is not condemned to act alone, but, with some luck and effort, will find others committed to the same task. There are, after all, traditions of struggling for freedom, collective enterprises and practices, which can make a rational claim on our allegiance. From this standpoint too, the 'I' of spirit turns out to be 'We', and it is 'We' who are responsible for sustaining history in its course and bringing it to an end in freedom.

Notes

1 Introduction

1 This attempt may itself seem question-begging to some readers in that it leaves a significant option out of account, the option of holding that Hegel has no metaphysics to outline. By far the most influential source of such a view in recent years is the work of Klaus Hartmann. There Hegel's philosophy figures as 'categorial theory, i.e., as non-metaphysical philosophy or as a philosophy devoid of existence claims' (Hartmann 1988: 274). Its aim, in Hartmann's view, is not to tell us what there is but to reconstruct the system of categories in terms of which any discourse about what there is, whatever that may be, must be conducted. On the face of things, a commentator on Hegel's philosophy of history can afford to deal briskly with this view. For it is plain that one cannot hope to accommodate, still less make coherent sense of, his dealings with history in the terms it permits, as Hartmann to his credit acknowledges. His simple and bold response is to excise them from the picture, putting them beyond the line which the categorial approach 'bids us draw', and even holding that Hegel 'can be censured' for his metaphysics of history (ibid.: 285–6). It would, however, be misleading to leave an impression that the present inquiry and Hartmann's reading of Hegel are in any way mutually indifferent and irrelevant. This is so for at least two reasons. In the first place the inquiry will serve to show that Hegel routinely and persistently makes 'existence claims', professing to know the world in its deepest reality and truth. Secondly, the inquiry will bear critically on the assumption that

the philosophy of history may simply be removed from the system, leaving the rest to flourish unimpaired. The argument will suggest rather that its integral, strategic role is such that the effect would be to threaten the system itself in its integrity and identity. How convincing these reasons are must, of course, be left to readers to decide. For sympathetic discussions of Hartmann, and indications of the nature and extent of his influence, they should consult the essays in Engelhardt and Pinkard (1994).

2   An introduction to the debate is provided by the various editors' explanations and justifications of their own procedure. Karl Hegel's Preface is translated in Sibree, while Nisbet translates Hoffmeister's Preface and the substance of Lasson's postscript 'On the Composition of the Text'. For readers of German a useful, though inevitably not neutral, overview is offered by Eva Moldenhauer and Karl Markus Michel in the *Anmerkung der Redaktion* of their edition which is based on Karl Hegel. Such readers should also consult the editors' *Vorbemerkung* and *Anhang* for the published lecture notes of the 1822–3 series (VPW). Details of these works are given in the Bibliography.

3   This need has also led to occasional alterations in the standard translations of Hegel's other works and of works by other writers. In all such cases a reference is given to the original passage.

4   For a discussion of the issues, see O'Brien 1975: 16–26 and Pompa 1990: 71–82.

3   Subject and infinite power

1   For a discussion of this issue, see Jaeschke 1990: 18–31, 297–303, 421.

Bibliography

Lectures and *Introduction*

The references to *Lectures* in this book are to Hegel's *Lectures on the Philosophy of History*, and the references to *Introduction* are to the Introduction to that work. The German text of the *Lectures* cited here is volume 12 of the *Theorie Werkausgabe* edition of Hegel's works, edited by Eva Moldenhauer and Karl Markus Michel. This text is based on Karl Hegel's edition, the edition also used by J. Sibree in the only complete English translation. The *Lectures* is cited as 'M', followed, in succession, by page references to the German text and to Sibree's translation.

In addition to Sibree, the Introduction to the *Lectures* has also been translated by Robert S. Hartman, H. B. Nisbet and Leo Rauch. Hartman and Rauch translate Karl Hegel, with, in Hartman's case, interpolations from the editions by Eduard Gans and Georg Lasson. Nisbet translates the more extensive edition by Johannes Hoffmeister. Citations of the *Introduction* are signalled by

'H', and also, for convenience of reference to the Karl Hegel text, by 'M'. The 'H' is followed, in succession, by page references to Hoffmeister and to Nisbet's translation. These are then normally followed by 'M' and, in succession, by page references to Moldenhauer and Michel and to the translations by Sibree, Hartman and Rauch. Where the 'M' or, very occasionally, the 'H' is missing in these sequences, it is because I have not been able to find the relevant portion of text in the editions in question. As Hartman translates somewhat less of Karl Hegel's edition than does Rauch or, of course, Sibree, a page reference to his translation has sometimes had to be omitted.

All translations from the *Lectures* and the *Introduction* that appear in this book are mine. Details of the various editions and translations referred to in the citations are as follows.

Hegel, G. W. F. (1953) *Reason in History: A General Introduction to the Philosophy of History*, trans. R. S. Hartman, New York: The Liberal Arts Press.

——(1955) *Die Vernunft in der Geschichte*, J. Hoffmeister (ed.), Hamburg: Felix Meiner.

——(1956) *The Philosophy of History*, trans. J. Sibree, New York: Dover.

——(1970) *Vorlesungen über die Philosophie der Geschichte*, E. Moldenhauer and K. M. Michel (eds). *Theorie Werkausgabe*, vol. 12. Frankfurt am Main: Suhrkamp.

——(1975) *Lectures on the Philosophy of World History. Introduction: Reason in History*, trans. H. B. Nisbet, Cambridge: Cambridge University Press.

——(1988) *Introduction to the Philosophy of History*, trans. L. Rauch, Indianapolis: Hackett.

Other works by Hegel referred to in the text

Werke	*Theorie Werkausgabe*, E. Moldenhauer and K. M. Michel (eds), Frankfurt am Main: Suhrkamp Verlag, 1970.
AW	'Aphorisms from the Wastebook', *The Independent Journal of Philosophy*, vol. 3 , 1979.

BS   *Berliner Schriften 1818–1831, Werke*, vol. 11.

CR   *Lectures on the Philosophy of Religion*, vol. 3: *The Consummate Religion*, P. C. Hodgson (ed.), Berkeley: University of California Press, 1985.

EL   *The Encyclopaedia Logic*, trans. T. F. Geraets, W. A. Suchting and H. S. Harris, Indianapolis: Hackett, 1991.

EPR   *Elements of the Philosophy of Right*, trans. H. B. Nisbet, Cambridge: Cambridge University Press, 1991.

EPW 1–3   *Enzyklopädie der philosophischen Wissenschaften im Grundrisse*

            1 *Die Wissenschaft der Logik, Werke*, vol. 8.

            2 *Die Naturphilosophie, Werke*, vol. 9.

            3 *Die Philosophie des Geistes, Werke*, vol. 10.

FK   *Faith and Knowledge*, trans. W. Cerf and H. S. Harris, Albany: State University of New York Press, 1977.

FS   *Frühe Schriften, Werke*, vol. 1.

GPR   *Grundlinien der Philosophie des Rechts, Werke*, vol. 7.

HA   *Hegel's Aesthetics: Lectures on Fine Art* vol. 1, trans. T. M. Knox, Oxford: Oxford University Press, 1975.

HL   *Hegel: The Letters*, trans. C. Butler and C. Seiler, Bloomington: Indiana University Press, 1984.

HPM   *Hegel's Philosophy of Mind*, trans. W. Wallace and A. V. Miller, Oxford: Oxford University Press, 1971.

HPN   *Hegel's Philosophy of Nature* vol. 1, trans. M. J. Petry, London: George Allen and Unwin, 1970.

HPW   *Hegel's Political Writings*, trans. T. M. Knox, Oxford: Oxford University Press, 1964.

ICR   *Lectures on the Philosophy of Religion*, vol. 1: *Introduction and the Concept of Religion*, P. C. Hodgson (ed.), Berkeley: University of California Press, 1984.

JS   *Jenaer Schriften 1801–1807, Werke*, vol. 2.

LHP1/LHP3   *Lectures on the History of Philosophy* vol. 1 and vol. 3, trans. E. S. Haldane and F. H. Simpson, London: Kegan Paul, 1892.

LNR   *Lectures on Natural Right and Political Science*, trans. J. M. Stewart and P. C. Hodgson, Berkeley: University of California Press, 1995.

LPR   *Lectures on the Philosophy of Religion* vol. 3, trans. E. B. Speirs and J. B. Sanderson, London: Kegan Paul, 1895.

NL   *Natural Law*, trans. T. M. Knox, Philadelphia: University of Pennsylvania Press, 1975.

PG   *Phänomenologie des Geistes, Werke*, vol. 3.

PM   *The Phenomenology of Mind*, trans. J. B. Baillie, London: George Allen and Unwin, 1931.

PRV   *Philosophie des Rechts: Die Vorlesungen von 1819–20*, D. Henrich (ed.), Frankfurt am Main: Suhrkamp Verlag, 1983.

PS   *Phenomenology of Spirit*, trans. A. V. Miller, Oxford: Oxford University Press, 1977.

SEL   *System of Ethical Life and First Philosophy of Spirit*, trans. H. S. Harris and T. M. Knox, Albany: State University of New York Press, 1979.

SL   *Science of Logic*, trans. A. V. Miller, Atlantic Highlands: Humanities Press, 1989.

VA   *Vorlesungen über die Äesthetik I, Werke*, vol. 13.

VGP1   *Vorlesungen über die Geschichte der Philosophie I, Werke*, vol. 18.

VGP2   *Vorlesungen über die Geschichte der Philosophie II, Werke*, vol. 19.

VGP3   *Vorlesungen über die Geschichte der Philosophie III, Werke*, vol. 20.

VPR   *Vorlesungen über die Philosophie der Religion II, Werke*, vol. 17.

VPW   *Vorlesungen über die Philosophie der Weltgeschichte: Berlin 1822–3*, K. H. Ilting, K. Brehmer and H. N. Seelman (eds), Hamburg: Felix Meiner, 1996.

WL1   *Wissenschaft der Logik I, Werke*, vol. 5.

WL2   *Wissenschaft der Logik II, Werke*, vol. 6.

Other works referred to in the text

Aarsleff, H. (1994) 'Locke's Influence', in V. Chappell (ed.) *The Cambridge Companion to Locke*, Cambridge: Cambridge University Press.

Blake, W. (1958) *A Selection of Poems and Letters*, J. Bronowski (ed.), Harmondsworth: Penguin Books.

Collingwood, R. G. (1946) *The Idea of History*, London: Oxford University Press.

Cooper, B. (1984) *The End of History: An Essay on Modern Hegelianism*, Toronto: University of Toronto Press.

Descartes, R. (1970) *Descartes: Philosophical Writings*, E. Anscombe and P. Geach (eds), London: Thomas Nelson.

Descartes, R. (1986) *Meditations on First Philosophy*, trans. J. Cottingham, Cambridge: Cambridge University Press.

Elster, J. (1978) *Logic and Society: Contradictions and Possible Worlds*, Chichester: John Wiley and Sons.

Engelhardt, H. T. and Pinkard, T. (eds) (1994) *Hegel Reconsidered: Beyond Metaphysics and the Authoritarian State*, Dordrecht: Kluwer Academic Publishers.

Engels, F. (1958) 'Ludwig Feuerbach and the End of Classical German Philosophy', in K. Marx and F. Engels, *Selected Works*, vol. 2, Moscow: Foreign Languages Publishing House.

Engels, F. (1962) 'Ludwig Feuerbach und der Ausgang der klassischen deutschen Philosophie', in K. Marx und F. Engels, *Werke*, Band 21, Berlin: Dietz Verlag.

Fackenheim, E. (1967) *The Religious Dimension in Hegel's Thought*, Bloomington: Indiana University Press.

Farrell, R. B. (1971) *Dictionary of German Synonyms*, Cambridge: Cambridge University Press.

Gadamer, H-G. (1981) *Reason in the Age of Science*, trans. F. G. Lawrence, Cambridge, MA: The MIT Press.

Habermas, J. (1968) *Technik und Wissenschaft als 'Ideologie'*, Frankfurt am Main: Suhrkamp.

Habermas, J. (1974) *Theory and Practice*, trans. J. Viertel, London: Heinemann.

Hartmann, K. (1988) *Studies in Foundational Philosophy*, Amsterdam: Rodopi.

Heine, H. (1948) *Self-Portrait and Other Prose Writings*, trans. F. Ewen, Secaucus: Citadel Press.

Hume, D. (1888) *A Treatise of Human Nature*, Oxford: Oxford University Press.

Hume, D. (1988) *An Enquiry Concerning Human Understanding*, New York: Prometheus Books.

Hyppolite, J. (1969) *Studies on Marx and Hegel*, trans. J. O' Neill, New York: Basic Books.

Inwood, M. (1992) *A Hegel Dictionary*, Oxford: Blackwell.

Jaeschke, W. (1990) *Reason in Religion: The Foundations of Hegel's Philosophy of Religion*, trans. P. C. Hodgson and M. Stewart, Berkeley: University of California Press.

Kant, I. (1922) *Kritik der Urteilskraft*, Leipzig: Felix Meiner.

Kant, I. (1952) *The Critique of Judgement*, trans. J. C. Meredith, Oxford: Oxford University Press.

Kant, I. (1968) *Critique of Pure Reason*, trans. N. Kemp Smith, London: Macmillan.

Kant, I. (1991) *Political Writings*, trans. H. B. Nisbet, Cambridge: Cambridge University Press.

Kant, I. (1993) *Critique of Practical Reason*, trans. L. W. Beck, Upper Saddle River: Prentice Hall.

Kierkegaard, S. (1941) *Fear and Trembling*, trans. W. Lowrie, New York: Doubleday.

Kojève, A. (1980) *Introduction to the Reading of Hegel*, trans. J. H. Nichols, Jr, Ithaca: Cornell University Press.

Kojève, A. (1993) 'Hegel, Marx and Christianity', trans. H. Gildin, in R. Stern (ed.) *G. W. F. Hegel: Critical Assessments* vol. 2, London and New York: Routledge. Reprinted from *Interpretation* (1970) 1: 21–42.

Locke, J. (1975) *An Essay Concerning Human Understanding*, Oxford: Oxford University Press.

McTaggart, J. M. E. (1918) *Studies in Hegelian Cosmology*, Cambridge: Cambridge University Press.

Marx, K. (1969) *Karl Marx on Colonialism and Modernization*, S. Avineri (ed.), New York: Doubleday.

Marx, K. (1973) *Surveys from Exile*, D. Fernbach (ed.), Harmondsworth: Penguin Books.

Marx, K. (1974) *Capital: A Critique of Political Economy* vol. 3, F. Engels (ed.), London: Lawrence and Wishart.

Marx, K. (1975) *Early Writings*, trans. R. Livingstone and G. Benton, Harmondsworth: Penguin Books.

Nietzsche, F. (1964) *Unzeitgemässe Betrachtungen*, Stuttgart: Alfred Kröner.

Nietzsche, F. (1980) *On the Advantage and Disadvantage of History for Life*, trans. P. Preuss, Indianapolis: Hackett.

O'Brien, G. D. (1975) *Hegel on Reason and History: A Contemporary Interpretation*, Chicago: The University of Chicago Press.

Ottmann, H. (1996) 'Hegel and Political Trends: A Criticism of the Political Hegel Legends', in J. Stewart (ed.) *The Hegel Myths and Legends*, Evanston: Northwestern University Press.

Paine, T. (1958) *The Rights of Man*, London: J. M. Dent and Sons.

Pompa, L. (1990) *Human Nature and Historical Knowledge: Hume, Hegel and Vico*, Cambridge: Cambridge University Press.

Roth, M. S. (1985) 'A Problem of Recognition: Alexandre Kojève and the End of History', *History and Theory* 24: 293–306.

Rousseau, J. J. (1973) *The Social Contract and Discourses*, trans. G. D. H. Cole, London: J. M. Dent and Sons.

Royce, J. (1901) 'Hegel's Terminology', in J. M. Baldwin (ed.) *Dictionary of Philosophy and Psychology*, New York and London: Macmillan.

Smith, A. (1991) *The Wealth of Nations*. London: Everyman Library.

Spinoza, B. de (1996) *Ethics*, trans. E. Curley, London: Penguin Books.

Toews, J. E. (1980) *Hegelianism: The Path Toward Dialectical Humanism, 1805–1841*, Cambridge: Cambridge University Press.

Walsh, W. H. (1971) 'Principle and Prejudice in Hegel's Philosophy of History', in Z. A. Pelczynski (ed.) *Hegel's Political Philosophy: Problems and Perspectives*, Cambridge: Cambridge University Press.

White, H. (1973) *Metahistory: The Historical Imagination in Nineteenth Century Europe*, Baltimore: Johns Hopkins University Press.

Wilkins, B. T. (1974) *Hegel's Philosophy of History*, Ithaca: Cornell University Press.

Williams, B. (1985) *Ethics and the Limits of Philosophy*, London: Fontana.

Wood, A. W. (1990) *Hegel's Ethical Thought*, Cambridge: Cambridge University Press.

Further reading

A small body of excellent work in English on Hegel's philosophy of history has appeared in recent years. The items listed below are particularly illuminating and accessible.

Berry, C. J. (1982) *Hume, Hegel and Human Nature*, The Hague: Martinus Nijhoff: 125–207.

Forbes, D. (1975) 'Introduction' in Nisbet, op. cit.: VII-XXXV.

Houlgate, S. (1991) *Freedom, Truth and History: An Introduction to Hegel's Philosophy*, London: Routledge.

Kain, P. J. (1993) 'Hegel's Political Theory and the Philosophy of History', in R. Stern (ed.) *G. W. F. Hegel: Critical Assessments* vol. 4, London: Routledge: 361–83. Reprinted from *Clio* (1988), 17 (4): 345–68.

Taylor, C. (1975) *Hegel*, Cambridge, Cambridge University Press: 365–461.

Index